CW01379276

Changing Political Economy of Vietnam

Based on years of painstaking research *Changing Political Economy of Vietnam: The Case of Ho Chi Minh City* offers a rarely seen view of the politics and political economy of Vietnam's second city during the reform era.

The book explores the way the state has become commercialised under reform as party and government officials have gone into business, and considers the impact this has had on politics within Ho Chi Minh City and on relations between the city and Hanoi. The book charts the way power has been decentralised to the lower levels of the party-state but argues that the central state retains significant power. These issues are explored through a variety of case studies, including the implementation of different reform policies, struggles over political and business appointments, clampdowns on speculative business activity, and the prosecution of two major corruption cases. Particular emphasis is placed on piecing together the myriad of informal practices that dominate business and political life in Vietnam.

This book challenges many of the preconceptions about reform in Vietnam. It will be invaluable to scholars interested in politics, economics and business in Southeast Asia.

Martin Gainsborough is a British Academy Post-Doctoral Research Fellow in the Department of Politics and International Studies at the University of Warwick. A specialist on Vietnam's politics and political economy, he has over ten years of experience in Vietnam. Martin Gainsborough also works as a consultant for a wide range of government, multilateral and private sector clients.

Rethinking Southeast Asia
Edited by Duncan McCargo
University of Leeds, UK

Southeast Asia is a dynamic and rapidly-changing region which continues to defy predictions and challenge formulaic understandings. This series will publish cutting-edge work on the region, providing a venue for books that are readable, topical, interdisciplinary and critical of conventional views. It aims to communicate the energy, contestations and ambiguities that make Southeast Asia both consistently fascinating and sometimes potentially disturbing.

This series comprises two strands:

Rethinking Southeast Asia aims to address the needs of students and teachers, and the titles will be published in both hardback and paperback.

RoutledgeCurzon Research on Southeast Asia is a forum for innovative new research intended for a high-level specialist readership, and the titles will be available in hardback only. Titles include:

1 **Politics and the Press in Thailand**
   Media machinations
   Duncan McCargo

2 **Democracy and National Identity in Thailand**
   Michael Kelly Connors

3 **The Politics of NGOs in Indonesia**
   Developing democracy and managing a movement
   Bob S. Hadiwinata

4 **Military and Democracy in Indonesia**
   Jun Honna

5 **Changing Political Economy of Vietnam**
   The case of Ho Chi Minh City
   Martin Gainsborough

Changing Political Economy of Vietnam
The case of Ho Chi Minh City

Martin Gainsborough

RoutledgeCurzon
Taylor & Francis Group
LONDON AND NEW YORK

First published 2003 by RoutledgeCurzon,
11 New Fetter Lane, London EC4P 4EE

Simultaneously published in the USA and Canada
by RoutledgeCurzon
29 West 35th Street, New York, NY 10001

RoutledgeCurzon is an imprint of the Taylor & Francis Group

© 2003 Martin Gainsborough

Typeset in Times by Steven Gardiner Ltd, Cambridge
Printed and bound in Great Britain
by MPB Books, Bodmin, Cornwall

All rights reserved. No part of this book may be reprinted or reproduced or utilised in any form or by any electronic, mechanical, or other means, now known or hereafter invented, including photocopying and recording, or in any information storage or retrieval system, without permission in writing from the publishers.

British Library Cataloguing in Publication Data
A catalogue record for this book is available from the British Library

Library of Congress Cataloging in Publication Data
A catalog record for this book has been requested

ISBN 0-415-36970-3

Contents

List of tables	viii
Preface	ix

1 From plan to market: the logic of decentralisation   1
  Introduction 1
  Decentralisation and reform 2
  Ho Chi Minh City 3
  Ho Chi Minh City under planning: the logic of control 5
  Ho Chi Minh City and reform: increased autonomy 6
  *Decentralisation versus centralisation: the controlling
    imperative 8*
  *Characterising local governments: from developmentalism to
    rent-seeking 9*
  Disaggregating the state: differing incentives 11
  Methodology and sources 13
  The structure of the book 14

2 In business: the hollowing out of the state sector   16
  Introduction 16
  *Ho Chi Minh City's political economy in the second half of
    the 1990s 16*
  New business opportunities with reform 19
  High growth sectors 21
  The emergence of diversified business corporations 24
  Changing property rights 24
  New management 28
  Bureaucratic and political background 28
  From speculation to smuggling 32
  Conclusion 39

vi *Contents*

3 Patterns of circulation: democratic centralism under strain   40
   Introduction 40
   Democratic centralism: the official picture 43
   Democratic centralism under strain 43
   Explaining change 46
   The changing character of elites 47
   Politics and business: three patterns 53
   Clientelist networks 53
   Democratic centralism undermined: the exception or the rule? 56
   Conclusion 58

4 Institutional conflict: the city, the centre and the lower levels   59
   Introduction 59
   Institutional rivalry: which institutions and what is at stake? 60
   The city People's Committee, the departments and the districts 65
   Some patterns: pressure from above and below 68
   Clampdowns: a backseat role for the People's Committee 70
   Where do clampdowns come from and why do they occur? 73
   Momentum lost 74
   The role of the city in clampdowns 74
   The city People's Committee's response to Decree 18: singing the tune of the lower levels 75
   Limits to the centre's writ in Ho Chi Minh City 76
   Conclusion 77

5 The politics of economic decentralisation: the Tamexco and Minh Phung–Epco Cases   78
   Introduction 78
   The rise of Tamexco, Epco and Minh Phung 79
   The fall of Tamexco, Epco and Minh Phung 83
   Explaining Tamexco's and Minh Phung–Epco's fall 90
   Proving guilt 94
   The politics of economic decentralisation 95

6 Rethinking reform: property rights and the dynamics of change   98
   Introduction 98
   Opposition to reform? 99
   Changes in property rights 100
   Government-centred property rights 101
   Enforcing property rights 101
   Ho Chi Minh City's property arrangements explained 102

What has changed? 104
What is the momentum of change? 104
The meaning of reform 105
Critiquing the Vietnam literature 106
Spontaneous change and reform 109

Appendix	110
Notes	135
Bibliography	174
Index	184

Tables

2.1	Top 100 companies and banks in Ho Chi Minh City by turnover in 1995: type of ownership	18
2.2	Ho Chi Minh City's top five limited liability companies by turnover in 1995: institutional and/or personal affiliations	20
2.3	Four diversified business corporations in Ho Chi Minh City in the late 1990s	26
3.1	Ho Chi Minh City party secretaries 1975–2000	47
3.2	Ho Chi Minh City People's Committee chairmen 1975–2000	49
5.1	Key facts about Tamexco	79
5.2	Key facts about Minh Phung	80
5.3	Key facts about Epco	81
5.4	Key figures linked to the Tamexco case	83
5.5	Key figures linked to the Minh Phung–Epco case	88

Preface

The gestation of this book now stretches back some years. At the heart of it lies three exciting and enjoyable years in Vietnam (1996–9). When I began field research in Vietnam, I had a general sense of the direction I wanted to travel, including a curiosity about the 'informal sector' in Vietnam, which for reasons that were rather ill-defined at the time I thought was important. However, I could never have imagined where my research would take me, the areas I would delve into and the conclusions I would draw. Research in Vietnam was never easy – on the contrary. The struggle involved in learning the language, the often sensitive nature of the kind of things I was trying to uncover and probably the weather, all combined to make it one of the more challenging periods of my life. Nevertheless, as insights came, they were inevitably the more rewarding for it.

Although it adopts a post-1975 perspective, *Changing Political Economy of Vietnam* is primarily about the 1990s in Vietnam from the vantage point of the country's business centre and second city, Ho Chi Minh City. While it is too early to be sure how the 1990s in Vietnam will be viewed by future generations, there is perhaps the beginnings of a sense in which, compared with subsequent decades, it may prove to have been a rather lawless one. At the beginning of the twenty-first century, Vietnam scholars are already starting to talk about there being a greater sense of 'order' in the country. Although its precise origins and make-up remain to be fleshed out, 'rule by law' as opposed to 'rule of law' seems a fruitful way to proceed. For this author, the term 'primitive accumulation' comes to mind as capturing something of the 1990s in Ho Chi Minh City. Certainly, there seemed to be a fair number of members of the elite – and others – getting rich on the back of such things as the emergence of the land market, the craze to establish banks, or generally exploiting their public positions in state enterprises and the bureaucracy for private gain. Some people also made spectacular losses as well. While officially regarded as exceptional, the Tamexco and Minh Phung–Epco corruption cases, which are explored at length in Chapter 5 of the book, epitomise much that lay at the heart of the 1990s. At the same time, the prosecution of these cases may in time be regarded as a turning point, when the central state sought to re-establish order over the activities of the lower levels of the party-state. This idea of recentralisation is a recurring theme in the book. This is in stark contrast to the dominant view of reform as decentralisation.

With its emphasis on the informal sector, it is my hope that this book offers a perspective on Vietnam's politics and political economy, which usually remains hidden, particularly from Western scholarship. Certainly, the book goes to some lengths to piece together how people really did business in Vietnam in the 1990s and the politics which underlies it. Ho Chi Minh City is also a city that attracts stereotypes: reformist city, vibrant private sector, disobedient towards the centre are the main ones. In the course of my research, much of what I observed fitted poorly with this received wisdom. Thus, it is also my hope that the book challenges many of the stereotypes surrounding Ho Chi Minh City. In particular, we have tended to assume that there is something distinctive about the southern political economy. In the future, we must try to prove it.

During my research I have incurred many debts. I would like to extend my sincere appreciation to the Department of Vietnamese Studies and Vietnamese Language for Foreigners at the University of Social Sciences and Humanities in Ho Chi Minh City for hosting my time in Vietnam. In particular I would like to thank the Department's director Nguyen Van Lich and all the staff who taught me Vietnamese. Learning Vietnamese was harder than the research itself but the many hours spent at 12 Dinh Tinh Hoang were one of the most enjoyable aspects of my time in Vietnam. I would also like to thank my Vietnamese friends who patiently explained the same things to me again and again and showed me how things 'really are'. Without their help this book would be infinitely poorer.

The book is a revision of a Ph.D. thesis in Politics undertaken at the School of Oriental and African Studies, University of London. In this regard, I would like to thank my supervisor John Sidel for his constant encouragement, clarity of insight and ability to push me that bit further. I would also like to thank my examiners, Jane Duckett and Jonathan Pincus. I am grateful to my fellow graduate students in Ho Chi Minh City who in the early days impressed me with their grasp of Vietnamese and, as people in a similar predicament, were a great source of intellectual and emotional support. I would like to thank Adam Fforde with whom I have benefited from many stimulating conversations over the years. Book revisions were completed while a British Academy Post-Doctoral Research Fellow in the Department of Politics and International Studies, University of Warwick. In this regard, I would like to thank Peter Ferdinand and Andrew Reeve for their support, and the British Academy and Leverhulme Trust for enabling me to conduct further research on Vietnam. I would also like to thank Craig Fowlie and Jennifer Lovel at Routledge who kindly guided me through the production process. I remain responsible for all remaining errors. Finally, I would like to thank my family, Mary, Annie and Francis Gainsborough, who were with me in Vietnam and thus experienced every twist and turn of the research and writing process.

1 From plan to market: the logic of decentralisation

Introduction

In Communist and former Communist countries, reform is commonly seen as embodying decentralisation and a consequent increase in local government power.[1] What is often less clear is the precise form this process has taken – in what ways has power been decentralised and to whom? – and particularly the consequences it has had for the type of state that has emerged at the local level. Moreover, the picture is not simply one of decentralisation. Moves in this direction are commonly met with a response, namely attempts to recentralise power. With reference to Ho Chi Minh City, it is this relative balance between centralisation and decentralisation that is explored in this introductory chapter. In turn it is also a major theme of the book as a whole.

This chapter first explores the shift from a situation of relative centralisation under the central plan to one of relative decentralisation under the market. In explaining the logic of this shift, emphasis is placed both on changes in Socialist development thinking towards a more favourable view of large cities – a process that had particular ramifications for Ho Chi Minh City – and on the informal way in which market activity has tended to emerge. The chapter also considers different ways of conceptualising the state at the sub-national level. Here, we draw on the rich literature in this field on China. By way of a pointer to ideas that will be developed later in the book, I suggest that Ho Chi Minh City has more in common with accounts that downplay the state's developmental proclivities in favour of greater emphasis on rent-seeking and an often debilitating rivalry between different state institutions. This observation, in turn, underlines the importance of breaking the state down into its constituent parts, which as I will explain is the approach adopted here. The chapter also questions the widespread tendency to view Ho Chi Minh City and its post-1975 leadership as 'reformist', in a kind of knee-jerk 'southerner therefore reformer' thesis. I argue that in relation to the findings of this piece of research, the 'reformist' label appears a poor fit not only in descriptive terms but also in terms of understanding the dynamics of change. As will become clear, this is a central tenet of the book.

2 *Changing political economy of Vietnam*

Decentralisation and reform

Economic reform has led to a decentralisation of power to the local level, resulting in a strengthening of local government in relation to the political centre. While scholars of Communist and former Communist countries disagree on many other issues, they are largely in agreement on this point. Decentralisation and a consequent increase in local government power can thus be regarded as a central theme running through the literature on transitional economies.[2] This has not always been the case. Some of the early literature on China took a rather different view. Writing in the late 1980s, Vivienne Shue argued that market reforms were enabling a greater penetration by the central state.[3] Victor Nee suggested that greater reliance on markets would have a corrosive effect on the power of local officials.[4] However, the growth in studies of local politics during the 1990s soon led to a different set of conclusions.[5] Contrary to expectations, the advent of the market has not seen local government withdraw or abstain from playing a role in the economy nor has its power withered.[6] Two scholars, again writing on China, have captured the dominant view as follows:

> Decentralisation has been the hallmark of economic reform, and this has not only meant dismantling the mechanisms of the planned economy such as central control of prices and materials but has also had implications as far reaching as depriving the central government of badly needed revenues.[7]

> The economic reforms of the last decade and a half have had a profound effect on local government. On the one hand, the reforms have increased the economic decision-making responsibilities of local governments. On the other hand, the reforms have reduced the financial support local governments receive from above. Although this represents potentially a crippling bind, in the context of marketisation this combination has effectively increased the economic power of local governments, while reducing their financial dependence on the centre.[8]

While reform is seen as having led to accelerated decentralisation in the transitional economies, the process is generally viewed as having a much longer historical gestation. In Vietnam's case, present-day decentralisation is seen in the context of a long history of regionalism. Douglas Pike likens geographic regionalism to caste in India, saying 'one cannot understand Vietnamese politics without forever bearing it in mind'.[9] In pre-colonial Vietnam, local autonomy was part of the accepted balance of power between the court and local village (*xa*) as is captured in the well-known saying 'the King bows to the customs of the village' (*phep vua thua le lang*).[10] The distinctive way in which the south was originally settled in pre-colonial times has been cited as creating a distinctly southern character and self-image, which in part manifests itself in a tendency towards regionalism.[11] Other scholars have suggested that regionalism became more entrenched as a result of the concentration of capitalist agriculture and commerce in the south with relatively little development occurring in the north under French colonial rule. Attention has also been drawn to the effects of the formal division of the country into north and south from 1954–75 following the Geneva agreements.[12] A number of scholars have emphasised the way in which the Constitution adopted in the Democratic Republic of Vietnam in 1960 created jurisdictional conflicts without institutionalised means to resolve them by granting provincial and city leaders equivalent powers to ministers at the centre. The relevant clauses of the 1960 Constitution were applied to the southern part of the country when the Constitution was revised after 1975.[13]

As with the literature on transition economies in general, scholars writing on Vietnam have also noted the inherent decentralising logic of the reform period, whether it be a spontaneous process or through formal policy decisions such as the liberalisation of price controls or the devolving of decision-making powers formerly held by planners to enterprises or individuals.[14] The rise of provincial representation on the party Central Committee from 1976–86 has also been cited as indicative of the trend towards decentralisation and increased local power that has occurred with reform.[15] At the same time, there is recognition in the literature that it is not simply a matter of ever-increasing decentralisation but rather that there is an ongoing tug of war between centre and periphery. A number of scholars have noted concerted attempts at recentralisation both during the 1980s and 1990s.[16] Attempted recentralisation in the 1990s has in turn been linked to a fall in provincial representation on the Central Committee after 1986 and especially during the period 1991–6.[17]

I shall now consider the implications of these issues for Ho Chi Minh City. First, however, we shall look at the city's administrative structure and its economic and political standing within the national economy.

Ho Chi Minh City

Ho Chi Minh City, or Saigon as it was known until the Communist victory in 1975, is Vietnam's largest city with a population officially estimated at 5.1 million or 6.8 per cent of the total population in 1998.[18] Situated 80 kilometres from the sea on the banks of the Saigon River, it is also the country's economic and commercial centre, contributing 18.7 per cent to nationwide GDP, 27.0 per cent to nationwide industrial output and 36.2 per cent to the country's total external trade (1998 figures).[19] The origin of the city's status as an economic centre dates back to the seventeenth century when it first emerged as a trading post. However, its economic development received a considerable boost with the arrival of the French in the early 1860s.[20] Today Ho Chi Minh City is also the richest city in the country, with annual per capita GDP in excess of 1000 US dollars compared with 350 US dollars nationwide.[21] Reflecting Ho Chi Minh City's higher level of economic development compared with the rest of the country, the structure of the city's economy is geared more to services and industry, which contribute respectively 55.8 per cent and 41.8 per cent to total GDP than to agriculture, which is responsible for just 2.4 per cent of total output.[22] Nationwide, agriculture contributes 23.7 per cent to GDP compared with 33.5 per cent of industry and 42.8 per cent for services.[23] Moreover, less than 0.01 per cent of Ho Chi Minh City's population is employed in agriculture compared with 68.8 per cent nationwide.[24]

Administratively, Ho Chi Minh City is one of three cities under direct central management (*thanh pho truc thuoc trung uong*).[25] This means that, like a province, there is no intervening level of authority between the city and the centre. The city is divided into 22 districts (*quan* or *huyen*). This follows the establishment of five new ones in 1997. These are split between 17 urban (*noi thanh*) and five suburban or rural (*ngoai thanh*) districts. The city's 22 districts are in turn broken down into a further administrative unit, namely the ward (*phuong*) or commune (*xa*) in the case of rural districts. There are a total of 303 wards and communes in Ho Chi Minh City. The wards are then broken down into two further sub-divisions: the sub-ward (*khu pho*) and People's Groups (*to dan pho*). At the level of the *to dan pho*, one is really talking about a collection of extended family units (*ho*).[26]

Like the country as a whole, Ho Chi Minh City is governed by a joint party–government structure in which the government is formally junior to the party. At the peak of the city administration is the city party committee (*Thanh uy*) headed by a party secretary (*bi thu Thanh uy*). The party committee comprises an Executive Committee (*Ban Chap hanh Dang bo*) and a smaller, inner Standing Committee (*Ban Thuong vu Thanh uy*). In Ho Chi Minh City, the Executive Committee has historically numbered around 50 at the city level while the Standing Committee has had between 13 and 18 members.[27] The party is also represented by a number of committees (*ban*) such as the economics committee (*Ban kinh te Thanh uy*), the ideology and culture committee (*Ban tu tuong van hoa Thanh uy*), and the organisation committee (*Ban to chuc Thanh uy*), which covers personnel. The government structure in Ho Chi Minh City comprises the People's Council (*Hoi dong nhan dan*) and the People's Committee (*Uy ban nhan dan*). The People's Committee, which is headed by a chairman (*chu tich Uy ban nhan dan*), is the executive organ (*co quan chap hanh*) of the locally elected People's Council. Beneath the People's Committee are a series of functionally specialised departments (*so*), covering areas such as industry, housing and land, and education.[28] Both the party and the People's Committee at the city level are linked into a hierarchical relationship extending upwards to the centre and downwards to the People's Groups (*to dan pho*) in the case of the party and to the quarters (*phuong*) in the case of the People's Committee. There are also party cells grouping just a few people beneath the People's Groups. Each level is formally subordinate to the level above.[29]

We shall now consider the situation that existed in Ho Chi Minh City under central planning. In this section, the emphasis is on the tendency towards tight central control. This contrasts with the shift towards greater autonomy in the city during the reform years, which is considered in the section immediately following this one.

Ho Chi Minh City under planning: the logic of control

When the Communists took control of Saigon in 1975, it was a hallmark of socialist development thinking at the time that large cities were to be discouraged. In its most idealised form, this way of thinking embodied the idea that socialism was about creating a radically 'new order', which was neither urban nor rural.[30] However, other considerations were also prominent. Urbanisation was disliked because of its spontaneous and disorderly character, which according to the thinking of the day ought to be subject to the control of planners. Cities were also viewed negatively because they were expensive, requiring such things as housing, streets and sewage facilities. Furthermore, urban populations were looked down upon as 'consumers' rather than 'producers'.[31] As a result, the aim was to achieve industrialisation without urbanisation or at least with minimum urbanisation. In its most radical form, it was this kind of thinking which underpinned the evacuation of Phnom Penh by the Khmer Rouge in Cambodia in 1975. It has also been a recurrent theme in post-1949 China up until the death of Mao Zedong and the end of the Cultural Revolution in 1976.[32]

In Vietnam, as the euphoria of victory gave way to the reality of the rebuilding task that lay ahead, the new regime was similarly influenced by this 'anti-urban bias'.[33] Writing in the early 1980s, the late historian Nguyen Khac Vien captured something of the official thinking (and venom) towards the former Saigon when he asked whether the now renamed Ho Chi Minh City was to become 'a parasitic metropolis, a consumer society, a colossal leech that will suck up the nation's wealth for its orgies and revelries' as opposed to a productive industrial, scientific and cultural centre.[34] Attempts from the late 1970s to create self-sufficient integrated agro-industrial zones at the district level similarly carry echoes of the Socialist development thinking of the time.[35] However, it was in the context of trying to minimise urbanisation that in 1975 the state instituted a policy of de-urbanisation, whereby a proportion of Vietnam's urban population was re-settled in New Economic Zones.[36] The result was that Ho Chi Minh City's population, which had grown rapidly on the back of the American-bankrolled war economy and had been swollen by refugees in the final years of the war, fell sharply in 1976 and continued to fall until 1984 (see Appendix Table A1.2).[37] The contraction in the city's population was despite the fact that victory in 1975 was accompanied by large-scale movement of cadres and their families from the north to Ho Chi Minh City (and the south in general) in order to run the new administration.[38] At the same time as re-settling people in New Economic

Zones, the state imposed restrictions on independent population movement to prevent fresh rural to urban migration.[39]

Paradoxically, despite the anti-urban bias, cities under socialism played a key role in financing the central plan.[40] To the extent that there was no tax system in a conventional sense under planning, the state was highly dependent on transfers from state-owned enterprises (see Appendix Table A1.6).[41] Despite the logic of the anti-urban development policy, state enterprises were still largely based in the main cities.[42] State enterprise transfers were assured by the Socialist pricing system, which maintained low prices for agricultural and mining products and high prices for manufacturing goods. However, to ensure that state enterprise profits were extracted for the benefit of the plan and were disbursed locally necessitated a high degree of central control over the urban economy. This included local governments under whose jurisdiction at least some of the state enterprises came.[43] While relying on the cities as the primary source of revenue, the period under planning also saw large urban areas, such as Ho Chi Minh City, starved of investment. Instead, investment was targeted at the development of smaller towns.[44]

A consequence of this approach was that traditional urban centres went into decline under planning. Writing about China, Barry Naughton describes how by the late 1970s the central districts of Shanghai, Tianjin and Guangzhou had a 'museum-like character' to them.[45] This comment also rings true for Ho Chi Minh City in the very early 1990s: uncrowded and relatively quiet streets, interior decor dating from the 1960s and 1970s, a low-lying skyline that had remained basically unchanged since 1975, little or no urban sprawl and no shanty towns typical of some other South East Asian cities.[46] Beyond external appearances, Ho Chi Minh City's comparative advantage as a commercial hub and port city was not brought to bear under planning as restrictions were placed on domestic trade and as trade with regional countries withered.[47] Against this backdrop, economic growth in Ho Chi Minh City was unremarkable in relation to the rest of the country.[48] Moreover, the city's share of nationwide output, although still significant, was below its potential (see Appendix Tables A1.3 and A1.4).[49]

Ho Chi Minh City and reform: increased autonomy

Neither planning nor the anti-urban bias were maintained indefinitely. Indicative of a weakening resolve towards de-urbanisation, plans to move urban residents to the New Economic Zones were scaled down mid-way through the Third Five Year Plan (1981–3).[50] Ho Chi Minh City's population started to grow again from 1985, averaging a rapid 4.8 per cent annually during 1985–90 (see Appendix Table A1.2).[51] Furthermore, no sooner was the plan in place in the period immediately after 1975 than state enterprises in Ho Chi Minh City, as elsewhere, began to engage in lucrative off-plan business activities. This often involved exploiting the differential inherent in the two-price system. Such activities gathered pace in the 1980s as they were complemented by sanctioned reforms that formally granted state enterprises greater autonomy.[52] As the planning system broke down and was replaced by greater reliance on the market, notably in the late 1980s, the requirement that the centre exercise tight control over local economies, such as Ho Chi Minh City, became less compelling.[53] This was particularly the case following fiscal reforms that saw a decline in the earlier dependence on state enterprise transfers as a source of revenue (see Appendix Table 1.6).[54]

At the same time, the shift to reform was accompanied by a change in thinking on the role of cities in economic development. This was especially the case for coastal or port cities, where access to regional and international markets was now perceived as being valuable, as was their position as an 'open door' through which foreign capital and technology could enter. In the case of Ho Chi Minh City, official articulation of this position is evident from the early 1990s, if still in a rather cautious fashion. By the mid-1990s, Ho Chi Minh City's position as key economic hub and perceived 'reform leader' was firmly established in the official lexicon.[55] This included the idea that city leaders had tolerated or even encouraged 'reform experiments', possibly without the knowledge of the central authorities and prior to their being adopted nationally. A notable example cited in this regard was the so-called 'Ba Thi model', named after the deputy director of the Ho Chi Minh City food department, in which rice was purchased at the market rather than the planned price.[56] However, for Ho Chi Minh City to be able to exploit its comparative advantage required that it be given the resources to increase investment, so it could improve infrastructure and become attractive to international business. To achieve this required that it be given greater autonomy. Thus, during the 1990s Ho Chi Minh City, along with other provinces and cities, was granted greater control over local expenditure, notably on infrastructure, and increased freedom to approve foreign investment projects.[57] Reflecting this greater autonomy, the size of the local government in Ho Chi Minh City was on a rising trend during the 1990s, as indicated by the number of state employees. Some of the largest increases were in the area of party and state management and construction, reflecting moves by the local state to 'gate-keep' the market economy and take advantage of the emergence of the land market (see Appendix Table A1.7).[58]

The shift away from planning to greater reliance on the market has impacted differently upon different parts of the country. For poorer parts of the country, greater scope to raise revenue locally in the face of declining central transfers could be distinctly disadvantageous given the perilous state of the local economy.[59] However, Ho Chi Minh City – a traditional commercial hub and international port served with relatively good infrastructure linking it with the fertile Mekong River Delta – was well-placed to take advantage of increased autonomy, including autonomy in fiscal matters. As a result, the city's economic growth rate soared during the 1990s, significantly outpacing the rest of the country.[60] The city's share of nationwide GDP also increased (see Appendix Tables A1.3 and A1.4).[61]

Although their claims have not been based on in-depth research on Ho Chi Minh City, most scholars to date have emphasised the city's enhanced power and authority under reform. Carlyle Thayer has argued that Ho Chi Minh City has emerged as a 'countervailing economic centre in its own right' with the result that political and economic power is 'no longer exclusively located in Hanoi'.[62] Fforde and de Vylder have noted Ho Chi Minh City's growing political power in the 1980s, which they link to the appointment to the Politburo in 1982 of the former party secretary in the city, Vo Van Kiet.[63] As further evidence of Ho Chi Minh City's increased authority under reform, the city is also commonly viewed as being influential in the 'reformist' direction that national policy took after 1986. This in turn is usually attributed to the rise of 'reformist' city leaders to key positions at the centre, notably Nguyen Van Linh who became party general-secretary in 1986.[64] The tendency to refer to Ho Chi Minh City's leaders as 'reformers' is widespread; in fact, in the academic literature, there are few scholars who do not do so.[65] This is despite a trend evident more generally in the literature towards questioning the validity of terms such as 'reformer' and 'conservative'.[66] As will be emphasised throughout the book, this author is doubtful that labelling city leaders as 'reformers' is helpful either in descriptive or explanatory terms. Other scholars have talked in terms of 'sectors' rather than factions, whereby membership of a particular sector (for example, a ministry, provincial government or the military) is seen as the unit of analysis in understanding leadership and policy change. This is beneficial insofar as it gets away from a focus on a limited number of factions (often just two). However, as will become apparent from the approach adopted here, reference to sectors still seems problematic in terms of its ability to capture the great variety that exists, not least within individual sectors themselves.[67]

Decentralisation versus centralisation: the controlling imperative

Up until now I have largely emphasised the decentralising logic of reform. However, getting the balance right between decentralisation and centralisation is not easy and thus merits some additional consideration.[68] Clearly the plan was never as centralised as the formal depiction would suggest.[69] The academic literature on Vietnam is full of examples of deviation from the plan. Moreover, as we have seen, local authorities and enterprise directors were never simply involved in implementing the plan and ensuring that revenues were transferred to the level above. Markets remained an enduring feature under planning. Horizontal trade links between Ho Chi Minh City and the Mekong Delta did operate as did trade with regional markets.[70] Thus, in practice, local governments were more autonomous under planning than the formal position might suggest.

Furthermore, while we can explain the rationale and logic that has underpinned decentralisation of power to the local level under reform, it is a mistake to see it as entirely a one-way process.[71] I have noted the increase in the size of the local government in terms of state sector employment during the 1990s, but employment growth among central institutions in Ho Chi Minh City was even more rapid. Moreover, while local governments, including Ho Chi Minh City, saw a decline in employment in the early 1990s, growth in the size of the central state was constant throughout the decade, reflecting the centralising and controlling thrust of reforms as well (see Appendix Table A1.7). In this context, Ho Chi Minh City's constitutional status equivalent to that of a province (i.e. without an intervening level of administration between it and the centre) can be viewed as potentially much more double-edged, as much about *central* control as increased power for the city, although this is obviously part of it.[72] In addition, the requirement that the centre exercise tight control over the local economy may have lessened but it has not disappeared. Compared with individual cities in China, Ho Chi Minh City is far more important in the context of Vietnam's national economy.[73] Tax revenue from state enterprises remained important even in the late 1990s, as ongoing struggles between Ho Chi Minh City and the centre for control over fiscal resources indicate.[74] Nevertheless, as state institutions and enterprises in Ho Chi Minh City both took and were granted greater autonomy during the 1980s and 1990s, what we are describing is a shift from a system of relative centralisation to one of rather more decentralisation, even if under planning the system was never as centralised as formally implied and under the market the centre has taken substantial steps to maintain control.

I shall now look at the different ways in which scholars have depicted local governments under reform. In doing so, I shall draw on the academic literature on China. These differing conceptualisations are useful insofar as they provide a benchmark against which to set my findings on the state of affairs in Ho Chi Minh City as they are presented throughout the book.

Characterising local governments: from developmentalism to rent-seeking

While there is broad agreement in the literature on transitional economies that reform has led to a decentralisation of power to the local level, there is less consensus on how local governments have responded to such changes and indeed how to characterise the nature of the local state that has emerged. Scholars writing on China have depicted local governments in quite diverse ways. One approach that has been common in the reform era is to view the Chinese state as having transformed itself into a 'developmental state' in the mould of state-capitalist countries such as Taiwan and South Korea. Here, local government is seen as intervening to coordinate local economic activity but with officials acting primarily to promote economic development rather than seeking profit for themselves.[75] Some scholars have seen the developmental state operating through corporatism.[76]

A second characterisation of local government in China is that of 'local state corporatism', which has been put forward by Jean Oi.[77] Like the developmental state, Oi also sees local government actively pursuing the economic development of the area under its jurisdiction. However, she characterises local government as taking on many of the characteristics of a diversified business corporation. Local officials, often led by the party secretary, are thus seen as acting like a board of directors, performing a coordinating role between different local institutions. This ability to coordinate is important: Oi says that local state corporatist systems are 'noted for their ability to mobilise not just one but all agencies and bureaus within local government'.[78] There is therefore cooperation between local institutions, even if there is competition for control over limited resources rather like there is in a business corporation.[79] In addition, Oi argues that the local corporatist state is generally not corrupt because the incentives, which are seen as deriving from fiscal reforms, mean both the economic well-being of officials and the financial health of the local economy are tied to successful economic development.[80] Moreover, while local government can be seen to be extracting resources from the economy by taxation and other means, she suggests that this is not rent-seeking because the money is then redistributed around the 'corporation' for the benefit of the local economy.[81]

A third characterisation of local government in China views it as 'entrepreneurial'.[82] In this approach, local government departments engage in profit-making business activity. The entrepreneurial state differs from both the developmental state and the corporatist state insofar as individual departments are seen as acting for their own benefit (i.e. seeking profits for themselves). In this way, the emphasis is more on competition rather than cooperation between local institutions. Although corruption is not ruled out under this model, the entrepreneurial state is seen as engaging in 'potentially productive' activities that are viewed as being qualitatively different from rent-seeking, corruption and speculation.[83] Jane Duckett suggests that entrepreneurial and developmental states are not mutually exclusive: entrepreneurial activity may exist alongside developmental behaviour. However, she quite rightly says that it is a key question as to whether entrepreneurial activity hinders or promotes wider economic development.[84]

The ways in which local governments have been depicted so far are on the whole quite flattering. They are not seen as especially predatory or corrupt. Rather they are generally regarded as engaging in activities that have the economic development of the locality as their primary aim. There is some doubt as to whether the entrepreneurial state aids or hinders wider development but the fact that the question is posed suggests there is a degree of ambivalence as to whether it is necessarily harmful.

Such generous views of local governments are not universally held in the China literature. Barrett McCormick, for example, argues that although the Chinese state is 'hard' in an authoritarian sense, it lacks the political autonomy and technical capacity required for it to merit the developmental label in the East Asian mould.[85] Echoing such views, Ling Liu views the state as a 'sporadic totalitarian state' with strong despotic power but weak infrastructural power. In Liu's depiction, which is derived from research on the local government in Wenzhou, there is none of the coordination or cooperation evident in the local corporatist model. Instead, he sees a 'functionally fragmented bureaucracy' ridden with tensions and conflicts between the different levels as they unilaterally pursue their own interests.[86] Such approaches are much more inclined to highlight rent-seeking or other corrupt practices on the part of local elites, which in turn casts further doubt on the ability of the local governments to engage in a coordinating role for the good of the local economy.[87]

In the much smaller literature on Vietnam, designated research on local politics is still in its infancy. However, a similar juxtaposition can be discerned (to some degree) in the Vietnam literature between those who at least implicitly veer towards seeing local government in a broadly developmental light and those who are less sure. As I have noted, much writing on Vietnam has emphasised the reformist credentials of Ho Chi Minh City, an accolade that has been extended to the city's leadership.[88] Such arguments tend implicitly to embody assumptions about local government capacity of a developmental nature. By contrast, other scholars writing on Vietnam have tended to emphasise the more predatory nature of local government. Focusing on the local level, Adam Fforde and Steve Seneque, for example, highlight a 'strong interlocking "triangle" of party, state and private interests' that tends to 'treat additional resources (state credit, aid funds, etc.) as a resource to be used for the group's benefit'. This, they argue, can greatly inhibit normal 'developmentalist' activities.[89]

As will become clear in subsequent chapters, the material presented in this book tends much more towards a less favourable view of local government. 'Productive' business activity as highlighted in Duckett's depiction of the entrepreneurial state does occur, although distinguishing between it and rent-seeking and corruption appears to be more difficult than she suggests. Moreover, the material presented here offers very little evidence for coordinated activity that is at the heart of the local state corporatist model put forward by Oi.

Disaggregating the state: differing incentives

Up until now, I have been referring to the state at the sub-national level as a unitary actor even though there have been passing references to its constituent parts. This is not the approach adopted in the book, where being clear about which institution or level of the state one is referring to is regarded as crucial.[90] In the same way that different provinces or cities in Vietnam have been affected differently by decentralisation, the impact on different levels of the state has also been different. Thus, in order to get to grips with the complexities of how decentralisation and the market mechanism has affected local government, it is necessary to break local government down into its constituent parts. It is a common criticism in the literature on transitional economies that many accounts fail to do this. Elizabeth Perry has written:

> By viewing the policy process as a tug of war between a unitary 'state' and an undifferentiated 'society', we run the risk of obscuring some of the most intriguing aspects of the reform experience.
>
> Terms such as 'state' and 'society' are simply too gross to capture the enormous variation that differentiates one Chinese region – or level of government – from another'.[91]

Writing on Tianjin, Christopher Earle Nevitt also provides insight into how decentralisation with reform may have impacted the state at the local level differently.[92] Focusing on the city and district levels in Tianjin, he argues that reform, or more specifically the new business opportunities that have emerged at the local level during this period, has broken the top–down monopoly of the state over the careers of officials. Under planning, opportunities for officials to do business were limited and as a result there was really only one career path for officials to follow, namely to try to rise up through the ranks of the party or state bureaucracy that peaked at the centre. With increased opportunities to do business, this has changed. Officials now have a choice in terms of potential career paths. As in the past, they can still follow the traditional career path. However, there is now an alternative path, namely to remain at the local level and focus on doing business – what Nevitt refers to as being the 'big fish in the small pond'.[93] In Tianjin, officials abandoning their official positions have not generally been seen, since business, especially private business, remains politically risky.

What is most significant, Nevitt argues, is that the incentives associated with the two career paths are very different. If officials pursue the traditional route, they are likely to be motivated towards pleasing the level above. Thus, cultivating a reputation for conscientiously implementing official policy can be expected to be high on their agenda. On the other hand, if officials intend to remain in the locality with an emphasis on doing business, they will be much less motivated to impress the level above. In fact, Nevitt argues that doing business effectively requires that they develop local networks of power and support, insulating themselves as far as possible from the level above because there is a high chance that their respective goals will conflict. Posing the question as to which path officials are likely to choose, Nevitt says that city-level officials are more likely to pursue the traditional path. Having risen to the rank of city official, a considerable investment has already been made in this path. Moreover, their position in the formal hierarchy – directly beneath the centre – means that they are likely to be under close scrutiny from the level above.[94] District-level officials, on the other hand, are much more likely to focus on a local business career. They are lower down the hierarchy.

From plan to market: the logic of decentralisation 13

There is no guarantee that they will rise up the slippery pole. Moreover, they are one step removed from the scrutiny of the centre.

Nevitt's research on Tianjin has been helpful in making sense of aspects of the material presented here on Ho Chi Minh City. A situation in which power was apparently scattered among institutions that were frequently if not perpetually in competition with each other has been an abiding feature of the research for this book. Moreover, problems between different levels in the formal hierarchy was also a recurrent theme.[95] In addition, it was striking – and initially rather puzzling – that although the business interests of district authorities could be discerned, it was much harder to do the same for the city authorities. Was this simply because city officials were less engaged in business activities than their district counterparts, or were they just better at concealing it? Nevitt suggests the former and offers a possible explanation why.

Methodology and sources

Research for this book was carried out in Ho Chi Minh City, where I lived from 1996 to 1999. I began fieldwork with the intention of studying the politics of banking. However, while the banks provided an initial and enduring focus, I also diversified into other areas. Over the course of three years, these included informal finance, the foreign exchange, gold and land markets, smuggling, state enterprise reform, and public administration reform. I also gathered biographical data on key political and business figures in Ho Chi Minh City, and made particular efforts to piece together the shareholding and ownership structure of banks and prominent companies in the city. All these different areas were investigated for what they revealed about Ho Chi Minh City's politics and political economy.

The period of fieldwork coincided with the onset of the Asian economic crisis in July 1997. Although its impact on Vietnam was somewhat delayed, it certainly made its presence felt. Foreign exchange shortages and problems in the banking sector were thus very much issues of the day. The emergence of the land market was still a relatively new phenomenon during the period of research. Banks, businesses and individuals were taking advantage of the emergence of the land market, engaging in activities they had not pursued for a generation.[96] In the weak regulatory climate that existed at the time, this led to all sorts of abuses and conflicts. It was against this backdrop that the period 1996–9 was dominated by a series of investigations into alleged misdemeanours by companies and banks in Ho Chi Minh City, some of which involved land. These cases resulted in lengthy investigations and courts cases in the city, culminating in the imposition of death penalties and extensive prison terms. In a rather macabre way, these cases capture very well an important part of the city's politics and political economy during the 1990s. They have hence provided rich material for the book.

The sources used to gain insights in these areas were primarily the Vietnamese press and informal, off-the-record conversations with close

14   *Changing political economy of Vietnam*

acquaintances. These sources were also used to collect biographical data on city politicians and business people, along with information on the shareholding structure of banks and companies, given that such information is not routinely published and is often considered sensitive. The people spoken to mostly held junior positions of lesser responsibility in government departments, business, banking, the law, the media and education. Formal interviews with officials were eschewed because they were found to be rather unhelpful.

In contrast to the tendency in the literature to emphasise the private sector in Ho Chi Minh City, the focus here is very much on state institutions and state companies. This is because those parts of the public sector are what came across as being most 'writ large' in late-1990s Ho Chi Minh City. Moreover, for all the talk of the city's private sector, it was still quite small during the period in which the research was being conducted.[97] Furthermore, in terms of politics, the dominant conflict appeared to be between institutions of the state, not a state–society struggle as depicted in some of the politics literature on Vietnam.[98]

The structure of the book

Including this chapter, the book has six chapters. Chapter 2 sets out the nature of Ho Chi Minh City's political economy as it had emerged by the second half of the 1990s. It explores who is doing business and how they are doing it, including an investigation of the changing nature of property rights. Considering the factors that lay behind the rise of these new business interests, the chapter argues that although business acumen was important, a company's political background was crucial because it offered both protection and opportunities for rent-seeking and other less salubrious activities. Chapter 3 looks at the involvement of Ho Chi Minh City politicians in business, arguing that such behaviour has become more common since the late 1980s. Focusing on political appointments in the city, the chapter suggests that the growth of business interests at the lower levels has begun to undermine the long-standing Leninist principle of democratic centralism. It is also suggested that it is these same business interests which lie behind Ho Chi Minh City's fractured politics. Examining this further, Chapter 4 looks at patterns of institutional collaboration and conflict in the city, drawing on material generated by the officially sanctioned programmes of state enterprise and public administration reform. In Chapter 5, I turn my attention to the downfall of a number of once-favoured companies in two landmark court cases in the city during the second half of the 1990s. Rejecting the standard depiction of the cases as undifferentiated clampdowns on corruption, the chapter argues that they should rather be seen in the context of attempts by the centre to discipline the lower levels of the party-state in the context of growing decentralisation. Chapter 6 notes that the book offers a starkly different depiction of Ho Chi Minh City from the more traditional image of it as a bastion of reformism. Arguing that it is informal changes rather than formal policy reforms which have had the greatest influence on the direction change has taken during the 1980s and 1990s, the chapter concludes by questioning the usefulness of the concept of reform both as a description of what has happened in the city since 1975 and also as an explanation of change.

2 In business: the hollowing out of the state sector

Introduction

In Ho Chi Minh City there are companies controlled by central state institutions. There are companies run by the military and the police. There are companies which come under the jurisdiction of local (i.e. city) state institutions. There are companies with foreign capital and there are also companies owned by private capital, including local Chinese capital. In this chapter, the focus is on the rise of companies linked to city party and government institutions, notably the city-level departments (*so*) and the districts (*quan*).[1] Over the course of the 1990s, some of these have developed into quite substantial business groups. These include companies and banks affiliated to firms such as Saigon Jewellery Company, Saigon Tourist and Phu Nhuan Jewellery Company. Others such as the Tan Binh Import–Export Company (Tamexco) and the District 3 Seafood Production Import–Export company (Epco) achieved prominence for a period, only to fall from grace later.[2] However, the rise of business interests connected to city institutions during the 1990s goes beyond these big names. In a business environment where there are distinct disadvantages associated with being prominent, many more companies have achieved substantial profits while remaining outwardly small and keeping a low profile. It is the emergence of these business interests – and the factors that lie behind their success – that form the subject of this chapter.[3]

While companies in Vietnam are routinely referred to as being 'state' or 'private', the chapter emphasises the importance of getting behind these labels. As we shall see, companies described as being 'private' often have state institutions among their shareholders while 'state' companies can in fact be found to be operating rather 'privately'. These issues can usefully be addressed in a discussion of property rights, which forms an important part of this chapter. However, we also return to the subject of property rights in Chapter 6.

Ho Chi Minh City's political economy in the second half of the 1990s

Officially published data, not surprisingly, offers few clues as to the nature of the property regime prevailing in Ho Chi Minh City in the second half of the

1990s. However, it provides a useful starting point for our analysis. Government statistics distinguish between four types of corporate management: central state, local state, non-state, and foreign. The latter includes 100 per cent foreign-owned companies and joint ventures between domestic and foreign firms. During the 1990s, joint ventures almost uniformly involved state companies.[4] In terms of a company's central or local state label, this refers to whether a company's controlling institution (*co quan chu quan*) is a central or a local institution, such as in Ho Chi Minh City's case a city institution.[5]

According to the official data (see Appendix Table A2.1), companies under state management contributed 46.5 per cent to Ho Chi Minh City's gross domestic product (GDP) in 1998. Central state companies were responsible for 27.7 per cent of the city's total output. Local state firms were responsible for a rather small 18.8 per cent. The non-state sector and the foreign-invested sector contributed 36.4 per cent and 17.0 per cent to the city's total GDP respectively. In the period 1994–8, the biggest change was an increase in the penetration of foreign capital. It more than doubled its share of GDP during this period. The consequent fall in the domestic share of GDP was spread fairly equally between companies under central and local state management and the non-state sector. In terms of industrial output, the pattern is similar (see Appendix Table A2.2). The foreign-invested sector's share of Ho Chi Minh City's total industrial output rose sharply during 1994–8. The other sectors have seen their share of industrial output in the city fall, although here the decline has been greater for the state sector than the non-state sector.[6]

What is understood by the term 'the non-state sector' merits some explanation. For example, it is sometimes used interchangeably with 'the private sector'. However, the non-state sector includes cooperative firms (*hop tac xa*), joint stock (*co phan*), limited liability (*trach nhiem huu han*) and private (*tu nhan*) firms, as well as family businesses (*doanh nghiep ca the*). The official data does not provide a breakdown of the non-state sector by type of enterprise in terms of share of GDP or industrial output. However, it does provide a breakdown in terms of the number of industrial enterprises and the total size of labour force for each category (see Appendix Tables A2.3 and A2.4). On this basis, it is evident that numerically the non-state sector in Ho Chi Minh City is dominated by family firms, of which there were 23,028 in 1998. Moreover, family firms employed some 60 per cent of the non-state sector labour force. By contrast, there were just 704 joint stock, limited liability and private firms in the same year, employing 38 per cent of the non-state labour force. Cooperatives numbered just 71 and employed less than 2 per cent of the labour force. It would therefore seem reasonable to assume that the larger share of non-state sector output comes from family firms rather than from joint stock, limited liability and private firms, although the necessary data is lacking to say this conclusively.

Such an interpretation is borne out if we look at the commanding heights of Ho Chi Minh City's economy. Taking the top 100 companies and banks in the city selected according to size of turnover in 1995, the non-state sector

18 *Changing political economy of Vietnam*

Table 2.1 Top 100 companies and banks in Ho Chi Minh City by turnover in 1995: type of ownership (%)

Companies	
Central state	40
Local state	26
Foreign joint venture	17
Limited liability (without local Chinese capital)	2
Limited liability (with local Chinese capital)	3
Banks	
Central state	0
Local state	9
Foreign joint venture	2
Local Chinese	1

Sources: *Chan Dung Nhung Doanh Nghiep Thanh Dat* [A Portrait of Business on the March], *Nha Xuat Ban Thanh Pho Ho Chi Minh* [Ho Chi Minh City Publishing House], Saigon Times Group, VAPEC, 1997; *Danh Muc Co Quan Xi Nghiep Tai Thanh Pho Ho Chi Minh* [List of Commercial Organisations in Ho Chi Minh City], *Cuc Thong Ke Thanh Pho Ho Chi Minh* [Ho Chi Minh City Statistical Office], 1 January 1996. While central state companies have been included in the top 100, the four state-owned banks have been excluded (hence the '0' for central state banks). However, this is rather misleading because their Ho Chi Minh City branches are significant members of the city business community in every respect, including turnover.

does not feature very prominently at all. (For summary see Table 2.1 above; for a complete list of Ho Chi Minh City's top 100 companies by type of management see Appendix Table A2.5.) There are no joint stock companies or private firms and just five limited liability firms: Minh Phung, Bitis, Tribeco, Epco, and Huy Hoang, which ranked 8, 66, 67, 68 and 78 respectively in the top 100. Limited companies are often viewed as representative of Vietnam's emerging 'private sector'. However, two of these firms (Tribeco and Epco) had state institutions among their shareholders while one (Huy Hoang) was headed by a former government official whose wife continued to be employed in the state sector.[7] Minh Phung, Bitis and Epco all had local ethnic Chinese links.[8] There were ten joint stock commercial banks among the top 100 but all but one were dominated by city state institutions. The exception was Viet Hoa Bank, which was controlled by local Chinese capital.[9]

The heavy presence in Ho Chi Minh City of companies controlled by central state institutions also comes across strongly from an analysis of the top 100 businesses, with 40 under the jurisdiction of central institutions. Centrally managed companies are typically controlled by government ministries. The industry and trade ministries are particularly well represented among the top 100.[10] Companies controlled by local state institutions in the top 100 numbered 26 while those listed as joint ventures account for 17 of the total.

If we look at just the top 50 companies, this pattern is reinforced. Among the top 50, there is only one limited liability firm. Centrally managed firms account for a substantial 28 of the top 50 while local state firms number 16, along with one bank controlled by local state business interests. Absent from the above analysis are companies controlled by the military and police. This is because details of their activities are not routinely published, either as part of the official statistics or elsewhere. However, no one would dispute that they were an important feature of Ho Chi Minh City's political economy in the 1990s.[11]

I shall now look more closely at companies controlled by local state business interests, including detailing their institutional affiliations and the sectors in which they have operated. Where appropriate I shall illustrate my argument with reference to companies that feature in the top 100.

New business opportunities with reform

Business interests associated with local party and government institutions have operated both as state and private companies during the 1990s. This underlines the fact that the terms 'state' and 'private' are simply labels under which different types of capital can choose to operate depending on circumstances. State companies linked to the departments and the districts were established throughout the 1980s. However, there was a surge in such companies being formed in the late 1980s. These include Saigon Jewellery Company and Phu Nhuan Jewellery Company, which were founded in 1988, and Tamexco, which was established in 1989.[12] Saigon Jewellery Company ranks 11 among the top 100. Other companies that were formed in the late 1980s and have since risen to prominence in Ho Chi Minh City include companies such as Eden Trading and Service Company, Ben Thanh Tourist and the First District Import Export and Service Company (Fimexco).[13] However, in terms of turnover, these firms are quite small and hence do not feature in the top 100.

Some state companies operated by the departments or district that have flourished in the 1990s were established as far back as 1975. One such firm is Saigon Tourist, which ranks 17 in the top 100. It took charge of a large number of Ho Chi Minh City's hotels and restaurants soon after liberation.[14] Another is Tan Binh Housing and Development Company, which was founded in 1976. It ranks 90 in the city in terms of turnover.[15] However, not all companies from this earlier period have successfully made the transition to the reform era. In fact, even companies formed earlier in the 1980s sometimes seemed to have lost their way by the second half of the 1990s.[16]

In Ho Chi Minh City, there is scarcely a city department or a district that does not have companies under its jurisdiction. This is normal and there is nothing illicit *per se* about the moves by such institutions to establish companies from the late 1980s. Departments with sizeable complements of companies include the Industry Department (*so cong nghiep*), the Cadastral, Land and Housing Department (*so dia chinh-nha dat*), the Public Transport Department (*so giao thong cong chanh*), the Construction Department (*so xay dung*) and the Trade Department (*so thuong mai*).[17] Saigon Jewellery

20 *Changing political economy of Vietnam*

Company and Eden Service and Trading Company both originated as companies under the Trade Department. Another Trade Department company is the International Beverage Company, which ranks 25 in the top 100. However, even the Health Department (*so y te*) and the Culture and Information Department (*so van hoa thong tin*) have companies under their control.[18]

Companies controlled by the districts sometimes appear more aligned to the district Party Committee and sometimes to the People's Committee. Saigon Tourist, for example, is associated with interests at the People's Committee in District One.[19] By contrast, Tamexco, which will be discussed in more detail in Chapter 5, is associated with party interests in Tan Binh district.[20] Other party companies include Saigon Petro, which ranks 90 in the top 100, and Phu Nhuan Jewellery Company.[21] In early 1999, there were a total of 33 companies that came under the authority of the city party.[22]

Local state business interests have also operated under a private label, usually as limited liability companies (*cong ty trach nhiem huu han*) (see Table 2.2 below). Of the limited companies that emerged most prominently during the 1990s, most were formed early in the decade. This is slightly later than their state counterparts such as Saigon Jewellery Company and Tamexco, formed at the end of the 1980s. However, this reflects the fact that hostility towards the private sector was such that it was not until the early 1990s that investors – even state business interests – felt it safe to contemplate forming a private company.[23] A good example is Epco, which we earlier noted ranks 68 in the top 100. It was founded in 1991. Epco will be discussed more in Chapter 5 but suffice it to say at this stage that among its shareholders were business interests connected to the District 3 People's Committee.[24] Tribeco, which we earlier noted as ranking 67 in the top 100, has Trade Department and District 1 companies (Saigon Jewellery Company, Saigon Finance

Table 2.2 Ho Chi Minh City's top five limited liability companies by turnover in 1995: institutional and/or personal affiliations

1 Minh Phung	Tang Minh Phung (local ethnic Chinese) and his wife Tran Thi Thuong (former traffic policewoman)
2 Tribeco	Local state interests (Saigon Finance Company; Saigon Jewellery Company; Saigon Tourist; Pham Hong Chuong)
3 Epco	Local state interests (District 3 People's Committee); Lien Khui Thin and Tang Minh Phung (both local ethnic Chinese)
4 Bitis	Local ethnic Chinese; Vu Khai Thanh
5 Huy Hoang	Le Van Kiem, former government official; wife deputy director of Trade Ministry company

Sources: *Chan Dung Nhung Doanh Nghiep Thanh Dat* [A Portrait of Business on the March], *Nha Xuat Ban Thanh Pho Ho Chi Minh* [Ho Chi Minh City Publishing House], Saigon Times Group, VAPEC, 1997; *Danh Muc Co Quan Xi Nghiep Tai Thanh Pho Ho Chi Minh* [List of Commercial Organisations in Ho Chi Minh City], *Cuc Thong Ke Thanh Pho Ho Chi Minh* [Ho Chi Minh City Statistical Office], 1 January 1996; interview 20 September 2000.

Company and Saigon Tourist) as its principal shareholders.[25] The limited liability company Huy Hoang, which ranks 78, was set up in 1990 by a former government official, Le Van Kiem, who came south in 1975.[26] Minh Phung, which at 8 is the highest-ranked limited company, was formed a few years later in 1993. It is commonly regarded as more genuinely 'private', although the wife of its founder, Tang Minh Phung, was a former traffic policewoman. Like Huy Hoang it expanded rapidly, although also like Tamexco and Epco it later fell from grace. Minh Phung will be discussed in more detail in Chapter 5.

As can be seen, private companies have been established by both serving and former officials. During the 1990s it was difficult to point to a law that unequivocally forbade serving officials from setting up private businesses. Party statutes state that party members cannot engage in exploitation (*khong bot lot*). However, this was so vague that it did not have a noticeable impact on behaviour.[27] Moreover, the practice of serving officials forming private companies often registered in the name of their wives or other family members has been so prevalent that any attempt to enforce a ban would have been bound to fail.[28]

High growth sectors

Companies associated with local state business interests have tended to operate in a well-defined set of areas. Sectors that occur with repeated regularity among the corporate success stories of the 1990s in Ho Chi Minh City include real estate, foreign trade, banking and finance, gold, retail trade, distribution, hotels, tourism, and entertainment. Some firms have also operated in light industry, notably textiles and garments, food processing and construction. The sectors in which these companies are concentrated have all seen rapid growth during the 1990s and as a result the potential for profits has been high.[29] They are also areas where reforms have created new opportunities that did not exist under central planning, such as in foreign trade, banking and real estate development.

The emergence of the land market

After 1975 the land and property market did not disappear but it declined and went underground. In the late 1980s this began to change.[30] The emergence of the land market in Ho Chi Minh City from the early 1990s was one of the most dramatic developments of the decade, resulting in soaring land and property prices amid a surge in both foreign-invested property development and domestic house-building. Many investors reaped high rewards, although not a few ran up spectacular debts as well. A staggering 43 per cent of all housing built in Ho Chi Minh City during 1975–99 occurred in 1991–5.[31] This activity was accompanied by a proliferation of housing and land companies, many of which were formed by business interests associated with the departments and districts. Indeed, there was hardly a department or a district in Ho

Chi Minh City which did not either form such a company or have companies operating in this area.[32] Furthermore, many of the companies controlled by local state business interests and which rose to prominence in the 1990s can be seen actively participating in this area. One such firm, Fosco or the Foreign Services Company, which originated under the auspices of the Youth Volunteer Force (*luc luong thanh nien xung phong*), profited by offering real estate services to foreigners. Fosco ranks 36 in the top 100 companies in Ho Chi Minh City.[33] Other firms that have been prominent in the property market include Huy Hoang, although it began life in the textiles and garments sector, and Eden Service and Trading Company. They have been involved in building luxury apartments in District 2. Phu Nhuan Jewellery Company has built villas in An Phu.[34] A number of companies, such as Saigon Tourist, Saigon Jewellery Company and Fimexco, successfully linked up with foreign property developers operating in the city. Saigon Jewellery Company was the leading local investor in the Diamond Plaza building on Le Duan street, for example, while Fimexco had a stake in the Sun Wah Tower on Nguyen Hue.[35] Both are prime commercial sites in the centre of Ho Chi Minh City.

The formation of banks

Reform also resulted in new business opportunities in banking and finance. The late 1980s saw the country begin its shift from the monobank system that had existed under central planning to a two-tier banking system.[36] This included the establishment of new joint-stock, shareholding commercial banks, a large proportion of which were formed in Ho Chi Minh City. Of the 50 or so joint stock banks formed nationwide in the late 1980s and in the 1990s, 20 either had their headquarters in the city or conducted a large proportion of their business there. The peak of new bank formations was reached in 1992–4 when no less than 14 new banks were established in the city.

Local state business interests, notably those connected to the departments and the districts, have been at the forefront of this activity (for information on the shareholding structure and personnel influences at Ho Chi Minh City's joint stock banks see Appendix A2.6). Saigon Jewellery Company has shares in three banks (Exim Bank, Asia Commercial Bank and Danang Bank) and a finance company (Saigon Finance Company).[37] Huy Hoang has a leading stake in VP Bank and Asia-Pacific Bank and is also a shareholder in Exim Bank.[38] Saigon Tourist is a leading shareholder in Oricom Bank along with Ben Thanh Tourist and Fimexco. It also has a stake in Saigon Bank for Industry and Commerce.[39] Phu Nhuan Jewellery Company has the dominant stake in East Asia Bank.[40]

Foreign and domestic trade

The shift to the 'open door' policy in foreign trade provided the opportunity for Ho Chi Minh City once again to exploit its comparative advantage as a regional trading hub. Strikingly, while the number of local state companies operating in the industrial sector fell during the 1990s, the number of local state trading companies increased sharply.[41] Companies controlled by the departments and the districts have been especially active in the foreign trade sector. Rather like the ubiquitous housing and land companies referred to earlier, general trading firms controlled by the departments and the districts are also very common. A particularly large one is the Trade Department's Sagimexco – or the Saigon General Trading and Import–Export Company – which ranks 13 in the top 100. Tamexco and Epco were also active in import–export.[42]

Other companies have tapped into Ho Chi Minh City's nationally preeminent position as a consumer market, engaging in retail trade and distribution. The rise of gold and jewellery companies such as Saigon Jewellery Company and Phu Nhuan Jewellery Company reflect the increase in disposable incomes in the city during the 1990s. With mistrust in the formal financial sector running high, gold has long been a popular way of saving.[43] Moreover, it was only in 1994 that the right of organisations and individuals to own gold was formally recognised in legislation.[44]

Saigon Jewellery Company has also engaged in retail trade. In 1991 one of Saigon Jewellery Company's subsidiaries, the International Trading Centre, purchased the Intershop on Nam Ky Khoi Nghia in District 1 from the bankrupt state firm Cosevina.[45] It has since turned it into a flourishing general store selling everything from groceries to electrical goods.[46] In addition to its construction and real estate interests, the District 1 company, Fimexco, also has interests in the retail business, with products as diverse as embroidered linen, babyware and videos for rent.[47] Motorbike and vehicle distribution has been another common business activity for local state companies in the 1990s. Phu Nhuan Jewellery Company is the distributor for Honda while Saigon Tourist performs a similar function for Ford.[48]

Tourism and entertainment

The 1990s also saw rapid growth in the tourism industry, notably foreign tourism.[49] Business interests in Ho Chi Minh City associated with the departments and districts have played a prominent part in exploiting this expansion. By far the dominant player in the sector is Saigon Tourist. While other companies have targeted budget or middle-range tourists, it has cornered the higher end of the market. Moreover, Saigon Tourist's position in the hotel sector is second to none. Nationwide it runs 53 hotels and 41 restaurants. Many of Ho Chi Minh City's most historic hotels, such as the Rex, the Continental and the Majestic, belong to Saigon Tourist.[50] Other companies with interests in tourism are Ben Thanh Tourist, Eden Service and Trading Company, and to a lesser extent Phu Nhuan Jewellery Company. However, none of them remotely rival Saigon Tourist. The 1990s have also seen a rise in night clubs and other entertainment outlets in Ho Chi Minh

24 *Changing political economy of Vietnam*

City. Many of the same companies that have prospered in the tourism sector have a stake in this area too.

The emergence of diversified business corporations

By the mid-1990s, some of the companies profiled in this chapter sat at the head of quite substantial business groups.[51] While most of the companies established by the city-level departments and districts had a core business, they generally diversified into a wide range of other areas, often with a bias towards services (see Table 2.3). Many also had sizeable stakes in banking. They were not large by international standards. Indeed, with the exception of firms such as Saigon Jewellery Company or Saigon Tourist, most were small even by the standards of centrally managed companies in Ho Chi Minh City. However, given that many did not exist little more than a decade previously, their rise is nevertheless striking.

Of companies linked to the departments and districts, Saigon Jewellery Company was arguably the most noteworthy. In 1995, just seven years after it was founded, it had emerged as number 11 in Ho Chi Minh City in terms of turnover. Compared with other companies controlled by local state business interests it was the largest.[52] During 1989–96 the company's turnover increased by an average of 43 per cent annually.[53] It was not only the dominant player in the gold industry in Ho Chi Minh City but also nationwide. Saigon Jewellery's gold taels, which have a distinctive dragon emblem, are considered the industry standard.[54] Moreover, as Table 2.3 indicates, it had diversified into a wide range of other areas. Other companies formed at the same time as Saigon Jewellery Company recorded similar or even faster growth during the 1990s. Phu Nhuan Jewellery Company, for example, averaged 67 per cent annual turnover growth during 1988–94.[55] It too had business interests in a wide range of areas (see Table 2.3).

Changing property rights

That companies such as Saigon Tourist and Saigon Jewellery Company, or even Epco and Tamexco for a period, have been successful is not unconnected with how they have been managed.[56] This in turn has to do with changes in property rights. Drawing on the work of Jean Oi and Andrew Walder, property rights are understood here in terms of Harold Demsetz's notion of property as a 'bundle of rights'. These are subdivided into three kinds of rights – control, income, and transfer – while there is also recognition that there are a variety of ways such rights might be enforced, ranging from formal law to social custom.[57] In terms of control, the rights refer to managerial control, including such things as major decisions about production and investment, and day-to-day operational decisions. In terms of income, they concern who claims a share of the income generated by a business or an asset. This potentially ranges from state interests outside of a firm to interests associated with the firm (possibly its management) to its employees. In terms of transfer, the interest is in who has the right to assign ownership to other parties.[58]

In terms of formally sanctioned property arrangements, scholars writing on China have identified five types of ownership arrangements. These range from traditional state ownership, where the autonomy of the enterprise is severely limited (government officials decide what an enterprise should produce and whom to sell it to: they arrange all financing and appropriate all profits or make up all losses), to the reformed state enterprise (where there is a partial reassignment of control and income rights to the company), through to the contracted public asset, the leased public asset and finally the fully privatised firm in which the government has no effective ownership rights, although it may make demands on it through regulation and taxation.[59] In Vietnam's case, including Ho Chi Minh City, the dominant formal arrangement has been the reformed state enterprise. This goes back to enterprise reforms introduced as early as 1979 and added to during the 1980s and 1990s. Under these arrangements, companies were given greater responsibility for production decisions. They were also given new rights over income generated by the enterprise, which enabled a firm to keep a percentage of the profits over and above that which had to be remitted to the government, including in the form of taxation. The underlying logic of these changes was that these new incentives would propel companies to perform better.[60]

However, while formal reforms have not gone much further than this, property arrangements have continued to evolve informally.[61] In Ho Chi Minh City, two forms seem to be most common. First, there is local elite privatisation, whereby those running state enterprises gradually, by stealth, assume greater control over company assets, with the result that they eventually exercise a much fuller set of rights than is consistent with the property regime pertaining to the reformed state enterprise. This includes far greater control over production and investment decisions, increased claims over income flows and even the decision to transfer ownership to other parties. That state enterprises have been informally sold off in this way was vividly illustrated during an investigation into a large-scale smuggling ring in Ho Chi Minh City in 1998, when it became clear that the limited liability company, Tan Truong Sanh, which had masterminded the smuggling ring, was operating eight former party and police companies.[62] In addition, some of the conflicts that have emerged in relation to the equitisation programme have arisen, one suspects, precisely because those running state enterprises have become used to viewing them as their own assets and now see themselves effectively being asked to buy back what is already their own. As might be expected, such difficulties have often arisen in relation to the valuation of enterprise assets.[63] I contend that it is this property form, referred to as local elite privatisation, which best captures the dominant property arrangements obtaining in the companies controlled by local state institutions, that have been profiled in this chapter.

Table 2.3 Four diversified business corporations in Ho Chi Minh City in the late 1990s

	Year founded	Type of management	Controlling institution	Personal affiliation	Core business	Subsidiary of affiliated companies	Affiliated banks
Saigon Tourist	1975	Local state	District 1 People's Committee	Director Do Van Hoang	Hotels and tourism	Heads the Saigon Tourist General Corporation incorporating 15 hotels, 7 companies, 4 restaurants/resorts and 5 independent financial businesses (including Eden Trading and Service Company); shareholder in limited company Tribeco; distributor for Ford	Oricom Bank; Saigon Bank for Industry and Commerce
Saigon Jewellery Corporation	1988	Local state	Member of Trade Department dominated Saigon Trading Corporation until 1998 when brought under city People's Committee umbrella	Director Nguyen Huu Dinh	Gold and jewellery retailing	Saigon Finance Company; Foodexco, includes the International Beverage Company; International Trading Centre, includes Intershop; shareholder in limited company Tribeco	Exim Bank; Asia Commercial Bank, Danang Bank

Phu Nhuan Jewellery Company	1988	Local state	Financial Management Department, city party committee	Director Cao Thi Ngoc Dung; Ngo Dinh Ngon, part founder	Gold and jewellery retailing	Phu Nhuan Construction & Housing Business Company; Tourism Service Company; Machine Export General Trading Company; distributor for Honda	East Asia Bank: took over Long Xuyen Bank in 1999
Huy Hoang	1990	Limited liability	n/a	Founder and director Le Van Kiem (former government official)	Textiles and garment manufacturing	Real estate and construction; KIA Huy Hoang Ceramic Tiles	VP Bank, Asia-Pacific Bank

Sources: *Thoi bao Kinh te Saigon* 5–11 May 1994; *Saigon Times Weekly* 12 June 1999; *Saigon Times Daily* 8 February 1999; *Vietnam Investment Review* 15–21 September 1997.

Second, there is the siphoning off of public funds or assets into newly established enterprises, which operate as private firms. The limited liability company Epco, established in part with a capital contribution from the People's Committee in Ho Chi Minh City's District 3, provides a good example of this. Another example is Tribeco, which has Saigon Jewellery Company, Saigon Finance Company and Saigon Tourist as shareholders. However, it is widely acknowledged in Vietnam that the establishment of private companies by state business interests is commonplace. Indeed, this is a scenario that potentially applies to any number of Ho Chi Minh City's 700 or so limited liability, joint stock and private firms, although by no means all of them will fit this category. Similar patterns have been identified in research on China, where these two property forms, local elite privatisation and the siphoning off of public funds or assets into private firms, have been referred to as the 'hollowing out of public ownership'.[64]

New management

While anti-competitive practices remained an everyday feature of the business environment in Ho Chi Minh City in the 1990s, adjustments in the property rights regime have injected a degree of competition, leading to changes in the way these companies are managed.[65] This can be seen in the glossy marketing brochures and annual reports that are now routinely produced by firms like Saigon Jewellery Company or Saigon Tourist in order to woo customers and investors. The new environment has also precipitated greater responsiveness to the market and a more dynamic approach to management. An article on the city party firm, Phu Nhuan Jewellery Company, although clearly a selective account, captures the nature of the changes well. Asking what is the secret of Phu Nhuan Jewellery Company's success, the article describes how the company began producing jewellery itself in 1993 when it judged the market to be ready: 'the standard of living of the people in the city had improved and little by little the government's policy of *doi moi* was having an effect'.[66] To ensure the quality of its products, the company imported machinery from abroad and sent its workers, many of whom were former soldiers (*bo doi*), overseas to study. Moreover, the language Phu Nhuan Jewellery Company used to describe its activity is thoroughly 'modem management'. It consciously rejects the ideological inducements offered to workers under planning in favour of material incentives or rewards (*don bay kinh te*).[67] In sum, it is all a far cry from the traditional view of an ailing state company.

Bureaucratic and political background

However, while the managers of companies such as Phu Nhuan Jewellery Company and Saigon Tourist have run real businesses and produced real products or services, better management or knowledge of their market are not the only reasons for their success. They are probably not even the most important reasons. In the 1990s being successful in business owed a great deal to a company's bureaucratic and political background. Some of this had to do with the superior initial resources endowment enjoyed by these companies (e.g. possession of property or land). However, it is also the case that a company's bureaucratic background carried with it certain additional benefits, such as political protection and easier access to licences, contracts and capital. Access to such benefits was no guarantee of success, as the experiences of companies like Tamexco and Epco illustrate. However, without them, a company's prospects for expansion were undoubtedly limited.

I shall now look at five different areas that have a bearing on business success. They are protection, licences, contracts, capital, and land.

Protection

In the 1990s, being well-connected to a department or a district offered a company at least a degree of political protection in an environment where business success could quickly result in jealousy or finger-pointing. For a more vulnerable company, this could very easily be the excuse for a punitive investigation by the police or tax department.[68] However, such bodies were inclined to tread more carefully if a company was believed to be associated with a powerful politician.[69] Companies involved in running night clubs and other forms of entertainment, including massage or hostess bars and prostitution, particularly need to be well-connected because given the nature of their business they are common targets for police raids on the grounds of stamping out 'social evils'.[70] As we have seen, companies such as Saigon Tourist, Ben Thanh Tourist and Eden Service and Trading Company have been prominent players in the entertainment business, as have military business interests.

A central umbrella (*o du*) is generally regarded as providing more protection than a local one, even in Ho Chi Minh City, so a city company that can boast good central connections – perhaps through the promotion to a central post of one of its own – has most guarantee of being able to operate without let or hindrance. During the 1990s, companies linked to the Department of Trade seemed potentially well-qualified in this respect.[71] Private companies have tended to be regarded as more vulnerable to the unwanted attention of investigating bodies than state companies. However, a limited liability company linked to state business interests is likely to be as well-placed as any to head off a potential investigation. During the 1990s, Huy Hoang avoided the fate of other large limited companies despite the fact that the knives were obviously out for it on a number of occasions. One source suggested that as a potential investigation was brewing Ministry of Commerce officials stopped it in its tracks by saying that Huy Hoang's director, Le Van Kiem, was 'their cadre'.[72]

Licences

Doing business in Ho Chi Minh City during the 1990s required the obtaining of a large number of licences covering every aspect of the business process.[73] Moreover, on account of the licensing system many sectors were effectively closed to new entrants. For instance, until 1998 only state companies were allowed to engage in direct foreign trade – a fact which clearly limited the competition faced by companies such as Tamexco. Non-state companies wishing to trade were normally required to use a state company as an intermediary. However, politically well-connected non-state companies could get round such restrictions. Epco's prominence in the import–export sector, for example, shows that it had no difficulty in this respect despite the fact it was a limited liability company.

Establishing a bank or obtaining a licence to trade in foreign exchange depended on a similar ability to negotiate the bureaucratic maze. As the prominence of companies linked to local state business interests in the banking sector testifies, this was clearly an area where these companies have excelled. Barriers to entry also existed in the gold industry which, as we have seen, is another sector where local state business interests operated very successfully in the 1990s. Saigon Jewellery Company and Phu Nhuan Jewellery Company were two of just six companies in the city permitted to issue gold taels.[74]

Contracts

Having gained the necessary licences to do business, the ability to secure contracts was also crucial. Once again, a company's bureaucratic and political background played an important part. This was particularly the case with the city-level departments, which as well as having companies under their control also had regulatory responsibilities (e.g. the Construction Department had regulatory responsibilities in the construction sector in Ho Chi Minh City, the Industry Department in industry, etc.). Given these responsibilities, the departments were frequently in receipt of information pertaining to forthcoming projects, which they were then able to channel to 'their' companies. Moreover, because of the close nature of the ties between the departments and business, there was often very little to distinguish between those with knowledge of a contract and the business interests interested in obtaining it. It is this pattern of interests that has prompted one scholar writing on China to talk in terms of a 'single-blended class' of business and cadredom.[75]

During the 1990s this method of obtaining contracts was also a key *modus operandi* for limited liability companies linked to state business interests. A limited company founded by serving or former officials could thus legally benefit from the full range of property rights pertaining to the fact that it was registered as a private company while being fed contracts by its well-connected owners. Epco benefited in this way through its links to District 3 People's Committee. Another example is Huy Hoang. While its founder, Le

Van Kiem, had left government office, his wife continued to hold a position at a centrally managed trading company with an office in Ho Chi Minh City. This is widely believed to be the source of contracts – and subsequent business success – for Huy Hoang.[76]

Capital

Access to capital is clearly the lifeblood of any business. The companies that flourished in the 1990s have not surprisingly therefore shown themselves very adept at mobilising capital, notably bank credit. A company's bureaucratic and political background does not provide a cast iron guarantee of access to capital, because there are examples of seemingly well-connected companies struggling in this respect. Nevertheless, it is difficult to imagine companies such as Saigon Jewellery Company, Phu Nhuan Jewellery Company and Saigon Tourist being so successful at mobilising capital if they were not so closely associated with business interests in the departments and districts.[77]

During the 1990s access to budget subsidies was much more restricted than in the previous decade.[78] However, access to credit via the state-dominated banking system was such that the credit constraint tended to remain soft during this period.[79] The political nature of the lending arrangements that prevailed during the 1990s can clearly be seen in relation to companies such as Tamexco and Epco.[80] Tamexco was able to continue obtaining credit from the state-owned Bank for Foreign Trade (Vietcombank) in Ho Chi Minh City even after it was clearly running up huge debts and in a way which overrode normal restrictions on bank lending. According to Vietcombank, it had no choice but to lend to Tamexco as a result of the intervention of various state institutions.[81] Moreover, it was not just state companies that were able to access capital in this way. Private companies controlled by state business interests or former officials have proved themselves just as adept at accessing bank credit. Epco, for example, had very good relations with Vietcombank and the state-owned Industrial and Commercial Bank (Incombank) from which it borrowed heavily.[82] These particular cases will be discussed in more detail in Chapter 5.

Furthermore, as we have seen, those companies in Ho Chi Minh City that have expanded rapidly in the 1990s were at the forefront of moves to establish banks. For companies that were shareholders in these banks, this offered an additional source of capital both for them and their subsidiaries. The holders of bank licences were usually also permitted to trade in foreign exchange, which, given frequent shortages of hard currency, notably dollars, could be particularly valuable.

Land

Like capital, access to land was a vital ingredient for doing business in Ho Chi Minh City during the 1990s. However, companies connected to state business interests were generally better endowed with land and property than others. This was often a legacy of the confiscation and redistribution of land and property that occurred in Ho Chi Minh City after 1975, much of which ended up in the hands of state business interests.[83] There was also a fresh round of land and property allocations in the early 1990s, in which state interests were again the main beneficiaries.[84] Saigon Tourist's rich land and property endowments date back to 1975. Substantial tracts of land were also allocated to the military and police at the end of the war. However, Huy Hoang also obtained significant land holdings despite the company's private status in the early 1990s.[85]

With the emergence of the land market during the 1990s, companies that had been allocated land or property or obtained it at low prices found themselves in possession of a rapidly appreciating asset. Moreover, given the way the property rights regime had evolved, companies were fairly free to sell or lease such assets as they saw fit, reaping healthy profits in the process. Companies in possession of land were also attractive propositions for foreign companies looking for a local joint-venture partner. Given the way land and property allocations have occurred since 1975 it is thus no coincidence that companies associated with the departments and the districts, such as Saigon Jewellery Company, Saigon Tourist and Fimexco, can be seen leading the way in link-ups with foreign real estate companies.

In addition, land and property offered an alternative way of obtaining bank credit in the 1990s because for the first time in a generation it could be mortgaged. In the mid-1990s, this reached such endemic proportions, notably in Ho Chi Minh City, that the central authorities, fearing the consequences for the banking sector if property prices were to fall, moved in February 1995 to impose restrictions, restricting the circumstances in which land could be mortgaged and requiring companies in possession of land to pay for using it. However, implementation was generally patchy and companies with good bureaucratic and political connections were on the whole far less affected than those that were less well-endowed. The imposition of restrictions on the land market in 1995 is discussed further in Chapter 4.

From speculation to smuggling

As we have seen, a company's bureaucratic and political position both conferred and was used to gain advantage in carrying out its mainstream business activities. However, the companies that have got ahead in Ho Chi Minh City in the 1990s also routinely engaged in other forms of activity, including taking kickbacks, profiteering, speculation, fraudulently obtaining bank credit, and smuggling. Some of this activity is sporadic and opportunistic (e.g. a traffic policeman pulling over a motorbike in order to extract a 'fine'). In such cases, the amount of money involved is generally small and simply ends up in the official's pocket. However, this kind of activity is often more institutionalised, with much larger amounts of money at stake. In cases such as this – revenue raised whether it is from kickbacks, profiteering or smuggling – is less likely to end up directly in the pocket of individual officials but rather tends to be regarded as 'institutional funds'.[86]

Taking kickbacks

The taking of kickbacks or other arbitrary fees occurs in the course of officials carrying out their normal bureaucratic duties. It most commonly involves demanding or accepting money for the issuing of licences or to ensure a less punitive tax assessment. Revenue is also raised through the sale of official forms or stamps even though they are not meant to incur any charge. Moreover, this kind of activity is not something that only occurs occasionally. It is the norm and examples come to light with persistent regularity. The introduction of a value-added tax (VAT) in January 1999 quickly led to the emergence in Ho Chi Minh City of a market in VAT invoices, concentrated in the stationery shops on Nguyen Hue and Le Loi streets and in Dan Sinh market in District 1. The demand for VAT invoices stemmed from the fact that companies were selling goods without having paid VAT at reduced prices compared with goods on which VAT had been paid. They were then 'legalising' their sale by buying an invoice on the black market. The market in VAT receipts existed at least in part because officials in the tax department were selling the receipts to interested parties, as this extract from *Sai Gon Giai Phong* newspaper makes clear:

> According to a number of tax officials, the receipts that are presently on the market are not exclusively forgeries. In reality, not a few receipts being sold on the market are the real thing issued by the Finance Ministry. How these receipts are coming to be sold on the market . . . is not difficult to understand.[87]

According to the article's author, the going rate for genuine VAT invoices was 3–5 million dong while forgeries were selling for 70–120,000 dong.[88] Another example of official documentation finding its way onto the market came to light following the introduction of a scheme to combat smuggling in November 1997. This saw three commonly smuggled products, namely wine and spirits, bicycles and electric fans, being stamped before they could legally be sold on the domestic market. However, the stamps were very quickly on sale on the streets of Ho Chi Minh City.[89]

Profiteering

Profiteering involved taking advantage of bureaucratic control over resources in short supply to secure a profit. While in the 1990s profiteering often involved commodities such as cement or fertiliser, it also frequently occurred in relation to foreign exchange, the price of which was administratively controlled throughout the decade.[90] Although banks were formally restricted as to the exchange rate they could charge, this was widely flouted. This was particularly the case at times of foreign exchange shortage, when it was common practice for bankers to sell dollars at the black market rate, taking the difference between the official and black market rates as profit:

> If an importer needs to buy $50,000, the formal sale price is $1:VND13,908 plus a transaction fee of 0.05%. However, in reality, businesses wishing to buy dollars do not pay this. Rather they must pay at a rate of $1:VND14,300 [the black market rate]. Thus, for a $50,000 transaction, businesses must pay the differential between the two rates, which comes out at VND19.6m ($1,400). This mount of money is paid in cash directly to the foreign exchange business personnel of the bank. Moreover, you don't get a receipt or sign any other sort of paper![91]

The buying and selling of dollars above the official rate was especially prevalent during the dollar shortage that followed the Asian economic crisis in 1997–8. Moreover, the finger was often pointed at the joint stock commercial banks in the city, many of which, as we have seen, were set up by business interests connected with the departments and the districts.[92] Banks frequently complained that they could not obtain dollars if they kept within the officially determined band.[93] Moreover, when foreign exchange controls were tightened in September 1998, requiring companies to sell 80 per cent of their surplus foreign exchange holdings to banks, many firms refused to do so unless they were offered an exchange rate higher than the formal one. Ironically most banks accepted this because they wanted the dollars.[94] However, there were also cases of prominent companies switching their accounts from less cooperative banks to more cooperative ones.[95]

Speculation

Speculation involved the buying and selling of commodities or other assets often in quick succession with the sole aim of making a profit. During the 1990s speculation involving land and foreign exchange was widespread. In the official media, those engaging in such activity are usually referred to simply as '*nguoi dau co*' (speculators). In conversation, people tended to refer to speculators in similarly anonymous terms such as a '*co*' (intermediary) or a '*dai gia*' (literally: rich and powerful person). Who these people really were remained concealed. Up to a point speculation was open to anyone. When a devaluation of the dong was widely anticipated, speculative activity became intense in Ho Chi Minh City as ordinary people sought to make a few hundred thousand dong by buying dollars on the black market. However, although anyone could engage in speculation, those best placed to do so were those with access to inside information regarding such things as the urban plan (*ke hoach do thi*) or the timing of a devaluation. As the following two examples illustrate, behind the anonymous label of 'speculator' very often stood state officials or their representatives.

Speculation in foreign exchange

As the fallout from the Asian economic crisis hit Vietnam in 1997–8, the dong was devalued three times. One such occasion occurred on 16 February 1998. That day, business began as usual with State Bank announcing the same exchange rate it had issued the day before. However, an hour or two after trading had begun, it announced a new official exchange rate, with the delay reputedly being designed to wrong foot the speculators. With the new rate announced, commercial banks reportedly stopped selling dollars but continued to buy. Meanwhile, the black market was silent (*yen ang*), as yet unaware of the official devaluation. Taking advantage of this, an unnamed speculator went to the black market with 130 million dong, which he exchanged into 10,000 US dollars at the old black market exchange rate of VND13,000:US$1. This money was then deposited in the bank and a further 9,000 US dollars were borrowed in dong using his deposit book as collateral. The 'speculator' then returned to the black market – which was still unaware of the morning's devaluation of the dong – and bought more dollars. This process continued for an additional third round until 12 noon. By this stage, news of the devaluation had filtered through to the black market, which became animated (*nhon nhao*) and the dollar price shot up. As an article in *Tuoi Tre* newspaper noted, not everyone is in a position to speculate in the way described:

> If you want to speculate like this person did, you need to have an edge on people in two ways: you need to get information before others and you need to be able to borrow money from the bank quickly in order to be able to shift your dong into dollars in your hand.[96]

With the timing of a devaluation naturally kept secret, the finger points clearly in the direction of banking sector personnel or people connected to them, such as family members or friends. Moreover, it is also the case that you would need to be a particularly special customer to be able to withdraw 130 million dong and borrow the dong equivalent of possibly as much as 18,000 US dollars on the basis of your deposit book, all in the course of a morning. This again suggests that the speculators came from within the banking sector or were closely connected to them.[97]

Land speculation

Rising land prices provided unprecedented opportunities for speculative activity during the 1990s. By the second half of the decade, the focus of the speculators had shifted more to outlying areas of Ho Chi Minh City, many of which were still semi-rural and where prices had yet to rise significantly. In 1998–9, the small island of Long Phuoc in District 9 was still experiencing what is popularly referred to as land fever (*sot dat*) both in anticipation of and following the construction of a bridge linking it to the mainland. The following extract captures well the speculative fever which frequently gripped the city during the 1990s:

> On the section of the road from the foot of Truong Phuoc bridge to the People's Committee of Long Phuoc quarter, a mass of new houses, cafes and bustling restaurants have sprung up. In particular, concrete posts have been planted on several plots of land adjacent to this road, marking them out, ready for sale to build houses. Every day, although Sunday is the most crowded, people from the urban areas of the city can be clearly seen pouring into Long Phuoc looking for 'land to buy' in order to put up a house with garden. . . . Nguyen Van Lon, a resident of Long Thuan hamlet, told us: 'In 1995 and 1996, the price of agricultural land adjacent to the principal roads cost only around 2–3 gold taels for 1,000 sq. m. However, once we had the bridge project, the price shot up to 10 taels. Now, it's not even certain that 30 taels would be enough'. Every time land changes hands, the price rises by about 7–10 gold taels per 1,000 sq. m.[98]

Given the covert way in which many land transactions occur, it is often very difficult to know who is buying land. However, the author of the article cited here eventually met two of the largest 'investors in the land business' in Long Phuoc. Although their precise identity was never revealed (their names were concealed), there is a strong hint that they got into the market early on the basis of inside knowledge and hence either were, or had close connections to, state officials.

> Going around, the old owners of the land (local people) told us they did not know who the new owners were because the land had changed hands so much. . . . Finally we were introduced to two of the largest investors in the land business in Long Phuoc, Mr Q of Long Thuan and Mr HN of Long Dai. These two men both had hundreds of hectares along the main road which they were holding on to, waiting for the land price to rise higher because they knew that this year two of the main roads are going to be tarmaced to connect up with Truong Phuoc bridge.[99]

The use of inside knowledge in this way to guide lucrative investments in the land market was commonplace in the 1990s. A significant proportion of the land acquisitions that occurred in the early 1990s were conducted by those privy to the drafting of the forthcoming 1993 Land Law who foresaw the impact that legalising the transfer of land use rights would have on prices.[100] Officials also commonly sold information about the urban plan if they did not want to use it themselves.[101] Moreover, there is circumstantial evidence suggesting that business interests associated with the departments and the districts behaved in this way. For example, when the central authorities moved to limit the scope for speculative land investment in 1995, it was noticeable that some of the most vocal critics of the policy were individuals directly associated with business interests in the Department of Trade.[102]

Fraudulently obtaining bank credit

During the 1990s companies commonly used deception or other sharp practices to secure bank credit. The fact that they were able to do this provides further illustration of the way credit constraints tended to be rather soft. Such practices included mortgaging assets that were in a company's possession but over which ownership was unclear or disputed; mortgaging the same asset more than once at different banks; and falsely inflating the value of land being used as collateral. The latter required an ability to persuade a notary official to certify the relevant documents. Another tactic involved companies using other firms to front for them in applying for credit. In this way a company could continue to borrow even after it had exceeded its credit limit or been blacklisted. A famous example of this involved Epco and Minh Phung, which is discussed in Chapter 5. However, a dispute between two joint stock commercial banks, Buildebank and Viet Hoa Bank, came to light in 1998 in which Viet Hoa Bank was alleged to have used three limited liability companies as a front to borrow money from Buildebank.[103] Credit was also obtained on the pretext of being needed for one particular purpose, such as for a letter of credit to pay for imports or for productive purposes, only to be used for another, such as real estate speculation.[104]

Smuggling

During the 1990s smuggling was widespread, and the smugglers included business interests connected to state institutions. Official accounts do not deny the involvement of party and state organisations in smuggling, as an editorial in *Nhan Dan* in 1997 illustrates:

> In order to bring in contraband, smugglers must turn to cheating, bribery or collusion with state officials. . . . Some enterprises of important state agencies also participate in smuggling or provide shelter to smugglers. . . . Anti-smuggling agencies have not coordinated closely together. . . . Some of their cadres have also protected or worked with smugglers. . . . All ministries, sectors and localities need to check on their subordinate import–export enterprises (including economic units of all party, mass organisations, public security forces, and the army) to ensure that all business activities are lawful. . . . It is unacceptable for anti-smuggling cadres to collaborate with smugglers.[105]

38 *Changing political economy of Vietnam*

However, while there is no blanket denial that party and state organisations participate in smuggling, official accounts strongly suggest that the cases that come to light are exceptional and prefer instead to place the emphasis on private business interests or individuals.[106] This is questionable not only because of the unrelenting way instances of official involvement in smuggling come to light but also because to engage in smuggling a company needs to be politically powerful or well-connected.[107] The example that follows provides powerful evidence to this effect in relation to the gold market.

Sourcing gold without import quotas: the need to smuggle

Given its foremost position as a major distribution centre and market, Ho Chi Minh City has long been a popular destination for smuggled goods.[108] Although a wide range of goods were smuggled in the 1990s, one that was smuggled with great persistency was gold. According to official estimates in 1997, around 40 tonnes of gold was smuggled into the city annually. At times of especially active gold smuggling, as much as 200–300 kg of gold was thought to enter the city each day.[109]

In the first half of the 1990s, gold imports were formally regulated by quotas issued by the State Bank to a limited number of companies authorised to import gold. However, the State Bank stopped issuing quotas in 1996, including to companies such as Saigon Jewellery Company and Phu Nhuan Jewellery Company.[110] Since this date no company has had the right to import gold: all gold entering the country on a commercial basis since 1996 has therefore been smuggled. Despite this, gold companies such as Saigon Jewellery Company and Phu Nhuan Jewellery Company have not seen gold supplies dry up, leading to the inevitable conclusion that they are at the very least tapping into smuggling networks. Moreover, such an interpretation is borne out in comments by industry officials:

> Nguyen Xuan Son, chairman of the management board of the Vietnam Gold, Silver and Gemstone General Corporation: 'In terms of unprocessed gold, the reality is that gold imports principally come from the informal route. According to business estimates, the volume of smuggled gold imports is rather large and clearly the main reason behind the strong demand for dollars'.[111]

> A senior official from the Vietnam Gold, Silver and Gemstone General Corporation ... admitted the company ... was being forced to buy gold from unknown sources. 'We have to buy gold in the domestic market to satisfy the needs of our customers and to maintain jobs for thousands of our employees', said the official, who refused to be named.[112]

> Nguyen Cong Tu, head of marketing at Saigon Jewellery Company, revealed that although the company has not got gold import quotas it was able to obtain 15 tonnes of gold for processing, which was about 50% of

what it imported in the previous year. We asked: When SJC obtained gold did it check its origin? Mr Tu said that SJC obtains gold for organisations and individuals across the country provided that they have permission to engage in the gold and silver business and that the gold . . . meets certain quality standards.[113]

Conclusion

This chapter has charted the rise during the 1990s of companies linked to local party and government institutions, notably the city-level departments and the districts. In particular, I have suggested that this has often involved a process referred to as the 'hollowing out of the state sector'. In little more than a decade, some of these companies have developed into quite substantial diversified business groups. Their interests are wide-ranging, although real estate, banking, and foreign and domestic trade have played an important part in most companies' business portfolios. However, the companies that rose to prominence during the 1990s have also been involved in a range of other activities including profiteering, speculation and smuggling. It is tempting to try to distinguish between 'productive' and 'rent-seeking' activity. Jane Duckett has characterised the state in China's Tianjin municipality as 'entrepreneurial', arguing that some companies founded by government departments are engaged in 'potentially productive activity', which she suggests is 'qualitatively different' from rent-seeking, corruption and speculation.[114] However, such a distinction appears difficult to sustain with reference to Ho Chi Minh City in the second half of the 1990s. Companies routinely engage in both types of activity. Moreover, it is a mistake to suggest that success in a company's 'productive' business activity is not dependent on its bureaucratic and political background. Whether it be gold and jewellery retailing, running a hotel, profiteering, speculation, or smuggling, such activities nearly always rely on a company's or individual's bureaucratic or political position to a greater or lesser extent. Sometimes the benefits that accrue can be rather indirect, such as being in possession of a large amount of property distributed many years earlier. On other occasions, it can involve a more direct exploitation of public position, such as channelling contracts to a favoured company or using inside knowledge to speculate. Furthermore, it is also difficult to distinguish between 'productive' and other forms of activity because very often the one seems to draw on the other. Thus, a company operating in the gold retail business after import quotas were stopped in 1996 had no choice but to rely on smuggled gold. Equally, a bank that provided routine banking services would also likely be involved in profiteering or speculation when the opportunity arose. Furthermore, it is inconceivable that profits derived from one type of activity would be kept separate from profits derived from another. In sum, therefore, what we are left with is a business culture where success and profits depend heavily on a company's bureaucratic and political background, whatever the area of activity.

3 Patterns of circulation: democratic centralism under strain

Introduction

Chapter 2 charted the rise of local state business interests since the late 1980s. Business success, I argued, was linked to changes in property rights combined with benefits derived from a company's political and bureaucratic position. In this chapter, I shift attention to the increasing involvement of politicians in business, looking in particular at the impact this trend has had on the appointments process.

In Communist countries, appointments have traditionally been governed by the principle of democratic centralism. This principle was first defined comprehensively at the Seventeenth Congress of the Communist Party of the Soviet Union in 1934 as follows: the election of all leading bodies in the party; their periodic accountability to their respective party organisations; strict party discipline and the subordination of the minority to the majority; and decisions of the higher bodies to be absolutely binding on lower bodies and on all party members. As can be seen from this definition, democratic centralism is as much a principle of state organisation as something that applies simply to the appointment process.[1] Lenin summed it up as 'freedom of discussion, unity of action'.[2] Nevertheless, it is widely accepted, including at various times by Communist parties themselves, that in practice the democratic element in the principle has tended to be ignored or paid lip-service only. In 1988, the Soviet leader, Mikhail Gorbachev argued that democratic centralism had been 'largely replaced by bureaucratic centralism', which entailed an 'excessive growth of the role played by the party apparatus at all levels' leading to 'power abuse and moral degeneration'.[3] From this critique – centred on excessive party dominance – emerged a call not just in the Soviet Union but in Communist parties around the world for political reforms whereby greater emphasis was to be given to the role of government and the rule of law even if at the same time the supremacy of the party was upheld.[4] While in Eastern Europe and the former Soviet Union this experiment was cut short by the collapse of Communist rule, elsewhere it has continued.

In Vietnam, reform may have seen the dismantling of the central plan, but democratic centralism remains in place, at least formally. In terms of the democratic component, this means that appointments to party and government positions are subject to a vote. In the case of party appointments, this is carried out by the Executive Committee (*Ban chap hang dang bo*) at the same level as that at which the appointment is taking place. Thus, for a party secretary at the provincial or city level, voting takes place at the provincial or city Executive Committee while for a district party secretary it is the district Executive Committee that votes. The same principle applies further down the hierarchy. In the case of People's Committee appointments, the appointment of the chairman and deputy chairmen is voted on by the People's Council, which is itself popularly elected.[5] As with party appointments, the People's Council also votes on People's Committee appointments at the same level. However, as we shall see, the vote is in reality just a formality, with the real decision being made elsewhere. Thus, in keeping with the critique cited above, the centralist element of the democratic centralism principle is more important, embodying the idea that decisions made by the higher level are binding. In the case of the appointment of a provincial or city party secretary, the decision is made at the central level. For a district party secretary, it is the city level that decides.

However, if this process – centred on the principle of democratic centralism – were working smoothly, we would expect the appointment process to be a straightforward and relatively uncontroversial matter. Furthermore, once appointed to a post, incumbents could be expected to be beholden to the level above – at least to a degree – which would be reflected in appropriately submissive behaviour. After all, it is the level above that appointed them and formally is empowered to dismiss them if they step too far out of line.[6]

In fact, in the case of Ho Chi Minh City in the second half of the 1990s, the reality was rather different. Of course, the outlines of democratic centralism could still be seen, notably in the official depiction of the appointments process. However, appointments were anything but straightforward in practice. Instead, what came across most strongly was the large number of institutions and offices potentially involved in making a single appointment, and a tendency for those officially responsible to consult widely before they committed themselves to a particular office holder. This went beyond what was formally required by a strict adherence to democratic centralism, suggesting that a greater variety of interests were being taken into account. Secondly, there was evidence of a greater tendency for appointments to be contested compared with the 1980s, and an associated unwillingness and inability on the part of the higher levels to impose their will. Moreover, the lower levels were anything but submissive. Indeed, if one maintains that democratic centralism still holds sway, it was profoundly puzzling how city-level departments in Ho Chi Minh City, which are headed by a director appointed by the city People's Committee chairman, so often appeared to be a law unto themselves, incapable of being galvanised into action by the chairman. Overall, then, there was a sense in which the principle of democratic centralism is coming under strain. A key question – and one that this chapter seeks to answer – is why.

One possible explanation is linked to the breakdown of the central plan and the growth of the market as outlined in Chapter 1. Under planning, the discipline inherent in the concept of democratic centralism was reinforced by the fact that the lower levels were dependent on the higher levels for the downward flow of financial and other resources. As the plan broke down and was replaced by the market as the principal means for allocating goods and services, the downward flow of resources became less important. Instead, local authorities increasingly developed their own resource bases. In Chapter 2, I charted moves by state institutions in Ho Chi Minh City to take advantage of new business opportunities afforded by reform from the late 1980s and 1990s. In particular, I noted the role played by the city-level departments and the districts in this process. Moreover, according to this interpretation based on the breakdown of the plan, it is not only that the lower levels are no longer so dependent on the higher levels in resource terms but also that their involvement in business and their emergent business interests impel them towards resisting outside interference and in particular any intervention which threatens these interests. With regard to the appointment process, being in a position to control or influence who gets appointed to which post, and especially who one's successor might be, is clearly crucial in terms of keeping business interests 'in the family' or maintaining access to resources associated with particular offices.

These issues have received little attention in the academic literature on Vietnam, although they have been addressed in writing on China. Looking at appointments made by the central party in China ('the central party nomenklatura') in 1990, John Burns argues that rather than it being a unilateral process, 'economic development and localism have given provincial leaders the resources to negotiate personnel changes with the Centre'. He also suggests that this reflects the fact that leaders at all levels need to build and maintain personal relations, which is not compatible with unilateral decision-making.[7] Although Burns' focus is on relations between the centre and the provinces, the idea that appointments which are formally the responsibility of the higher level may be subject to negotiation with the lower level would appear to have salience within the locale as well, including in Ho Chi Minh City. His ideas also offer a possible explanation why the higher levels often find it difficult to keep the lower levels in line. Burns' assertion regarding the importance of building and maintaining personal relations concurs with other research as well. A number of China scholars have drawn attention to the existence of clientelist networks at the local level.[8] Writing in 1989, Jean Oi noted that the presence of such networks has not always been recognised in the study of Communist countries:

> It has often been assumed that communist rule is impersonal, impartial, and effective. This was in part, no doubt, because of the influence of the totalitarian image of communist rule. Only recently have studies shown

that clientelism is not an aberration but an outgrowth of the communist system.[9]

Drawing on this literature, this chapter explores the extent to which it is possible to establish the existence and identify the structure of clientelist networks in Ho Chi Minh City held together by commercial interests. I then consider whether such interests can be seen to exercise influence on the appointment process in a way that is out of step with the old logic of democratic centralism. However, I first look at ways in which democratic centralism appears to be coming under strain, contrasting the official depiction of the appointments process with what is occurring beneath the surface.

Democratic centralism: the official picture

To judge from official announcements of appointment changes in the Vietnamese press it appears that very little has changed, for the language deployed is fully in keeping with democratic centralism. When Nguyen Minh Triet replaced Truong Tan Sang as party secretary in Ho Chi Minh City in 1999, that the decision had come from the Politburo in Hanoi could not have been made clearer. The party general secretary visited the city to convey the news:

> Party General Secretary Le Kha Phieu held a meeting with the Ho Chi Minh City Party Standing Committee on January 12 to convey two decisions made recently by the Party Central Committee Political Bureau. The first decision relates to the appointment of Nguyen Minh Triet . . . to the position of secretary of the Ho Chi Minh City Party Committee. . . . The second decision stipulates that Truong Tan Sang . . . will be relieved from the post of secretary of Ho Chi Minh City Party Committee.[10]

The role of the city party Standing Committee in Ho Chi Minh City can also clearly be seen in relation to district party appointments. This too is also fully in line with democratic centralism.[11] Moreover, in press reports and public utterances, lip service continues to be paid to the democratic element of the principle. When Truong Tan Sang and Vo Viet Thanh were made city People's Committee chairman in 1992 and 1996 respectively, both initially in an acting capacity, it was emphasised on each occasion that their appointment would be subject to a vote by the city People's Council in keeping with the law (*theo dung luat dinh*).[12] Party appointments in the city also continue to be subject to a vote by the same level of the party Executive Committee.[13]

Democratic centralism under strain

While the official depiction appears quite straightforward in reality it is more complex. This is partly because of the overlapping party/government jurisdiction under which the party as 'the force leading the State and society' (*luc luong lanh dao Nha nuoc va xa hoi*) is the senior institution with the dominant say in all appointments.[14] Thus, in the case of the city People's Committee chairman appointment it is the city party committee in consultation with the party at the centre that is instrumental in choosing the chairman. One source related how the city party committee gives a name to the People's Council even though in the official account it is the People's Council that is afforded the foremost role in the appointment of the People's Committee chairman.[15] Party oversight of government appointments is a feature throughout the political system.

The appointments process is also more complex because of the involvement of a greater number of organisations than is usually suggested. These include organisations like the Central Party Organisation Department (*ban to chuc trung uong dang*), the City Party Organisation Department (*ban to chuc thanh uy*) and the People's Committee Organisation Department (*ban to chuc chinh quyen*). Their role is to act as a central point where the names of candidates are put forward and subjected to preliminary vetting. Another organisation that has an input in the appointments process is the Economic Department (*Ban kinh te*) of the party, which exists at both the central and local level. At the local level its participation is mainly in relation to the appointment of directors of departments and important state business positions.[16]

However, the participation of these organisations in the appointments process is usually omitted from the official account. This partly reflects the tendency to downplay the party's oversight of the government in day-to-day public discourse. It also reflects the fact that it is at the level of these departments that disagreements may occur when multiple names are put forward for consideration. By the time an appointment is announced publicly, or subject to a vote by the party Executive Committee or the People's Council, the aim is to present a façade of unanimity and suggest that the lines of jurisdiction are clear. In fact, appointments are only put forward for a vote when everything is resolved.[17]

The involvement of multiple organisations in a single appointment – and a greater potential for conflict as a result – can also be clearly seen in the appointment of directors of city-level departments in Ho Chi Minh City. The formal position is that a departmental director is appointed by a decree signed by the city People's Committee chairman (*chu tich uy ban nhan dan thanh pho ky quyet dinh bo nhiem*). However, even leaving out the role played by the central and city party and their associated committees, the central ministry (*bo*) from the same branch as the department in question also has a hand in the appointment process. The involvement of the ministry reflects the fact that although the city departments are formally an organ under the People's Committee (*cac co quan chuyen mon thuoc uy ban nhan dan*), by virtue of their functional speciality (industry, construction, education, etc.) they are also in a close relationship with a central ministry.[18]

However, the origins of the complexity go beyond simply the involvement of a large number of organisations. Problems arise because the issue of who really has jurisdiction over appointments is much less clear-cut than is formally said to be the case. That such jurisdictional problems arise is first and foremost because power is no longer strictly dependent on the formal position institutions hold in the hierarchy. This state of affairs is something that affects the system from top to bottom, leading to rivalry between party and government, between the centre and city, as well as between every conceivable combination of offices within the city itself. These issues are discussed further in Chapter 4. However, one consequence of the rivalry is greater uncertainty in the appointments process, which manifests itself in increased consultation and negotiation, and an inability to impose appointments from on high.

Below are two examples that capture these difficulties well. They involve appointments to the People's Committee at the city level and in state business.

1 Delays in confirming the People's Committee chairman

One Ho Chi Minh City appointment that appears to have been more contested during the 1990s is that of People's Committee chairman. In the early 1990s an attempt was made to give the prime minister the power to appoint (*bo nhiem*) the chairman. Illustrative of the way local interests can sometimes block central initiatives, this was defeated in the National Assembly in 1992, although the prime minister has the right to approve (*phe chuan*) the People's Council election of the chairman and can dismiss him (*mien nhiem*).[19] Greater interest in who becomes People's Committee chairman in Ho Chi Minh City makes sense in terms of the idea that in the context of political reform, government positions in general may have become more important during the 1990s.[20]

The struggle over the People's Committee chairman's appointment also appears to have been further played out in relation to incumbents themselves. However, in such cases, the appointment may have been contested because of local differences as well as central ones. Both the last two People's Committee chairmen, Truong Tan Sang (1992–6) and Vo Viet Thanh (1996–present) were appointed initially in an acting capacity while none of their predecessors were. Moreover, they both spent quite long periods as acting chairman – eight months in the case of Sang and fourteen months in the case of Thanh – before a vote of the People's Council was called to confirm them in the post.[21] This also points to a greater degree of contestation than in the past. In particular, Thanh's difficulties were the subject of comment in local political circles.[22]

In neither case is it possible to be certain as to the precise source of the opposition. However, what seems most likely is that it reflected both political differences in Ho Chi Minh City and between senior party figures at the centre.[23] A lack of support for Thanh in certain quarters was evident in his failure either to retain his Central Committee place in 1991 or regain it in 1996.[24] A whispering campaign against Thanh was also clearly discernible in Ho Chi Minh City during the second half of the 1990s.[25]

2 An inability to impose a controversial appointment

There is evidence of increased contestation in state business appointments where there is also a tendency to appoint people initially in an acting capacity. In one such case in the late 1990s, involving the city party company, Saigon Petro, it was evident that the city party committee was not in a position simply to impose the appointment of a new director. Its weakness in this respect was despite the fact that as the company's controlling institution, responsibility for the appointment formally rested in its hands.[26] In contrast to the previous example, this appointment appears to have been contested primarily – if not exclusively – because of differences at the local level, which pitted the city party committee against certain local business interests.

In 1998 the deputy director of Saigon Petro, Ho Hong Son, who had been with the company for 15 years, was appointed acting director after the previous incumbent was implicated in the Minh Phung–Epco case (see Chapter 5). For Son to be confirmed as director, he would need the support of the dominant interests within the company itself and also the city party committee. However, after a period of months, Son was not confirmed in the post and his candidacy was allowed to lapse. According to sources interviewed in Ho Chi Minh City at the time, he had the necessary support from the city party committee as well as from a majority within Saigon Petro (around 80 per cent reportedly supported his candidature). However, various business interests in the city opposed his appointment. This opposition, as my informant suggested, was significant enough to result in his candidacy being withdrawn despite the backing of the city party committee.[27] The opposition to Son would appear to go back to the period soon after he was appointed acting director when he clashed publicly with the state-owned bank Vietcombank in Ho Chi Minh City over difficulties his company had been experiencing in securing foreign exchange.[28]

Explaining change

If, as it has been argued, there was greater consultation, negotiation and contestation in the appointments process during the 1990s than the formal logic of democratic centralism implied, a key question is what might have brought about such a change. One possibility is that a more fluid, less predictable appointments process is a consequence of the rise of state business interests at the local level since the 1980s and the associated growth of clientelist networks capable of undermining old-style democratic centralism. However, can such interests be identified? Or, more specifically, can such interests be linked to politicians?

In an attempt to answer this question, the chapter will now look at different appointments in the city since 1975, asking whether the background and experience of those who held key office in the 1990s differed in any significant way from their predecessors. I shall begin by looking at those who have held the post of party secretary, continuing with the posts of People's Committee chairman and deputy chairman. Later, the discussion will be widened to include departmental directors and district chiefs.

The changing character of elites

Party secretaries

Five people have held the post of city party secretary in Ho Chi Minh City since 1975: Nguyen Van Linh, Vo Van Kiet, Vo Tran Chi, Truong Tan Sang and Nguyen Minh Triet (see Table 3.1 below; for full biographical details see Appendix Table A3.1). Nguyen Van Linh and Vo Van Kiet both went on to hold high political office at the centre: Linh as party general-secretary (1986–91) and Kiet as prime minister (1992–7).[29] All Ho Chi Minh City's party secretaries have been southerners by birth except Nguyen Van Linh, who was born in the northern province of Hai Hung.[30] However, Linh came south when he was 24 years old and is almost regarded as a southerner on account of his long service in the south, notably during the war years.[31] All the city's party secretaries remained south after 1954 and were politically active during the war. However, given their wide age range, their experience naturally varied. The last two party secretaries (Truong Tan Sang and Nguyen Minh Triet) were only in their late 20s and early 30s in 1975. Their experience was respectively as youth and labour union organisers, while their predecessors held much higher office.[32] Nguyen Van Linh and Vo Van Kiet both held senior leadership positions in the Central Office for South Vietnam by the end of the war.[33] Kiet was the party's special representative on the Military Management Committee that took control of Saigon at Liberation.[34] Vo Tran Chi, who served as party secretary in Ho Chi Minh City from 1986–96, was a provincial militia leader in his native Long An during the war.[35]

As time has elapsed since the end of the war, those being appointed party secretary have come to the post with more experience than their predecessors of working in the city's districts or departments during the 1980s and 1990s. This is particularly evident with Truong Tan Sang who served as party secretary in Binh Chanh district (1986–8) and as director of the Agriculture

Table 3.1 Ho Chi Minh City party secretaries 1975–2000

Nguyen Van Linh	1976
Vo Van Kiet	1976–81
Nguyen Van Linh	1981–6
Vo Tran Chi	1986–96
Truong Tan Sang	1996–2000
Nguyen Minh Triet	2000–

Sources: *Tuoi Tre* 28 April 1998; *Sai Gon Giai Phong* 25 September 1992, 6 November 1986 and 15 May 1996; BBC SWB FE/3738 B/6 15 January 2000.

Department (1990–1) in the city before being appointed city party secretary.[36] However, Vo Tran Chi had similar experience, having served as party secretary in District 5 and head of the city party's agricultural department (*phan ban nong thon thanh uy*) before being appointed city party secretary.[37] In the case of Nguyen Minh Triet, his experience was gained in southern provincial politics, serving as deputy party secretary and secretary in Binh Duong province (former Song Be) from 1988–97.[38]

Since 1991 the party secretary in Ho Chi Minh City has always also been a Politburo member. Previously they had just been Central Committee members. The change occurred when Vo Tran Chi was party secretary. Chi became a Politburo member halfway through his time in office at the Seventh Party Congress in 1991.[39] The last two party secretaries have also appeared to have greater central experience or exposure than their predecessors. Truong Tan Sang, for example, was selected in 1989 to study at the party's ideological school, the Nguyen Ai Quoc Institute (now the Ho Chi Minh National Political Academy) in Hanoi.[40] This is very much associated with someone being groomed for high office.[41] Nguyen Minh Triet served as the head of the central party's Mass Mobilisation Committee before being appointed party secretary in Ho Chi Minh City.[42]

Taken in conjunction with growing decentralisation under reform, the fact that the party secretary in Ho Chi Minh City is now routinely a Politburo member may represent an attempt by the central party to ensure that the city's party secretary is more firmly locked into the centre. This fits with other evidence presented in this book that suggests increased moves to recentralise power during the 1990s (see especially Chapters 4 and 5). In this respect, it is noticeable that Nguyen Minh Triet – the most recent holder of the party secretary post – has had less direct involvement in Ho Chi Minh City politics than any of his predecessors.[43] This could even suggest that the party secretary post is shifting to one held by a 'trustworthy outsider' rather than necessarily a local man.

People's Committee chairmen

Since 1975 there have been six city People's Committee chairmen in Ho Chi Minh City: Vo Van Kiet, Mai Chi Tho, Phan Van Khai, Nguyen Vinh Nghiep, Truong Tan Sang and Vo Viet Thanh (see Table 3.2 below; for full biographical details see Appendix Table A3.1). Of these, two went directly on to be party secretary in the city (Vo Van Kiet and Truong Tan Sang).[44] Phan Van Khai went on to be prime minister (1997–present), succeeding Vo Van Kiet.[45] Mai Chi Tho went on to be interior minister (1987–91).[46] Five out of the six people who have held the People's Committee portfolio have been southerners by birth. The exception is Mai Chi Tho, who served as People's Committee chairman from 1976–85. Tho was born in the north, although like Nguyen Van Linh he spent considerable time in the south during the war.[47] The majority of those who have held the People's Committee chairman's post

Table 3.2 Ho Chi Minh City People's Committee chairmen 1975–2000

Vo Van Kiet	1976
Mai Chi Tho	1976–85
Phan Van Khai	1985–9
Nguyen Vinh Nghiep	1989–92
Truong Tan Sang	1992–6
Vo Viet Thanh	1996–

Sources: *Sai Gon Giai Phong* 1 May 1977, 27 October 1991, 25 September 1992 and 26 September 1997; Thoi Bao Kinh te Saigon 20–6 August 1992 and 27 June–3 July 1996.

remained south during the war. Mai Chi Tho finished the war as head of security in an area known as T4, which incorporated Saigon-Gia Dinh and a number of southern provinces.[48] Vo Viet Thanh, who was appointed People's Committee chairman in 1996, worked in military intelligence during the war.[49] The only People's Committee chairman who did not serve in the south in the war is Phan Van Khai, who as a 21-year old went north (*tap ket ra bac*) in 1954. During the war he held various departmental positions in the State Planning Committee and in the Reunification Committee, which was set up on the eve of victory in the south. From 1960 to 1965 he studied at the People's Economics University in Moscow.[50] With the exception of Thanh, who was made a member of the Central Committee in 1986 only to lose his position in 1991, all People's Committee chairmen in Ho Chi Minh City have been Central Committee members.[51] The People's Committee chairman is also always the deputy secretary of the city party committee and a member of the city party Standing Committee.

Business interests

From the preceding discussion it is clear that we can discern both elements of continuity and subtle changes in the background and experience of those who have served as party secretary and People's Committee chairman in Ho Chi Minh City since 1975. In terms of continuity, we can point to their common southern heritage and the fact that even in the late 1990s war service carried considerable weight. It is striking in this respect how Phan Van Khai's official biography emphasises his fact-finding mission to the war zone to carry out research on the southern economy (*1973 vao chien truong B2*) even though he spent the war principally in Hanoi and Moscow.[52] In terms of subtle changes, we can point to growing district and departmental experience among the ranks of the city's party secretaries and People's Committee chairmen, and the fact that the party secretary is now always a Politburo member.

However, what it is not possible to do is to link Ho Chi Minh City's party secretaries or People's Committee chairmen to business interests, either directly or indirectly. While this is perhaps not surprising for those who served in the 1970s and early 1980s, such interests cannot be discerned even for those who have held office since the late 1980s, when changes of this nature might conceivably have become apparent. There is clearly a potential difficulty here, namely that the city's top leaders may have business interests but they are simply well concealed. In Chapter 2 I noted the way in which the political and business culture in Vietnam is such that people seek to hide their business activities, often registering companies in the names of relatives and close friends. These difficulties notwithstanding, there is a sense in which if prominent political figures are involved in business their interests tend to come to the surface only in the form of rumours or off-the-record remarks. However, in the case of Ho Chi Minh City's party secretaries and People's Committee chairman there was very little even by way of rumours.[53]

Research on China would suggest that an absence of well-developed business interests among the top city-level elite in Ho Chi Minh City is possibly not so puzzling. Writing on Tianjin, which like Ho Chi Minh City is a centrally managed city, Christopher Nevitt has argued that those who hold city office have less room for manoeuvre than those lower down the chain, given their closer proximity to the centre and the resulting expectations that go with their position.[54] This limited room for manoeuvre, Nevitt argues, also affects their ability actively to pursue business interests. While inevitably those who reach the relative heights of city office have worked their way up the hierarchy – and thus once held positions one-step removed from the centre and arguably more conducive to doing business – one could also argue that those who have risen up the chain of command to date have tended from the outset to have followed quite rarefied career paths. Truong Tan Sang, for example, was one of very few deputy People's Committee chairmen also to be a Central Committee member, suggesting he was already on a different career trajectory from that of his counterparts.[55] He was also selected to study at the prestigious Nguyen Ai Quoc Institute. The 'proximity to the centre' argument would also apply to Nguyen Minh Triet, given his position as a provincial party secretary, while Vo Viet Thanh was appointed deputy People's Committee chairman having already held deputy ministerial office and been a member of the Central Committee.[56]

The sense that this problem is not simply one of failing to uncover the business interests of Ho Chi Minh City's party secretaries and People's Committee chairmen is strongly reinforced by the fact that business interests can be identified quite clearly for officials lower down the formal chain of command, beginning with the city's deputy People's Committee chairmen.

Deputy People's Committee chairmen

City-level deputy People's Committee chairmen are elected by the People's Council at the same level although, as with the People's Committee chairman appointment, there is the normal party supervision in the appointment process. In addition, the People's Committee chairman is empowered to recommend candidates for deputy chairman to the People's Council. Such powers are only a recent phenomenon and are the result of changes to the Law on the Organisation of People's Councils and People's Committees introduced in 1994.[57] In Ho Chi Minh City, there are five deputy chairmen and they are usually delegated specific areas of responsibility within the city by the chairman.[58]

The background of those who have served as deputy People's Committee chairman in Ho Chi Minh City since 1975 is in some respects quite similar to that of the city's party secretaries and People's Committee chairmen (for full biographical data on People's Committee deputy chairmen see Appendix Table A3.1). Like those above them, they too are predominantly from the south.[59] Many were also active during the war, and in the case of those who held the deputy chairman's post during the 1990s, often as youth or student organisers.[60] Only two deputy People's Committee chairmen have been Central Committee members while in office (Le Van Triet and Truong Tan Sang) compared with Central Committee membership being the norm in the case of the city chairman.[61] The city's deputy People's Committee chairmen have always been a member of the city party Executive Committee and occasionally a member of the party Standing Committee.[62]

Regarding the background of deputy People's Committee chairmen since 1975, two have come with deputy ministerial experience (Le Van Triet and Vo Viet Thanh).[63] Others have had experience in planning or in party work (Phan Van Khai and Pham Phuong Thao).[64] The second half of the 1990s has also seen the emergence of deputy People's Committee chairmen who might loosely be said to have a more technocratic background (Tran Thanh Long and Nguyen Thien Nhan).[65] However, by far the most common background among deputy People's Committee chairmen in Ho Chi Minh City includes experience gained in the city's districts or departments as district party secretaries, People's Committee chairmen, or as directors or deputy directors of city-level departments. Prior to 1989, this background does not appear to be so common.[66] By the 1990s it was the norm. These include people such as Pham Chanh Truc and Le Thanh Hai, who held the post of deputy People's Committee chairman in the 1990s.[67] Both were former party secretaries in District 5.[68] Hai also served as director of the Housing and Land Department and later as director at the Department of Planning and Investment.[69] Other deputy People's Committee chairmen in the 1990s include (*Ba*) Le Thi Van, who previously served as People's Committee chairman in Binh Thanh District, and Le Minh Chau, who came up through District 6, where he was party secretary before serving as the director of the Department of Trade and Industry and later as director of the Department of Trade.[70] Both Van and Chau – particularly Chau – were important local politicians during the second half of the 1980s and 1990s. Chau features strongly later in the chapter, where he is located at the centre of a key business empire. Van resurfaces in Chapter 5 where I discuss two major corruption cases.

The pattern that emerges for Ho Chi Minh City's deputy People's Committee chairman with respect to identifiable business interests contrasts heavily with that of the city's party secretaries and People's Committee chairmen. Among those who have been deputy People's Committee chairmen during the 1990s, it is quite common for them to have held a position in state business, or from the late 1980s and early 1990s to have served on the management board of one of the new joint-stock commercial banks. During the 1980s, Nguyen Van Chi, for instance, served as the general-director of the Trade Department company, Imexco, before moving to the Department of Labour and subsequently becoming deputy People's Committee chairman.[71] Le Thanh Hai, who became deputy People's Committee chairman in 1996, served for a period as chairman of the management board of Buildebank, which was established in 1989. At the time, Hai was also the director of the Housing and Land Department.[72] Meanwhile, in 1995 Le Minh Chau became the chairman of the management board of the newly created Saigon Trading Company (Satra), which grouped together 29 companies covering a diverse range of business sectors. At the time of his appointment, Chau was still serving as deputy People's Committee chairman.[73]

Department directors and district chiefs

Similar business interests can also be seen among those who have held positions in the departments or districts but have not risen to be deputy People's Committee chairmen. One of the most striking careers in this respect is that of Do Hoang Hai. After serving as deputy director in the Department of Land and Housing, and as deputy party secretary and party secretary in District 6, Hai began a career in state business in 1985 that spanned 12 years. During this time he served as the director or general director of four companies (Imexco, Fideco, Saigon Frozen Food Company, Saigon Trading Company), as the chairman of the management board of two companies (Tomasca and Cofidec), as a member of the inspection board of Saigon Finance Company, and as a management board member of Exim Bank. In 1996 he was made a member of Ho Chi Minh City's party Executive Committee and in 1998 he emerged as the head of the city party's Economics Committee.[74] This pattern of shifting from political to business office and back again appears to be a new phenomenon. During the 1990s, others appear to have left their formal political career behind, more clearly pursuing a business path. Do Van Hoang, who in 1996 became the general director of Saigon Tourist and the management board chairman of Oricom Bank, is the former chairman of District 1 People's Committee.[75] Furthermore, departmental and district politicians have not just been active in state business; they have also formed limited liability companies, as documented in Chapter 2 for Tribeco and Epco.[76]

Politics and business: three patterns

Looking at the involvement of politicians in business during the 1990s, three patterns can be identified. (For an overview of Ho Chi Minh City politicians with identifiable business connections see Appendix A3.2.) The first is for politicians to run companies directly serving as directors or general directors. In such cases, they usually do not hold political office concurrently, although they might have held it previously and may hold it again in the future. Do Hoang Hai is a good example of this. However, there are exceptions. The Chief Architect, Le Van Nam, is the former general director of Saigon Export Processing Zone. At the time, he was also the director of the city's Construction Department.[77] The previous director of Saigon Tourist, Duong Van Day, held the post while also serving as People's Committee chairman in District 1.[78] For others a period in state business might be the precursor to a political career. Nguyen Van Chi is an example of this.[79]

The second pattern is for politicians to serve on management boards of banks or companies. Here, the tendency is for them to hold political office concurrently. Le Thanh Hai is an example of this, holding as he did both a position at Buildebank and the Department of Housing and Land.[80] Another example is Nguyen Ngoc An, who served as management board chairman of Saigon Bank for Industry and Commerce in the first half of the 1990s. At the time he was a member of Ho Chi Minh City's party Standing Committee, where he eventually enjoyed a 13-year period in office (1983–96). He was also the head of the party's Economics Committee.[81] In such cases, there is a sense in which the politician's role is to provide protection and access.

A third pattern is for politicians to be involved in business by virtue of their position as the head of a company's controlling institution. This job most commonly falls to the director of departments or districts. In his capacity as director of the Trade Department, Le Minh Chau provides an example of this tendency.[82]

Much more difficult to document is the way any of these people extract personal benefit from their involvement in business, although the discussion in Chapter 2 of the spontaneous and often illegal way property rights evolved in Ho Chi Minh City during the 1980s and 1990s provides some pointers. Moreover, that business office, including state business office, confers material advantage for those who hold it comes across strongly in interviews and, periodically, in candid remarks in the press.[83]

Clientelist networks

Much of the time it is difficult reliably to identify clientelist networks in Ho Chi Minh City or such phenomena as political 'groups', backers or protégés. This is in stark contrast to the seeming readiness with which the academic literature on Vietnam has identified apparent 'factions' at the national level based on different policy positions or 'sectoral' groups based on institutional or territorial affiliation.[84] Among Ho Chi Minh City's top leaders, Phan Van Khai has been widely seen as a protégé of Vo Van Kiet on account of his serving under him in Ho Chi Minh City as deputy People's Committee chairman and succeeding him both at the State Planning Committee in 1989 and later as prime minister in 1997.[85] However, there is very little analysis in the literature as to what this association has meant for Khai's career.

People's Committee chairman Vo Viet Thanh (1996–present) spent his early career following in the footsteps of Mai Chi Tho (People's Committee chairman 1976–85), who along with his brother, the leading national politician, the late Le Duc Tho, would appear to have been an important factor in his promotion.[86] Like Mai Chi Tho, Thanh also served as director of police in Ho Chi Minh City. Moreover, when Mai Chi Tho was appointed interior minister in 1987, Thanh also left Ho Chi Minh City, becoming deputy interior minister. Thanh's seeming political weakness during much of the 1990s has also been linked to the death of Le Due Tho in 1991 and the fading of the Tho family star.[87]

However, generally it is rare that we can identify such associations so clearly. The relationships that lay behind Vo Tran Chi's rise to party secretary, for example, are far from clear, while informants openly recognised that it was unclear whether Truong Tan Sang was close to Kiet or Do Muoi.[88] After the death of Le Duc Tho and the formal retirement of Mai Chi Tho, there was similar uncertainty during the 1990s as to who Vo Viet Thanh's backers were.[89] Lower down the formal chain of command such patterns become even harder to discern.

Who is linked to whom is, of course, the subject of much speculation. However, a great deal of what is said is usually based on hearsay, is sometimes politically motivated, and over time can be seen to be unreliable. Furthermore, although we can observe who succeeds whom in terms of political appointments, which in conjunction with other information (place of birth, war record or more anecdotal material) might suggest some kind of association, it is difficult to be definitive.[90]

Nevertheless, it would be a mistake to conclude that such networks and associations do not exist. What little we know suggests that they do exist, if in a more fluid and shifting fashion than is often supposed. From the way people talk it is evident that the idea of the group and backers are at the heart of Vietnamese political culture. One source summed it up succinctly, saying that for Vietnamese people if you have got an umbrella you are fine but if you have not you are liable to come to harm (*neu co khoe roi neu khong co bi hai*).[91]

Despite the obstacles to piecing together such networks, it is possible to point to instances in Ho Chi Minh City where the weight of evidence is such that it is difficult to conclude otherwise that what we are seeing is an agglomeration of entrenched local personal and business interests. Moreover, in such cases, the pattern of appointments can be clearly seen to reflect those interests, with decisions strongly influenced from below rather than by the formal application of democratic centralism.

Le Minh Chau and the Trade Department

Le Minh Chau was born in Can Tho in 1935. As was noted earlier, he began his career in District 6, after which he became director of the Department of Trade and Industry and later director of the Trade Department. Chau was succeeded at District 6 by Do Hoang Hai, who, as also noted earlier, has pursued a career in both business and politics. Born in Ben Tre in 1941, Hai is six years Chau's junior. However, they served together in Saigon during the war and both spent time in prison on Poulo Condore.[92] They are also linked by the fact that their wives are sisters.[93] (For biographical data on Chau and Hai see Appendix Table A3.1.)

When Chau was at the Department of Trade, Hai was still active in state business. However, a number of the companies in which Hai held the post of director or served on the management board were linked to the Trade Department by the fact that it was their controlling institution.[94] In effect, therefore, Hai was on occasions running companies where the controlling institution was headed by his wartime comrade and brother-in-law, namely Chau. The formal position is that the city People's Committee chairman signs the decree appointing someone director of a company belonging to a department.[95]

Chau's seeming ability to manipulate the appointments process in this way thereby keeping key positions 'in the family' can be seen on other occasions. When Chau became the chairman of the newly created Saigon Trading Corporation (Satra) in 1995, it was Hai who was appointed its first general director (*tong giam doc*).[96] Moreover, when Hai relinquished his position as Satra general director in 1997, becoming head of the city party Economics Committee, he was succeeded by Pham Hao Hon.[97] Hon had earlier succeeded Chau as director of the Trade Department, having previously been his deputy director.[98] Once again, the appointments would appear to have Chau's stamp on it.

By all accounts, the setting up of Satra was Chau's personal initiative. One source referred cynically to its creation as 'creating jobs for retiring officials'.[99] Moreover, given that Chau had by now relinquished his formal position at the Trade Department, Satra's establishment appears very much to be a tactic aimed at shoring up his influence over companies affiliated to the Trade Department.[100] By far the majority of Satra's member companies were originally under the Trade Department.[101] At its founding, Satra incorporated a number of lucrative assets, including a number of companies and banks that were profiled in Chapter 2. These include Saigon Jewellery Company, the Foreign Services Company (Fosco), Eden Service and Trading Company as well as Exim Bank, Saigon Industrial and Commercial Bank and Saigon Finance Company.[102]

Chau's ability to manipulate the appointments process may also have been helped by the fact that he had friends on the city party's Economics Committee. As was noted earlier, the Economics Committee plays a behind-the-scenes role in department and business appointments in the city. From 1991–7, the head of the Economics Committee was Nguyen Ngoc An, who as noted earlier was the one-time management board chairman of Saigon Bank for Industry and Commerce. This bank is also one of those claimed by Satra as suggesting a possible conflation of interests between him and Chau. This interpretation is strongly supported by the fact that An was succeeded at the Economics Committee in 1997 by no less than . . . Do Hoang Hai.[103] Given An's seniority compared to Chau and Hai and the notable fact that he held high office in the city party Standing Committee, it is plausible to suggest that he acted as their umbrella in the early years.

The political and business interests linked to Chau and Hai and concentrated on companies affiliated to the Trade Department extend further still. Hai is married to a politician of national distinction, namely (*Ba*) Truong My Hoa. Hoa became an alternate Central Committee member in 1986 and a full member in 1991, when she was also appointed to the party Secretariat.[104] In 1997 she was appointed vice-president of the National Assembly.[105] Like Hai and Chau, Hoa also served in Saigon during the war.[106] She was also imprisoned on Poulo Condore.[107] Hoa's early career was spent in Ho Chi Minh City's Tan Binh district, where she was first deputy party secretary and later secretary.[108] Tan Binh district was originally the controlling institution of Tamexco, the company that was at the heart of the Tamexco corruption case, detailed in Chapter 5. Given Hoa's good central credentials, she too may have acted as an umbrella for Chau's and Hai's activities in Ho Chi Minh City. Other business groups profiled in Chapter 2 focused on Saigon Tourist, Phu Nhuan Jewellery Company, Huy Hoang, and Epco appear to fall outside the sweep of Trade Department business interests.

Democratic centralism undermined: the exception or the rule?

Although neither Chau nor Hai held particularly high political office, that they were a powerful political and business force in Ho Chi Minh City in the late 1980s and 1990s is difficult to dispute. However, the question remains whether they are representative or exceptional.

Certainly this author was unable to piece together anything quite so extensive for other political figures in Ho Chi Minh City, although this does not mean that equivalent networks do not exist. Nevertheless, the impression gained was that the Chau–Hai–Hoa clique began to raise eyebrows in Ho Chi Minh City in part because there was nothing else quite like it.[109]

Nevertheless, while the clique may be exceptional in its size and the sheer extent of its reach, there is other evidence to suggest that entrenched local

Patterns of circulation: democratic centralism under strain 57

interests, particularly at the departmental and district level, were the norm in the second half of the 1990s and that this was having a debilitating effect on democratic centralism.

First, it is striking how during the second half of the 1980s and 1990s it became increasingly common for people to spend long periods in office in a single district or department, suggesting a tendency towards entrenched positions of power. Le Thi Van, for example, held the post of People's Committee chairman in Tan Binh district for eight years beginning in 1986. Earlier it was noted how Tan Binh district was originally the controlling institution of Tamexco, which was very much a rising company in the late 1980s and first half of the 1990s when Van held office in the district.[110] Another politician who spent a long time in a single post was Tran Ngoc Con, who became deputy People's Committee chairman in 1999. Prior to this he had spent nearly a decade in the Industry Department. The Industry Department has a large number of companies under its jurisdiction, including recognised assets such as Legamex and REE.[111] Con first served as deputy director in the Department before becoming its director. Nguyen Van Chi, meanwhile, spent five years at the Department of Labour, War Invalids and Social Affairs before becoming deputy People's Committee chairman in 1996.

Second, informants frequently stated that outgoing office holders play an important part in choosing their successor. This is distinctly out of step with the officially stated position and by extension with democratic centralism. However, informants presented this insight as if it was very much the norm. In the case of the appointment of a departmental director, therefore, not only does the People's Committee and the ministry (of the same branch as the department) have an input but the outgoing director also plays a part. At the Trade Department in the 1990s, the outgoing director's input would appear to have been the key to who took over. A similar pattern of entrenched local interests seemingly able to manipulate the appointments process was also in evidence in District 1, where the last two directors of Saigon Tourist were also chairman of the district's People's Committee.[112]

Third, we can also point elsewhere to what appears at the very least to be a certain deference to the lower levels by the higher levels. In 1997, when the posts of People's Committee chairman and deputy chairman in Ho Chi Minh City's District 3 were being decided after the incumbents had been removed from office on account of their involvement in the Minh Phung–Epco corruption case, the city People's Committee was described in the press as entrusting the job of preparing personnel (*giao cho uy ban nhan dan quan chuan bi nhan su*) to present to the People's Council and the district People's Committee. The city People's Committee appeared to be relegated to the role of approving (*phe chuan*) what the lower level came up with. (The Vietnamese word for 'approve' here is the same as that used to describe the role of the prime minister in the selection of the People's Committee chairman following the failure of the prime minister's office to gain more control over the appointment.) Even assuming that the city People's Committee retains a significant degree of authority in district-level appointments, there is very little sense here of imposition from above in the way the appointment process is formally described. It is also striking how on this occasion even the language used in the official account of how the appointment process works seems to depart from classic democratic centralism.

Conclusion

In this chapter, I have documented the changing character of Ho Chi Minh City's post-1975 political elite. The picture is one of continuity and change. Continuity can be seen in terms of the continued prominence of wartime experience among the city's elite and the way possession of such credentials was still considered important in the 1990s. Meanwhile, change is evident from the way those who held high office (People's Committee deputy chairman and above) during the 1990s have spent the greater portion of their early career in the districts and departments, in contrast to their predecessors for whom wartime experience dominated these early years. A further area of change relates to the growing involvement of politicians in business, especially from the late 1980s. Developments in this area have taken a variety of forms but it is clear that politicians are involved in both state and private business, and it is not uncommon for individuals to hold both political and business office simultaneously. Business interests appear most developed at the lower levels – especially in the departments and districts – although they are also in evidence among those who have risen to the rank of People's Committee deputy chairman.

I have argued that the growth of business interests at the lower levels is having a detrimental impact on the application of the principle of democratic centralism, whereby the higher levels are supposed to exert control over the appointment process. This can be seen both in the tendency for appointments to be contested and in the seeming ability of incumbents to determine who succeeds them. Thus, while the outlines of democratic centralism can still be seen there is a strong sense that it is increasingly coming under strain.

4 Institutional conflict: the city, the centre and the lower levels

Introduction

In the previous chapter I noted the increased involvement of politicians in business in Ho Chi Minh City since the late 1980s. In particular I drew attention to the fact that while such business interests are clearly discernible at the departmental and district level, and also among deputy People's Committee chairmen, they are much less in evidence among those who have risen to the rank of city party secretary or city People's Committee chairman. I argued that the old logic of democratic centralism, whereby appointments were decided by the level above, was being undermined. This development I linked to the growth of business interests at the lower levels, which has led to power becoming decentralised, enabling the lower echelons to play a greater role in the appointments process than formerly was the case.

In this chapter I broaden the scope of the enquiry, exploring the ways the development of local business interests has had an impact on institutional relations in Ho Chi Minh City more generally. Institutional rivalry in the city is widespread, both between institutions at the same level in the hierarchy and at different levels. A key task of this chapter is to explore the extent to which there are patterns to this rivalry and, to the extent that there are, gain a better understanding of what lies behind it. Supporting material is drawn from episodes relating to state enterprise and public administration reform, because it is in relation to control over state enterprises and the carrying out of certain bureaucratic functions that institutional rivalry appears to be particularly intense.

The chapter also considers one of the main paradoxes of the state in Vietnam – and it would appear Communist states more generally – namely that for all its seeming ability to monitor the population and suppress opponents, the state's ability to direct and promote socio-economic change (or 'reform'), as opposed to it occurring in a more spontaneous fashion, is limited. This is something that appears to be particularly acute during the reform era, although revisionist scholarship would also suggest it was a feature of the pre-reform years.[1] Writers on China have frequently drawn attention to this paradox. Writing on Wenzhou, Liu adopts the idea of a 'sporadic totalitarian state', with strong despotic power but weak infrastructural power.[2] These terms are drawn from Michael Mann's analysis of state power, expounding the idea that while the state is able to suppress opposition (strong despotic power), its organisational capacity is poorly developed (weak infrastructural power).[3] Lieberthal and Oksenberg talk in terms of a 'fragmented authoritarian regime'.[4] Such conceptualisations – where the state retains an ability to control but not transform – would appear to have salience in relation to Ho Chi Minh City, notwithstanding all the reformist accolades commonly attached to it. As the material presented in this chapter indicates, the state in Ho Chi Minh City bears very little resemblance to a 'developmental state', wherein the idea of change occurring as a result of conscious state intervention rather than by a spontaneous process is uppermost.[5] It also appears to have little in common with the conception of local state corporatism, wherein local officials, often led by the party secretary, are seen as acting like a board of directors, performing a coordinating role between local institutions.[6]

Nevertheless, while a lack of capacity is the norm, state-initiated clampdowns do periodically occur in Ho Chi Minh City. In the second half of the 1990s, these were directed at activity such as speculative land acquisitions, the black market trade in foreign exchange or smuggling where, as we saw in Chapter 2, the involvement of state institutions and their representatives is widespread. Given the difficulties state organs have in organising coordinated action the tendency is for the impact of such clampdowns to be fairly short-lived: those involved suspend their activities for a period, resuming it when the heat is off. However, what is striking about the clampdowns is the relative ferocity with which they are initially launched and the fact that for a period – admittedly a limited one – they have some effect. Given the way power has become scattered, this is not what one would expect. To further our understanding of the institutional dynamics that underpin such processes, the chapter looks at two clampdowns that occurred in the city in 1995 and 1998, asking where the impetus for them came from and what role the city authorities played in their execution. First, however, we consider what lies behind institutional rivalry in the city.

Institutional rivalry: which institutions and what is at stake?

Notwithstanding official efforts to create the impression of seamless unity, institutional rivalry is endemic in Ho Chi Minh City. Quite simply, it is something that plagues all institutions. There is rivalry between central and city institutions, between institutions at the same level in the city, between institutions at different levels, and between departments within the same institution. The problem is first and foremost one of jurisdiction: that is, where the jurisdiction of one body ends and another begins is frequently unclear and commonly subject to dispute.

There are many reasons why this is the case. One relates to the overlapping jurisdiction between the party and the government. The formal position, that the party leads (*dang lanh dao*) while the government manages (*nha nuoc quan ly*), has long shed more heat than light on who does what. Moreover, a key component of the critique articulated in the political report presented to the Sixth Party Congress in 1986 was that 'party committees at various levels run the whole show', including doing the work of government organs.[7] In response, the political report argued for a strengthening of the role of government institutions. This has been a formal component of reform ever since. Moreover, it appears to have had at least some impact in strengthening government institutions. In Chapter 3, I noted the way the appointment of the People's Committee chairman in Ho Chi Minh City during the 1990s appeared to attract greater controversy compared with the previous decade. Local informants also referred to the way the People's Committee in Ho Chi Minh City was relatively unimportant during the period of Mai Chi Tho's tenure as chairman (1976–85).[8] By contrast, off the record people spoke constantly in the late 1990s of the rivalry between the city party committee and city People's Committee.

In what one actually sees, evidence for party–government rivalry is often absent from the picture.[9] Indeed, the examples cited in this chapter mainly deal with rivalry that ostensibly is between government institutions. If we conceive of the party as seeking to manipulate and control from behind the scenes, this may in part reflect the way party activity tends to be more hidden from view. However, with the party represented in all government organisations, it is also the case that what may come across simply as intra-government rivalry is likely to reflect differences in the party as well.

Second, institutional problems occur because of the fact that there are organisations in the city – namely the departments – which although formally under the city People's Committee (*cac co quan chuyen mon thuoc uy ban nhan dan*) also have relations with the central ministry in their specific area of responsibility.[10] One source highlighted the potential for problems caused by overlapping jurisdictions in this respect, describing the departments as 'belonging' to the People's Committee while at the same time as 'reporting to the Ministry but not subject to order from it'.[11] This principle of dual accountability (*song trung truc thuoc*) is frequently the cause of jurisdictional disputes.[12]

Third, there are organisations in Ho Chi Minh City that, although they operate within the geographical locale of the city, answer directly (*nganh doc*) to the centre. These include the army, police, tax, treasury, and state asset management.[13] There are also companies in the city that answer to the centre, as we saw in Chapter 2.[14] Jurisdictional disputes occur as a result of this. Furthermore, as indicated in Chapter 3 in relation to political and business appointments, even in situations where formal jurisdiction is clearly set out, old certainties no longer apply as a result of decentralisation linked to the

62 *Changing political economy of Vietnam*

growth of business interests with reform. The result is that who prevails in a given situation has to be worked out on a case-by-case basis.

At the root of most jurisdictional disputes lie issues such as who controls the running of state enterprises or which institution has the right to carry out certain bureaucratic functions. Both activities represent a source of income for the institutions and individuals involved, with revenue earned by any combination of business prowess, rent-seeking or corruption. During the 1990s disputes frequently arose in relation to changes put forward in connection with the formally sanctioned programme of state enterprise and public administration reform, both of which threatened to shake-up long established arrangements. State enterprise reform officially embodied the idea that access by state enterprises to budget subsidies and cheap credit via the banking system should be restricted. It also included a programme of equitisation (*co phan hoa*), whereby companies designated as not needing to remain in the state sector sold shares.[15] Public administration reform was formally conceived of as a way of streamlining the bureaucracy and improving administrative efficiency.[16]

Beyond the general picture of a situation of endemic institutional rivalry in Ho Chi Minh City in the 1990s, a number of more specific patterns can be discerned. One of the most prominent – and one which is often lost amid the tendency in much of the Vietnam literature to emphasise Ho Chi Minh City's relative independence or free-spiritedness – is that of the power of central institutions in the city. The two following examples, drawn one each from the fields of public administration and state enterprise reform capture this well. They also illustrate clearly the way the city People's Committee is often distinctly powerless in relation to central interests in the city, at best able to do no more than engage in a debilitating, blocking action.

1 The Chief Architect's office

The Chief Architect's office (*Van phong Kien truc su truong*) was created in Ho Chi Minh City in 1993.[17] It was founded in order to give the prime minister greater control over the urbanisation process in the city, which since the early 1990s had rapidly gathered pace. One source described its purpose as being to stop institutions in the city 'doing whatever they liked'.[18] The idea that the Chief Architect's office is in many ways a special organ belonging to the prime minister is evident from the way the Chief Architect is appointed. While the 'name' originates in the city, it must be approved (*phe chuan*) by the prime minister.[19] This puts the Chief Architect on a par with the city People's Committee chairman, who is also approved by the prime minister. However, it also elevates him in relation to the city's departmental directors, who are appointed by the People's Committee chairman.[20] However, the ambiguity of the situation is evident from the fact that the Chief Architect's office is considered to be at the same level as a department and therefore junior to the People's Committee, from whom its budget also comes.[21] From 1993, when the Chief Architect's office was founded, and for the remainder of the decade, the Chief Architect was Le Van Nam. He is a southerner with long experience in Ho Chi Minh City. However, he also re-located north (*tap ket ra bac*) in 1954, suggesting that he had good central connections too.[22]

Based on conversations at the Chief Architect's office, it was certainly evident that people at the office regarded themselves as endowed with special powers. According to their account, the Chief Architect has the right to overrule the Housing and Land Department, the Construction Department, and the Planning and Investment Department, if they proposed developments that did not fit the urban master plan it had drawn up. One official even said that the Chief Architect could overrule the People's Committee chairman if he was out of step with the master plan. The People's Committee, in turn, was required to appeal to the prime minister if it disagreed with a decision coming from the Chief Architect's office, the official said. In addition, if a company wished to secure land use rights or build on a site, it had to get the approval of the Chief Architect's office first – and before it liaised with the Land or Construction Departments. The Chief Architect also has the right to issue construction licences.[23]

However, this view of the extent of the Chief Architect's authority has never been accepted by the city People's Committee or the departments, and as a result the institutions have constantly sparred with each other.[24] Reflecting this, the city People's Committee has favoured reining in the powers of the Chief Architect's office. In 1998 it called for the Chief Architect's office to be made an organ directly under the People's Committee chairman (*mot bo phan truc thuoc Chu tich Uy ban nhan dan thanh pho*). It also wanted its right to issue construction licences removed.[25] This right has long been a source of conflict with the Construction Department.[26]

Despite the wishes of the city People's Committee, the powers of the Chief Architect's office have not been formally reined in. In June 1999, one source described it as 'just a suggestion', saying that the People's Committee still needed to submit a formal proposal to the Prime Minister's Office and the Construction Ministry. In the view of the same source, the Prime Minister's Office was against the change, as was the Construction Ministry, which it said had issued a report in 1998 recommending that the existing situation be maintained.[27] As a result the feuding in Ho Chi Minh City has continued. Possibly reflecting the intensity of the rivalry surrounding the Chief Architect's office, the office was being investigated by the Finance Department in March 1999 over reports that it had illegally collected 2.1 billion dong in the course of its appraisal of zoning plans.

As an illustration of the general pattern of central encroachment in Ho Chi Minh City, the case of the Chief Architect's office is revealing. With the backing of both the prime minister's office and the construction ministry, the Chief Architect's office proved able to resist the efforts of the city People's Committee and the departments to have its power reined in.

2 Equitisation and the road vehicle inspection stations

Disputes over where the jurisdiction of one institution ends and another begins can also be seen in the equitisation process. The following example provides further illustration of the strength of centrally backed institutions in Ho Chi Minh City during the 1990s. In November 1998 an article appeared in the Ho Chi Minh City party newspaper, *Sai Gon Giai Phong* (Liberated Saigon), which led with the headline 'Can we equitise the chicken that lays the golden egg?' (*Co the co phan ha 'con ga' de trung vang?*).[28] It concerned a proposal by the Ho Chi Minh City People's Committee that three road vehicle inspection companies, referred to as stations, operating in the city be put forward for equitisation. The article is illustrative both in the light it sheds on the complex interests that have grown up around the vehicle inspection stations, and moreover on the particularistic and defensive nature of these interests. Furthermore, since the vehicle inspection stations were only founded in 1996, it is evident that these interests have become entrenched after just two years of operation.

As the article in *Sai Gon Giai Phong* makes clear, the companies effectively have two owners, the central Vietnam Department of Inspection and Regulation (*Cuc Dang Kiem Viet Nam*), and interests connected to the public transport branch (*nganh giao thong cong chanh*) in Ho Chi Minh City:

> From 1996, as part of the Ministry of Transport and Communication's expansion . . . , the Vietnam Department of Inspection and Registration (*Cuc Dang Kiem Viet Nam*) founded three stations, the setting up and management of which it entrusted to the Ho Chi Minh City public transport branch (*nganh giao thong cong chanh*). Legally speaking, the stations belong to the Vietnam Department of Inspection and Registration. Indeed, the Department contributed the machinery and equipment used for vehicle inspections. However, the land and the employees belong to the city public transport branch. The turnover of the stations is divided between the two institutions according to the ratio of their respective capital contributions.[29]

That the inspection stations have proved profitable – and hence are something over which it is worth fighting – is underscored by the reference in the article to them as the 'chicken that lays the golden egg'. In 1998 their combined turnover was 8.4 billion dong (600,000 US dollars) having recorded average growth of 73.5 per cent annually in the two years since 1996.

Against this backdrop, the proposal by the city People's Committee that they should be equitised did not go down well. *Sai Gon Giai Phong* describes the stations as 'rather surprised' (*kha bat ngo*) at the city's intervention saying that, in the light of the ownership arrangements, it is not for the city authorities to put the stations forward for equitisation (*cac tram . . . , khong*

Institutional conflict: the city, the centre and the lower levels 65

phai la doanh nghiep cua thanh pho de dua vao dien co phan hoa). There was also friction between the stations' dual owners, the Vietnam Department of Inspection and Registration, and public transport interests in the city, with the latter favouring a smaller management role for the Department. In order for equitisation to be possible, the article suggests that one side needs to buy out the other but adds that even then it is doubtful that the Department (*cuc*) will agree.

The situation prevailing with the vehicle inspections stations, whereby the central interests to whom they belong strongly resist any encroachment by the city authorities into what they regard as their domain, is very common in Ho Chi Minh City.[30] With equitisation, the tendency was simply for the process not to progress if such problems were encountered. This lack of progress is discussed further in Chapter 6 in pursuit of a better understanding of the dynamics of continuity and change.

The city People's Committee, the departments and the districts

Another recurring theme in institutional relations in Ho Chi Minh City in the 1990s were problems between the city People's Committee and the departments. As was noted above, the departments are organs of the city People's Committee but they also have relations with the central ministry in the area in which they specialise. Below are two examples that clearly illustrate the problems between the city People's Committee and the departments. Moreover, in both cases, the beneficiary of the People's Committee's moves against the departments appears to be the districts.

1 One stop, one stamp

In 1996 there emerged in Ho Chi Minh City a reform of administrative procedures, known as 'one stop, one stamp' (*mot cua, mot dau*). It was first introduced on an experimental basis in a limited number of the city's districts with a view to it being applied more widely if it proved successful.[31] Its stated aim was to end the situation whereby people wishing to carry out administrative procedures, such as legalising the documentation on their house or getting a licence to renovate it, had to run the gauntlet of countless offices collecting numerous official stamps. Apart from being time-consuming and inefficient, this also created an environment in which bribery and corruption flourished.[32] To put an end to this, 'one stop, one stamp' involved the creation of a single office (*phong tiep dan*) in each district, where the public would go to complete procedures. Moreover, the idea was that this would be the only place they had to go. 'One stop, one stamp' was clearly backed by the city People's Committee, which can be seen emphasising its successes and calling for renewed efforts to address the problems.[33] If successful, centralising authority in the hands of the districts as envisaged by 'one stop, one stamp' would naturally create both winners and losers. In this case, the potential winners were the city and district authorities. The potential losers were the departments the public no longer needed to visit.

When 'one stop, one stamp' was applied in District 1 in 1997–8 the proposed changes did not go exactly as planned. The district authorities were quite successful in regaining control over their own offices, which previously had acted rather unilaterally in administrative procedures.[34] Where problems emerged was in relation to the departments. Under 'one stop, one stamp', documentation was still required to cross department desks but it was the responsibility of the district authorities, not the people themselves, to liaise with the departments. However, the departments proved reluctant to give up their role in the process. According to district sources, the departments took so long to return documentation that people continued to go directly to the departments themselves, thereby defeating a central plank of 'one stop, one stamp'.[35]

One interpretation of the problems between District 1 and the departments suggested that it was the departments' relationship with the centre that was to blame. The head of the Committee for Administrative Reform in Ho Chi Minh City, Mai Quoc Binh, described the departments as being 'caught up with' requirements imposed by the ministries at the centre (*so nganh vuong quy dinh cua cac bo, nganh o Trung uong*). However, District 1 also articulated its own problems with the centre itself, notably over the right to print the forms needed to carry out the administrative procedures, which it said the ministries refused to relinquish. It described this situation as 'extremely absurd' (*het suc vo ly*). Against this backdrop, District 1's feeling of powerlessness in relation to the departments and the centre was very evident. The deputy head of Committee for Administrative Reform in District 1, Nguyen Van Lang, said in an interview in 1998 that it was not the districts that had the power to 'throw out' the laws, only those who had issued them, namely the centre (*cap quan lai khong co quyen bo ma 'nguoi' co quyen chinh la 'nguoi' da ban hanh quy dinh*). He also called on the government to lean on the ministries to pay more attention to the administrative reform (*de nghi Chinh phu chi dai cac bo day manh va chu y hon nua den cong cuoc cai cac hanh chinh*).[36]

In the sources on public administrative reform, references to problems between the departments and the People's Committee are extremely common. The difficulty is often encapsulated in a phrase, which talks about the 'complicated relationship' between the vertical leadership and local management by departments (*quan he phuc tap giua lanh dao nganh doc va quan ly theo dia phuong doi voi cap so*).[37] Embodied in this is the idea that the principal cause of the problem is the fact that the departments have dual accountability to both the city People's Committee and the centre.

2 *The reorganisation of the Saigon Trading Corporation*

Rivalry between the city People's Committee and the departments can also been seen in relation to who controls certain state enterprises. In Chapter 3, the Saigon Trading Corporation (Satra) was described, and it was noted that it is closely associated with interests at the Trade Department, in particular its former director Le Minh Chau. (For biographical data on Le Minh Chau see Appendix A3.1.) Chapter 3 also drew attention to the fact that among Satra's original 29 member-companies, there were a number of particularly lucrative assets, notably Saigon Jewellery Company, the Foreign Service Company (Fosco) and the less well known but rather successful Eden Trading and Service Company. However, notwithstanding the strength of the Trade Department interests that lay behind Satra, its control over these assets did not go uncontested during the late 1990s. Moreover, the ensuing struggle appeared to pit interests in the city People's Committee against those in the Trade Department.

That there were problems at Satra first came to public attention in 1998. An article in *Thoi Bao Kinh te Vietnam* (Vietnam Economic Times) in August described Satra as a 'giant with clay legs' (*nguoi khong lo chan dat set*), adding that lines of management within the corporation were 'unclear' and power was 'disbursed' between individual companies not concentrated as was intended (*nhap nhang trong quan ly phan tan quyen han*). In particular it said it was proving very difficult to move capital around the corporation from where there was a surfeit to where there was a deficit – again a fundamental goal of the general corporation concept. Furthermore, the key fault-line, according to the article, was between individual company directors and Satra's board of management (headed by Le Minh Chau), with company directors apparently resentful of what they perceived as interference in its day-to-day affairs by the management board.[38]

In October 1998, two months after the article appeared in *Thoi Bao Kinh te Viet Nam*, a meeting of the Ho Chi Minh City party Standing Committee proposed that the city People's Committee directly oversee the 'consolidation and reorganisation' of Satra (*de nghi Uy ban Nhan dan thanh pho truc tiep chi dao xay dung phuong an cung co, to chuc lai*). This included a decision that Satra should concentrate more on its core business – namely trading – and that companies that did not fit with this should be hived off (*tach nhung doanh nghiep khong cung chuc nang nhiem vu trong tam*). Firms mentioned at this stage were Saigon Jewellery Company, the Foreign Service Company (Fosco) and the Petroleum Service Company.[39] Whatever the real reason for the reorganisation, the subsequent departure of these companies was clearly a blow to Satra, a fact which was reflected in lower turnover figures for the corporation the following year.[40] Moreover, only a few months before an article had emphasised the importance of Fosco to Satra.[41]

Although a loss to Satra, the corporation's reorganisation clearly had the support of the city People's Committee. Very soon after the decision to reorganise Satra was made public, the People's Committee deputy chairman, Nguyen Van Chi, announced the People's Committee backing for the establishment of a new tourism general corporation centred on Saigon Tourist. (For biographical data on Nguyen Van Chi see Appendix

68 *Changing political economy of Vietnam*

Table A3.1.) Among the ranks of companies affiliated to the Saigon Tourist General Corporation was a one-time Trade department and Satra company, namely Eden Trading and Service Company.[42] As was noted in Chapter 2, Saigon Tourist is controlled by business interests in District 1 and hence Eden's departure from Satra and its joining of the Saigon Tourist General Corporation would appear to be another example of a move supported by the city People's Committee which benefited one of the districts.

The People's Committee's support for hiving off Satra affiliates did not stop with the creation of a new tourism corporation. In March 1999, deputy chairman Chi announced plans to establish another general corporation, focused exclusively on gold and jewellery. At its core would be another one-time Satra affiliate, namely Saigon Jewellery Company. Saigon Jewellery Company also seemed to favour this course of action. According to an official in the company's planning department, Doan Thanh Thoai, it had at the time of Chi's announcement already submitted for People's Committee approval a plan for establishing the new corporation.[43] The attitude of Saigon Jewellery Company to the planned changes is discussed further in Chapter 6. However, that there were those within the People's Committee wanting to wrest Saigon Jewellery Company from Trade Department influence was also evident from a comment in the city People's Committee's English-language magazine, *The Saigon Times Weekly*, which said that because the company represented the 'seed' of a future business group, the present management arrangements were not suitable:

> Therefore the State should allow [it] to operate under more liberal mechanisms, for example, putting them under the management of Ho Chi Minh City government instead of the Ho Chi Minh City Department of Trade to avoid multi-level management, which restricts . . . , self-mastery in business and personnel organisation and limits . . . business opportunities.[44]

Some patterns: pressure from above and below

The material presented so far in this chapter suggests a number of patterns. First, it illustrates clearly the heavy presence of central interests in Ho Chi Minh City and the relative weakness – generally speaking – of the city People's Committee in relation to these interests. In the cases explored above, such as those involving the Chief Architect's office and the vehicle inspection stations, what we are seeing is the People's Committee's authority being compromised from above. Moreover, the creation of the Chief Architect's office in 1993 occurred just a year after efforts to win greater powers for the prime minister in appointing the People's Committee chairman had been rebuffed, as was discussed in Chapter 3. This suggests a pattern of attempted central encroachment in Ho Chi Minh City in the 1990s spearheaded by the prime minister's office.[45]

Institutional conflict: the city, the centre and the lower levels   69

Second, the material presented in this chapter highlights the way conflict between the city People's Committee and the departments is commonplace despite the fact that the departments formally come under the jurisdiction of the People's Committee chairman. This represents pressure on the People's Committee from below. Sometimes, the People's Committee appears to get the better of department interests, such as in the reorganisation of Satra. However, on other occasions, department interests prove harder to dislodge. A good example is provided by the case of 'one stop, one stamp'.

Third, the material presented so far suggests a certain affinity between the city and the district People's Committees, with the city authorities backing district interests at the expense of the departments. There are echoes of this in both the way Satra was reorganised and in the logic of 'one stop, one stamp'. Furthermore, this also ties in with material presented in Chapter 3, which pointed to a certain deference on the part of the city People's Committee towards the appointment of a district People's Committee chairman.

This contrast – in the relationship between the city People's Committee and the departments, on the one hand, and the districts on the other – seems at first sight rather puzzling. On the face of it we would expect there to be similar jurisdictional disputes or conflicts in both cases. After all, as was illustrated in the previous chapter, the rise of business interests at the lower levels can be seen equally in the districts as in the departments. So how do we explain the difference?

Research on China, which has also noted a degree of accommodation on the part of the city authorities towards the districts, explains it as follows:

> . . . the general pattern of economic reform favours local activism and innovation. From the very beginning of the reform period, official state policy has often lagged behind policy innovations introduced in the localities. . . . This gives the district officials a strategic advantage on behalf of increasing local power and autonomy at the expense of their ostensible city-level superiors. City officials must deal cautiously with aggressive district governments for fear that district activities will ultimately be endorsed by Beijing.
>
> . . . however much district governments may undermine city-level authority, the economic success in the districts that such activity generates casts a flattering reflection on city officials as well.[46]

The idea that a rather ambivalent relationship between the city and district authorities may be the result – a sense on the part of the city authorities that they need to compromise in order to maintain a degree of authority – may also be present in Ho Chi Minh City. On the other hand, it is less clear that it is necessarily the districts that have been at the forefront of 'reform-oriented' experimentation, or that their activities have later been endorsed by Hanoi.

On the difficult relations between the city People's Committee and the departments – something not specially commented on in the China literature

– we have emphasised the way problems are caused by the departments' dual accountability to the People's Committee, on the one hand, and the centre on the other. This is a dynamic clearly absent in the districts and hence may explain why relations between the city People's Committee and the departments have tended to be difficult. It may also be that the activities of the district authorities occur in a distinctive enough locale for them not to be so troubling to the city authorities. In the case of the departments, by contrast, their city-level status means their sphere of operation is very much that where the city People's Committee is also operating and is also formally empowered to coordinate. Moreover, in the context of a general pattern of central encroachment in the city, the departments' relations with the centre may make them doubly threatening: in effect amounting to a threat from above at the same time as they represent a threat from below.

While these patterns can be discerned, there is also quite a lot of variation in Ho Chi Minh City. In certain circumstances the departments may clash with the city People's Committee, as illustrated by the cases of 'one stop, one stamp' and the reorganisation of Satra. However, on other occasions, they can be seen more to be working together: their shared antagonism towards the Chief Architect's office provides a good example. Furthermore, while the centre may at times work with departmental interests against the city authorities, as suggested by 'one stop, one stamp', on other occasions it plays little or no role. This would appear to be the case in regard to the reorganisation of Satra.

I now turn to the subject of clampdowns in Ho Chi Minh City. These shed further light on relations between the city authorities and the centre, and the city authorities and the lower levels.

Clampdowns: a backseat role for the city People's Committee

Earlier in this chapter I noted how effective clampdowns are the exception rather than the rule in Ho Chi Minh City.[47] As I have sought to show, this can be attributed to the fact that power is spread over a large number of institutions rather than being concentrated. This is a consequence of the particularistic pursuit of commercial interests by state institutions, either directly through the running of companies or indirectly through carrying out certain bureaucratic functions. The existence of such activity makes it difficult for any institution to galvanise others into acting in a common direction. It is also the case, as we saw in Chapter 2, that some of the same institutions that have regulatory or oversight responsibilities are engaged in the very activities, whether it be speculation in land or foreign exchange or smuggling, that they are formally required to guard against.

However, clampdowns do occur from time to time. Moreover, what is striking is how they sometimes occur with a startling degree of ferocity. Those on the receiving end are left in no doubt that they are being clamped down upon and at least for a period stop what they were doing. The following two examples involving clampdowns on speculative activity in the land market in 1995 and in the foreign market in 1998 respectively capture something of this ferocity and illustrate the way in which initially the clampdowns were quite effective in reining in the behaviour in question.

1 Decree 18 and the land market

Decree 18 (*nghi dinh 18*), which was introduced in February 1995, occurred in the midst of a speculative boom in which land and property were changing hands at a rapid rate and local banks were lending heavily on the back of inflated asset prices. To this day, Decree 18 is remembered by Ho Chi Minh City's business community and those with interests in real estate as a 'defining moment' in the same way that a stock market crash might be recalled in other countries. That it caused such a shock to the land market was because it undermined a belief that companies had private property rights in all but name. By 1995 this belief had become well-established in local business circles, despite the fact that the formal position remained that individuals and companies had land use rights with all land owned by the state.[48] The idea that there was *de facto* private ownership had gained ground in the wake of the passage of the 1993 Land Law, which had recognised the right of households and individuals to exchange, transfer, rent, inherit, and mortgage (*chuyen doi, chuyen huong, cho thue, thua ke, the chap*) – the so-called five rights. However, it was rather vague as to the rights of urban land users, saying that this would be set out in subsequent regulations.[49] In the absence of the promised clarification, businesses and banks proceeded as if companies had the five rights. The issue of who really owned the land was regarded as mere semantics. The result was that there was a surge in land and property trading. Banks also willingly accepted property and land as collateral for lending. Prominent among those trading in the land market were state institutions. As was noted in Chapter 2, they had disproportionately benefited from allocation of land after 1975 and again in the early 1990s. Moreover, they were now in a position to reap profits from an asset they had usually paid little or nothing for. An editorial in *Sai Gon Giai Phong* (Liberated Saigon) and an article in *Lao Dong* (Labour) published shortly after Decree 18 was issued captured neatly what had been going on:

> Until now . . . some businesses have used the system of land allocations as a way of doing business – invest a bit of money, complete the required procedures, pay some land use fees (at a low price) along with the necessary 'fees' to oil the wheels, and you'll get yourself allocated some land which you can divide into lots and sell for a ten-fold profit.[50]
>
> . . . businesses . . . outwardly claim that they need land use rights in order to build a factory or other establishment when in reality they want to acquire land to sell on or to do business, gaining super profits in the

72 *Changing political economy of Vietnam*

process, or to mortgage it so as to borrow an even larger amount of money.[51]

All this, however, was undermined by Decree 18, which announced that land use rights had to be converted into leases with restricted mortgaging rights.[52] The sense in which people active in the land market at the time felt that the ground had been removed from beneath their feet comes across very clearly in comments in the press. One journalist described businesses as feeling they had been 'dispossessed of power' (*bu tuoc doat quyen loi*).[53] Moreover, not only did Decree 18 cause an outcry: it stopped transactions involving land, including the mortgaging of land use rights, in their tracks. Speaking in March 1995, one Ho Chi Minh City banker said that Decree 18 had 'caused disorder to business in urban centres', adding that if it was not amended banks would only take collateral on houses and 'absolutely not against land use rights'.[54]

Although fully aware of the disruption that Decree 18 had caused, those behind the clampdown were wholly unsympathetic: 'Of course banks must examine their ability to recover capital', said the head of the General Department of Land, Ton Gia Huyen, expressing incredulity that banks had agreed to take land as collateral given that it belongs to the state.[55] However, it also remains the case that prior to Decree 18 neither the General Department of Land nor anyone else had sought to remind companies or banks of this fact, nor had they intervened to stop it.

2 Decree 37 and the foreign exchange market

Decree 37 (*quyet dinh* 37), which was promulgated in February 1998, was issued against a background of an intense foreign exchange shortage caused by speculative hoarding on the black market in the aftermath of the Asian economic crisis. Like Decree 18, it had a dramatic effect on the market. In early February, just before the clampdown, the differential between the official interbank market exchange rate and the black market rate had reached an unprecedented 1,200 dong per dollar.[56] The speculative fever in Ho Chi Minh City at this time was intense, with large numbers of the general population seeking to position themselves in order to profit from the widely anticipated devaluation. At this time, black market trading was talked about openly in the press with the black market dollar price quoted alongside the official exchange rate, a practice which tended to fuel the speculative psychology (*tam ly*). The following extracts capture the prevailing mood well:

> Banks are holding on to dollars rather than selling them to businesses which have payments to settle on letters of credit. . . . People are worried that the Vietnamese dong is going to continue to lose value so they have bought dollars in order to save. . . . A number of banks and business organisations, which don't yet have a need for dollars, are also on the look out for hard currency. This is leading to an increase in demand and

Institutional conflict: the city, the centre and the lower levels 73

creating a false demand. This situation had made the supply and demand of dollars all heated up (*gay gat*).[57]

A number of businesses which have overseas payment commitments but are unable to buy dollars from the bank, have to get dollar cash from the free market. However, this makes the price there hotter still (*cang them nong*). In truth, a lot of raw material importers complain that they transfer money into the banks but they are not immediately able to buy [dollars]. A week later when the bank does sell, the [dollar] price has gone up by a further few hundred dong, causing them loss.[58]

It was against this background that Decree 37 was introduced. Its centrepiece was a 5.6 per cent devaluation in the dong, along with various other stipulations requiring companies to sell dollars to banks. In contrast to earlier efforts, the impact of Decree 37 was substantial. Following the devaluation of the official exchange rate, the dong immediately began to appreciate on the black market. Just a few days after Decree 37, the differential between the formal and black market price had fallen to as low as 150 dong in some cases. Moreover, the gap narrowed further in subsequent weeks before settling marginally above the official rate, where it remained for the next six months. Dollars were by no means plentiful during this period but the worst of the speculative hoarding had been broken, with the market no longer anticipating a further devaluation.[59] One of the most striking illustrations of state power associated with Decree 37 was the way in which – at a stroke – press coverage of the black market disappeared or became distinctly subdued. Moreover, most publications stopped quoting the black market exchange rate altogether.

Where do clampdowns come from and why do they occur?

On closer examination, the impetus for both the clampdowns on land and foreign exchange speculation can be seen to have come from the centre – as indicated by the fact that they were launched with the issuing of government decrees. Moreover, Decree 37 was preceded the day before it was introduced by a central government appeal to provincial and city leaders to step up their efforts against the smuggling of goods, gold and dollars.[60] The hand of the central authorities was also very much in evidence in the sudden scaling back of press coverage of the foreign exchange black market. According to sources in Ho Chi Minh City, this followed the intervention of the central party Culture and Ideology Department (Ban Van Hoa Tu Tuong trung uong) – coordinated with the launch of Decree 37 – ordering newspaper editors to cease reference to the black market.[61] As their revised coverage indicated, editors took note of this. In the case of Decree 18, it was also very much central institutions, notably the General Land Department (*Tong cuc Dia chinh*), which came out and defended it.[62]

74 *Changing political economy of Vietnam*

In both cases there is a sense in which the clampdowns occurred amid a perception among certain central institutions that a boundary had been crossed in a way that called for intervention. Where this boundary lies relates in part to the degree of day-to-day disruption speculative activity was causing to normal business activity, but also to the affront to the centre caused by lower level state institutions behaving in this way. In addition, the speculative activity was also perceived to present a systemic threat: if such activity went unchecked there was a risk that it would undermine the banking system itself because of the vulnerability of banks to a fall in real estate prices or the danger that with the shortage of dollars banks would be unable to honour deferred payment letters of credit when they became due. In the aftermath of the Asian financial crisis, such concerns were not just hypothetical, as a number of banking defaults indicated.[63]

Momentum lost

Notwithstanding these concerns and the way Decrees 18 and 37 initially stopped market activity in its tracks, the momentum was not maintained for long. In the weeks and months that followed, references to the black market gradually crept back into press coverage, while it was not too long before there was a resurgence in speculative foreign exchange trading.[64] Moreover, after the initial shock caused by Decree 18 subsided, activity in the land market resumed, particularly as it became clear that the Decree was being selectively applied.[65]

As with the difficulty in launching clampdowns, the seeming inability of state institutions to sustain them can be understood in terms of the compromised authority of both the city and the central-level institutions in Ho Chi Minh City. In both cases, the limits to their power can be linked to the existence of entrenched business interests in the city, particularly at the lower levels.

The role of the city in clampdowns

In contrast to the central institutions that provided the impetus behind both Decree 18 and 37, the city authorities appear to have played rather a back-seat role. Whereas central institutions could be seen calling meetings and defending the clampdowns, city officials remained largely silent. Indeed, it was scarcely conceivable that the city authorities could lead any such clampdown on its own. Instead, the impression gained was that the city authorities only decided to get tough when they were under pressure from the centre to do so.[66] In the case of the foreign exchange market, two sources independently referred to a list held by the city party committee containing the names of the leading black market traders. One informant even suggested those on the list would soon by rounded up.[67] However, arrests were rare. One occurred in Ho Chi Minh City just prior to Decree 37 in January 1998, when there was mounting pressure on the city authorities to stem the speculative tide. The arrest, which had no impact whatsoever on speculative activity, had all the hallmarks of a token effort, although it was made to look as if a 'big fish' had been hauled in. In language reminiscent of that used to describe big businessmen in Saigon before 1975, the person arrested was described in the press as a 'king'. However, in reality, it was hard to see a resemblance.[68]

The city People's Committee's response to Decree 18: singing the tune of the lower levels

Hesitancy on the part of the city-level authorities comes across strongly in the clampdown associated with Decree 18. As noted earlier, Decree 18 resulted in a tirade of critical comment from business interests in Ho Chi Minh City. Moreover, it is possible to be quite precise as to where the opposition was coming from. *Nguoi Lao Dong* (The Worker) newspaper drew attention to a configuration of departmental and district city interests, including the Department of Land and Housing, the Cadastral Department, the Go Vap district People's Committee and the Tan Binh Housing and Development Company, which is controlled by interests connected to the Tan Binh District People's Committee. According to the newspaper, they had made their views known to a group of city delegates on their way to the National Assembly meeting in Hanoi, referring to the 'blocked up and illogical situation' (*tinh trang ach tach, bat hop ly*) in the land market.[69] Ho Chi Minh City National Assembly delegates were also outspokenly critical of Decree 18. This included both Le Minh Chau and Do Hoang Hai, who as we saw in Chapter 3 are at the centre of business interests linked to the Trade Department and Satra. Chau and Hai called for Decree 18 to be watered down in a variety of ways, including that it not be applied retroactively.[70] The strength of the opposition was underlined by the fact that the views of these individuals and institutions were made known in such a public way.

With such a concentration of district and departmental interests firmly opposed to Decree 18, the reluctance of the city authorities to back the centre and throw its weight behind the Decree was understandable. Moreover, in the years that followed the promulgation of Decree 18, the city People's Committee actively campaigned for its key provisions to be revoked. At a meeting in the city in July 1998, the deputy People's Committee chairman, Le Thanh Hai, delivered a report on behalf of the Ho Chi Minh City government to the party general secretary, Le Kha Phieu, and the prime minister, Phan Van Khai, in which he called for a change in the regulations to allow land to be allocated to businesses rather than leased.[71] In this respect, the city authorities can be seen to be 'singing the tune' of the lower levels. Nevertheless, the centre was not easily swayed by their representations, for it was not until December 1998 – nearly four years after Decree 18 had been issued – that the right to allocate land to businesses was granted to Ho Chi Minh City, and then only on an experimental basis.[72]

Limits to the centre's writ in Ho Chi Minh City

The fact that in certain circumstances central institutions are able to precipitate clampdowns in Ho Chi Minh City suggests they retain a degree of authority that is less in evidence in the case of the city party committee or People's Committee. However, clampdowns in Ho Chi Minh City do not just lose momentum because of weakness or hesitancy on the part of the city authorities. Clampdowns also lose momentum because of limits to the extent of central authority in the city. This too can be linked to the existence of entrenched local business interests.

The following example simultaneously illustrates a lack of faith on the part of a local state company in the authority of its city-level controlling institution, and also the way central institutions are not always able to secure a result either. In this case, the entrenched local interests appear to reside in the Ho Chi Minh City branch of the state-owned Bank for Foreign Trade (Vietcombank).

Saigon Petro and Vietcombank: appealing to the centre

In October 1998 an episode came to light involving the city party company, Saigon Petro, and its attempts to secure foreign exchange from the Ho Chi Minh City branch of the state-owned Vietcombank. Saigon Petro was one of five importers of refined petroleum products, which it then sold on the local market. As a result, the company had large dong holdings but generally lacked the foreign exchange it needed to pay for its imports. It was in this context that Saigon Petro approached Vietcombank to try to meet its foreign exchange needs. At the time, these needs were estimated to be in the region of 11–14 million dollars monthly. However, for reasons that are not entirely clear, Vietcombank turned it down.[73]

In an effort to change Vietcombank's mind, Saigon Petro sent a series of official letters (*cong van*) to its controlling institution, the city party Financial Management Department (*Ban Tai chinh Quan tri Thanh uy*), and also to the central party Financial Management Department (*Ban Tai chinh Quan tri Trung uong*), the central party Economics Department (*Ban Kinh te Trung uong*), the director of the State Bank of Vietnam in Hanoi and the prime minister, Phan Van Khai. The prominence of central institutions among the recipients of Saigon Petro's official letters is striking insofar as it suggests that it did not have much confidence in the ability of its own city-level controlling institution to be able influence Vietcombank on its own. However, when its representations to the centre failed to elicit a positive result, the acting director of Saigon Petro, Ho Hong Son, told his story to *Sai Gon Giai Phong*. The article which followed – 'Is it right to lack foreign exchange for essential imports?' – brought the incident to a head although still not in Saigon Petro's favour.[74] According to sources close to Vietcombank consulted at the time, Vietcombank was furious at the implied criticism of it aired publicly in the press and appealed directly to the city party committee. The city party committee, meanwhile, did not take Saigon Petro's side but instead called on the company to apologise to the bank.[75] The outcome is revealing in what it says about the authority of Vietcombank in Ho Chi Minh City, both in relation to the city party committee and to various central institutions, which would also appear to face control problems there.

Conclusion

This chapter has highlighted a variety of different themes. In the first instance, institutional rivalry can be seen to be structurally rooted, whether it is overlapping jurisdiction between the party and the government, the departments' dual accountability, or the fact that there are institutions operating in Ho Chi Minh City that answer directly to the centre. However, these structural roots of institutional rivalry pre-date reform. What appears to have happened is that changes introduced with reform, such as greater emphasis on the role of government, along with more spontaneous developments such as the growth of business interests among state institutions with the shift from the plan to the market, have aggravated these earlier structural problems, both as the authority of government institutions has increased and as power has shifted more to the lower levels. Thus, while the People's Committee in Ho Chi Minh City is a more significant institution in relation to the party in the 1990s compared with the 1980s, it has also been weakened by the growth of business interests at the lower levels. This loss of control at the city level has been accompanied by increased efforts by the centre to increase the scope of its authority in Ho Chi Minh City. It is this that lies behind the attempt by the prime minister's office to gain greater control over the appointment of the People's Committee chairman in 1992 and the creation of the Chief Architect's office in 1993. Because of the centre's distance from the lower levels in Ho Chi Minh City – and because of the persistence in the city of a certain old-style deference towards central authority – the centre is better placed to clamp down on local business interests when they act in ways that threaten systemic stability – such as that of the banking system – as we saw in the cases of speculation in land and foreign exchange in 1995 and 1998. In doing so, the centre does not receive much support from the city-level authorities, who as was noted in relation to Decree 18 are much more inclined to tailor their stance to the interests of the lower levels in the city, particularly if those interests are powerful and their views are strongly put. However, from the perspective of the centre, this does not necessarily matter if the clampdown succeeds in bringing rent-seeking behaviour back to within acceptable limits and reinforcing who is the real power in the land.

5 The politics of economic decentralisation: the Tamexco and Minh Phung–Epco cases

Introduction

In the previous chapter, we looked at institutional rivalry and conflict in Ho Chi Minh City. One of the ways we did this was through the example of clampdowns. In this chapter, attention shifts to two cases in the city spanning 1996–9, in which businessmen, bankers and officials were investigated for various acts of alleged corruption, taken to court and in seven cases sentenced to death. Although not the only such episodes during the 1990s, the Tamexco and Minh Phung–Epco cases, as they have become known after the names of the principal companies involved, have left an indelible imprint on the second half of the decade, attracting widespread popular interest and massive newspaper and television coverage. Moreover, these were not just any companies. These were jewels in their time: privileged, politically connected firms, that expanded rapidly during the early 1990s and were held up as examples to be emulated. Those who ran them were nothing less than prominent members of the elite.

Compared with the clampdowns discussed in the previous chapter, I shall argue that Tamexco and Minh Phung–Epco represent an entirely different phenomenon. When a clampdown occurs – as was indicated – it may be rough but no one dies and indeed it is often the case that few people are arrested. Tamexco and Minh Phung–Epco, by contrast, involved the total and utter destruction of certain individuals, some of whom were ultimately put before a firing squad. As an insight into Vietnam's politics, why those involved were so viciously brought down is worth considering and is the main focus of this chapter. In an attempt to find an answer, I consider a range of different explanations for these companies' fall and also scrutinise the process by which the key participants were 'found guilty'. Ultimately, I argue that this kind of episode is symptomatic of the decentralisation of economic power that occurred with the growth of the market during the 1980s and 1990s, but also of how this is an environment in which the centre increasingly feels the need to strike back. In this respect, far from being undifferentiated clampdowns on corruption, the cases serve to divert attention from the real nature of Vietnam's political economy.

Economic decentralisation: the Tamexco and Minh Phung–Epco cases 79

First, I look at the rise of the three companies at the centre of the cases – Tamexco, Epco and Minh Phung – focusing on the interests that lay behind the firms and the extent of their business activities. As was noted in Chapter 2, Epco and Minh Phung are two of just a handful of limited liability companies that made it into the list of Ho Chi Minh City's top 100 companies in the second half of the 1990s.

The rise of Tamexco, Epco and Minh Phung

Tamexco

The Tan Binh Production Service Trading and Export Company (*Cong ty san xuat kinh doanh va don vi xuat khau*), or Tamexco as it is widely known, was founded in 1989 by state business interests in Ho Chi Minh City's Tan Binh district. From 1986–91, the party secretary in Tan Binh district was a woman called Truong My Hoa, who we encountered in Chapter 3 as married to Ho Chi Minh City politician and businessman Do Hoang Hai. As we also noted, Hoa later went on to be vice-chairman of the National Assembly.[1] Her deputy was another woman, Le Thi Van, who was the People's Committee chairman and deputy party secretary in the district. Van later became deputy People's Committee chairman in Ho Chi Minh City.[2] (For biographical data on Truong My Hoa and Le Thi Van see Appendix A3.1.) Although at the end of 1993 Tamexco was brought under the formal control of the city party authorities – specifically its Financial Management Committee (*Ban tai chinh quan tri thanh uy*) – Tan Binh district interests remained important.[3] Certainly the names of Hoa and Van crop up with persistent regularity as the controlling influence behind Tamexco whenever anyone talks about the company's owners.[4] Tamexco's director was Pham Huy Phuoc, who was born in the Mekong Delta province of Tra Vinh in 1955.[5]

Table 5.1 Key facts about Tamexco

Full name	Tan Binh Production Service Trading and Export Company
Year established	1989
Type of management	Local state company
Controlling institution	Ho Chi Minh City Party Financial Management Committee
Real owners	State business interests in Tan Binh district
Director	Pham Huy Phuoc
Assets	Leading shareholder in Tacombank; Cosimex; Tan Binh Investment Development Company; Joint venture partner in Neetaco

Sources: *Tuo Tre* 25 January and 25 March 1997; *Thoi Bao Kinh te Saigon* 5–11 May, 26 May–1 June and 6–12 October 1994; interviews 6 May 1998 and 8 March 1999.

80 *Changing political economy of Vietnam*

In terms of its business focus, Tamexco was not very different from many other well-connected companies formed in the late 1980s (see Chapter 2). An advertisement for the company in 1991 described it as being involved in import–export, real estate and tourism.[6] Products commonly imported by Tamexco included fertiliser, construction materials and cars. Tamexco was also an exporter of seafood.[7] By all accounts, the company did well in the early 1990s. Figures for 1992 show it recording an increase in import–export turnover of 60 per cent year on year, contributing 18.6 billion dong to the state budget and achieving after-tax profits of 7 billion dong.[8] In the same year, Tamexco set up Tan Viet joint stock commercial bank, better known as Tacombank, becoming its leading shareholder. Phuoc was made chairman of the bank's management board (*hoi dong quan tri*).[9] Moreover, Phuoc was in demand elsewhere, serving as the deputy chairman of a Japanese–Vietnamese joint venture company, Neetaco.[10] Tamexco's business interests did not stop there. An article in *Thoi Bao Kinh te Saigon* (Saigon Economic Times) in 1994 singled out Tamexco alongside seven other up-and-coming companies, saying it had 'good prospects of becoming a future business group' (*co nhieu trien vong chuyen sang tap doan tuong lai*). As well as linking Tamexco with Tacombank, the article also listed Cosimex and the Tan Binh Investment and Development Company (*Cong ty Dau tu va Phat trien Tan Binh*) as belonging to its group. Ranked alongside Tamexco in the *Thoi Bao Kinh te Saigon* article were companies such as Saigon Tourist, Saigon Jewellery Company and Phu Nhuan Jewellery Company.[11]

Minh Phung

Minh Phung's origins go back to 1985, although it was not until 1993 that it was licensed as a limited liability company. Headquartered in Ho Chi Minh City's predominantly Chinese district, District 11, Minh Phung was founded by an ethnic Chinese, Tang Minh Phung. Slightly younger than Tamexco

Table 5.2 Key facts about Minh Phung

Full name	Minh Phung
Year established	1993
Type of management	Limited liability company
Owners	Tang Minh Phung Tran Thi Thuong
Director	Tang Minh Phung
Assets	Shareholder in Exim Bank and Vung Tau Bank; 39 subsidiary limited liability companies

Sources: *Thoi Bao Kinh te Saigon* 21 January–3 February 1993; *Tuoi Tre* 20 May 1997 and 10 July 1999; *Chan Dung Nhung Doanh Nghiep Thanh Dat* [A Portrait of Business on the March], *Nha Xuat Ban Thanh Pho Ho Chi Minh* [Ho Chi Minh City Publishing House], Saigon Times Group, VAPEC, 1997, p. 16; *Thoi Bao Ngan Hang* no. 127, 1994; *Sai Gon Giai Phong* 24 June 1999.

director Pham Huy Phuoc, Tang Minh Phung was born in 1957. It was he, along with his wife, Tran Thi Thuong, a former traffic policewoman, who put together the company's registered capital in 1993. Minh Phung began as a producer and exporter of garments before developing lines in shoes, lacquerware and toys. Later the company diversified into general import–export, construction and real estate development.[12]

The early years were not without difficulty. In 1993, Minh Phung was investigated on suspicion of real estate irregularities, which resulted in a small fine.[13] However, in retrospect, the investigation proved to be a minor disruption that did not prevent the company's continued rise. Minh Phung's expansion included the development of interests in banking. In 1994 Minh Phung was listed as being among 13 leading shareholders in the predominately state-owned Exim joint stock bank.[14] The company also had a stake in Vung Tau bank.[15] By 1995, Minh Phung employed over 8,000 people and had an annual turnover of 1,169 billion dong, making it the eighth largest company in Ho Chi Minh City.[16] For a private company, with avowedly private owners, this was unprecedented. Moreover, Tang Minh Phung was very much an established member of the city's business community. In 1993 he was made a member of the executive committee of a business association for companies in the processing sector, while in 1997 he was among the delegates of a business roundtable meeting organised by the Saigon Times Group in Ho Chi Minh City.[17]

Epco

Like Minh Phung, the District 3 Seafood Production Import–Export Company (*Cong ty san xuat che bien xuat nhap khau quan 3*), better known as

Table 5.3 Key facts about Epco

Full name	District 3 Seafood Import–Export Company
Year established	1991
Type of management	Limited liability company
Owners	District 3 People's Committee; state-owned Bank for Foreign Trade (Vietcombank); Lien Khui Thin; Tang Minh Phung
Director	Lien Khui Thin
Assets	Huu Nghi Hotel; Song Than industrial park; two processing factories; eight subsidiary limited liability companies

Sources: *Thoi Bao Kinh te Saigon* 12–18 December 1991, 5–11 May and 8–14 December 1994; *Chan Dung Nhung Doanh Nghiep Thanh Dat* [A Portrait of Business on the March], *Nha Xuat Ban Thanh Pho Ho Chi Minh* [Ho Chi Minh City Publishing House], Saigon Times Group, VAPEC, 1997, p. 69.

Epco, was also a limited liability company. However, its owners have always had a more overtly statist background. Founded in 1991, Epco's first shareholders were the District 3 People's Committee and four individuals, one of whom was an ethnic Chinese called Lien Khui Thin, who became the company's director.[18] The People's Committee capital contribution came direct from the District 3 budget.[19] In 1994, two new shareholders came on board, namely the state-owned Bank for Foreign Trade (Vietcombank) and Minh Phung's director, Tang Minh Phung. They effectively bought out three of the four original individual shareholders – all except Lien Khui Thin, who remained as Epco's director. In December 1994, Epco was described as being 40 per cent owned by the District 3 People's Committee. Vietcombank had a 25 per cent stake, while the remaining 35 per cent was said to be in the hands of private individuals (*thanh vien ben tu*), which we now know were Thin and Phung.[20] By 1994, District 3 People's Committee was the single largest shareholder, a fact reflected in the appointment of one of its personnel, Nguyen Tuan Phuc, as chairman of Epco's management board. Moreover, cementing District 3's influence, Phuc and another District 3 official, Nguyen Dang Lien, were assigned to work at Epco on a day-to-day basis. Tang Minh Phung, meanwhile, was made deputy director of Epco and also deputy chairman of its management board.[21]

Soon after its founding, Epco ran an advertisement in a Ho Chi Minh City newspaper, describing itself as offering import–export services to Hong Kong, notably the provision of live seafood and freshly cut flowers.[22] However, it also developed interests in hotels, tourism, real estate development and construction.[23] Epco expanded rapidly. In 1995, just four years after its founding, it had turnover of 145 billion dong and employed some 790 people. Epco was not as large as Minh Phung but it was still ranked 68 among companies in Ho Chi Minh City.[24] That same year, Epco opened offices in Los Angeles and Sydney.[25] Like Tamexco, Epco was heralded as a future 'business group', described as owning two processing factories and the Huu Nghi Hotel.[26] Moreover, Epco was frequently held up as a company worthy of emulation, receiving numerous government awards, including certificates of commendation from the Ministry of Trade and General Customs Department, a labour award and a gold medal for meeting international quality standards.[27] Further underlining the fact that it was held in high regard politically, Epco played host to a visiting Cuban Communist Party delegation in November 1996.[28] That same year, it also set out its expansion plans until 2000, listing construction of a steel plant along with hotel and real estate development in Ho Chi Minh City, Hanoi and Vung Tau.[29]

Having charted the rise of Tamexco, Epco and Minh Phung, attention now turns to their fall, looking at what the accused were alleged to have done and highlighting the main contours of the investigation and trial process. I argue that from a fairly early stage in the investigation process it was never really in doubt that the accused would be found guilty.

The fall of Tamexco, Epco and Minh Phung

Tamexco

It first became evident in May 1996 that Tamexco was in difficulty. (See Appendix A5.1 for chronology of key developments in the Tamexco case.) An article in the English-language *Vietnam Investment Review* reported that Tamexco director, Pham Huy Phuoc, had been arrested in 'March/April' on charges of corruption in connection with losses at Tamexco estimated to be in the region of 350 billion dong.[30] According to the article, news of Phuoc's arrest had prompted a run on Tacombank. However, the article sought to reassure customers by saying – misleadingly in fact – that 'Tamexco is in fact independent of Tacombank and Pham Huy Phuoc's capital in the bank is held in pledge in compliance with the regulations'. It added that Tacombank had managed to 'overcome the crisis'.[31]

Over the next few months, the investigation into the events at Tamexco, led by the Ho Chi Minh City police investigation authority (*Co quan can sat dieu tra tong an thanh pho Ho Chi Minh*), gathered momentum. Among the main parties in the case, Phuoc and the director of a limited company called Dolphin that had worked closely with Tamexco, Le Minh Hai, were charged with 'corruption involving socialist assets' (*tham o tai san xa hoi chu nghia*), 'offering bribes' (*dua hoi lo*), 'intentionally contravening state regulations

Table 5.4 Key figures linked to the Tamexco case

Pham Huy Phuoc	Director Tamexco
Le Minh Hai	Director Dolphin Limited Company
Tran Quang Vinh	Director Binh Gia Limited Company
Le Duc Canh	Head Notary Office No. 1 Ba Ria Vung Tau
Nguyen Duy Lo	Deputy general-director Vietcombank
Nguyen Van De	General director Vietcombank
Nguyen Manh Thuy	Banker Vietcombank
Tran Linh	General director Vietcombank Vung Tau
Le Thi Van	People's Committee chairman Tan Binh District
Pham Van Hoa	Deputy party secretary Tan Binh District
Pham Ngoc Suong	Deputy head city party Financial Management Committee
Nguyen Chi Phuong	Party secretary Tan Binh District
Nguyen Thi Minh Tam	Deputy People's Committee chairman Tan Binh District
Dang Van Cuong	Deputy party secretary Tan Binh district
Pham Minh Duc	Head city party Financial Management Committee

Sources: *Tuoi Tre* 10 and 26 October 1996; *Thoi Bao Kinh te Saigon* 19–25 June 1997.

84 *Changing political economy of Vietnam*

causing serious consequences' (*co y lam trai qui dinh cua Nha nuoc ve quan ly kinh te gay hau qua nghiem trong*), and 'gambling' (*danh bac*). Hai had reportedly been instrumental in bribing the head of Notary Office No. 1 in Ba Ria-Vung Tau, Le Duc Canh, to verify artificially inflated land values. This enabled Tamexco to borrow more from the bank. Canh, in turn, was charged with 'taking bribes' (*nhan hoi lo*) and for 'exploiting his public position for private gain' (*loi dung chuc vu quyen han trong khi thi hang cong vu*). Another one of the prominent figures in the case, Tran Quang Vinh, who was the director of a limited company called Binh Gia that had also collaborated with Tamexco, was accused of corruption and intentionally contravening state regulations.

On 8 October 1996 the net was cast wider, with three senior bankers being charged with 'intentionally contravening state regulations' for continuing to lend to Tamexco despite its debts. These were Nguyen Duy Lo, the deputy general director at the state-owned Vietcombank, Nguyen Van De, a general director at Vietcombank and management board chairman of the joint venture bank, First Vinabank, and Tran Linh, who had headed Vietcombank's branch in Vung Tau and was also the deputy general director at First Vinabank.[32] Vietcombank was the main Vietnamese shareholder in First Vinabank. On 26 November another senior Vietcombank banker, Nguyen Manh Thuy, was charged with the same crime of 'intentionally contravening state regulations'. The levelling of the charge against Thuy brought to 20 the total number of people facing charges.[33]

During the investigation, steps were also taken to remove from office serving politicians implicated in the case before their involvement became widely known. In late May, just a few weeks after the problems at Tamexco first came to light, *Sai Gon Giai Phong* (Liberated Saigon) reported personnel changes in Tan Binh district, including the departure of the People's Committee chairman and deputy party secretary in the district, Pham Van Hoa. Hoa, who had succeeded Le Thi Van when she had become deputy People's Committee chairman in 1994, was later questioned when the case came before the Court of Appeal. He was also censured in June 1997 along with six other city and district officials by the Standing Committee of the Ho Chi Minh City party for 'being connected to the [Tamexco] case' (*co lien quan den vu an*). Back in May 1996, *Sai Gon Giai Phong* described Hoa as going to a different job (*di cong tac khac*). However, in the circumstances, the new job never materialised.[34]

Another politician who left office as the case against Tamexco was being prepared was the former Tan Binh District People's Committee chairman, Le Thi Van. She resigned as deputy People's Committee chairman in August 1996, reportedly on 'health grounds'.[35] Like Hoa, she too was summoned to appear at the appeal court and was also later censured by the city party Standing Committee.[36] When the case came to court, Phuoc said that he had given Van 11,000 US dollars to fund foreign trips, although Van denied this. There was also a dispute over two Nissan cars that Phuoc reportedly gave to

Van's family. Here, the issue was not about whether the transaction had taken place but whether both cars had been paid for. Van insisted they had.[37]

As the investigation gathered momentum, efforts were also made to revitalise Tacombank. A completely new management team was installed at the bank in October 1996. Phuoc was replaced as management board chairman by Luong Van Yen.[38] Furthermore, after having suffered a run on deposits, the bank also attempted to raise its registered capital to 60 billion dong.[39]

On 12 December the People's Court of Investigation in Ho Chi Minh City (*Vien kiem sat Nhan Dan TPHCM*) transferred the Tamexco file to the People's Court in Ho Chi Minh City (*Toa an Nhan Dan TPHCM*). This marked the formal end of the investigation stage. At the same time, the People's Court announced that the plan was to 'settle the case' by the end of January.[40]

The Tamexco trial began on 23 January 1997. It was a relatively short affair, lasting just nine days until 31 January. It took place in an environment of widespread public and media interest. Large crowds, including family members of the accused and other onlookers, gathered daily outside the courtroom to catch a glimpse of those in the dock. There was also daily coverage in the press and on television. Even before the case came to court, it had been trawled over quite extensively in the media. During the early stages of the investigation, press coverage was light. However, as the investigation gathered momentum during October prior to reaching its climax in December, newspaper articles appeared with greater frequency. There seemed to be very little in the coverage of the precept 'innocent until proven guilty' or of concern among officials that such coverage could prejudice the accused receiving a fair trial. On 29 October, even before the investigation was complete, the deputy head of the People's Court of Investigation, Dang Cong Tam told journalists categorically that Phuoc had bribed 38 or 39 organisations but that his main crime was corruption involving over 20 billion dong.[41]

The trial itself also included the release of a fair amount of salacious detail about Phuoc's alleged playboy lifestyle. Phuoc was said to have personally embezzled 144 billion dong, spending money on lavish foreign trips and gambling. On one occasion, Phuoc was said to have gambled away five of Tamexco's cars in a card game. He was reputed to have given gold to his mistress to buy a luxury villa in Ho Chi Minh City worth over 200,000 US dollars. The attention of the court was also drawn to the fact that Tamexco operated different accounting books – something Phuoc was said to have personally ordered his chief accountant, Ngo Van Ho, to do. The manner in which Phuoc bought shares in Tacombank using Tamexco money and registering the shares in the names of his relatives was also scrutinised.[42]

Rather revealing in terms of the actual web of responsibility that surrounded Tamexco's activities was the questioning in court of former Vietcombank deputy general director, Nguyen Duy Lo. While the official purpose was to shift the burden of guilt on to the bankers, the episode also highlighted the involvement of other institutions in ensuring Tamexco's access to credit. Lo was asked to explain why Vietcombank had continued lending to Tamexco despite its debts:

Court: By December 1992, Tamexco's total debt at Vietcombank was $15.6m, wasn't it?
Mr Lo: It was only $10m.
Court: Why then did you continue to lend a further $3m?
Mr Lo: At this stage, we did not want to lend but because Tamexco was a fertiliser importer – importing fertiliser for the winter–spring harvest – this was a duty entrusted to us by the office of the government.
Court: Why did they not entrust it to a firm that could do business profitably?
Mr Lo: The court ought to ask this question to the Ministries of Agriculture and Trade; why did they give [fertiliser import] quotas to Tamexco?[43]

When Lo was pressed further as to whether he was aware that lending to Tamexco, given the circumstances of its debts, contravened bank regulations (*sai so voi phap luat ngan hang*), he said that lending to the company was guided by Document 8 (*van ban 08*), issued on 8 April 1991. Document 8 apparently permitted certain bank clients to borrow beyond the normal ceiling set at 10 per cent of a bank's legal capital for a single client. According to Lo, it was the result of collaboration between different institutions in Ho Chi Minh City, including the local party committee:

> Document 8 was signed by [deputy State Bank governor] Chu Van Nguyen, and was the result of a collaboration between the State Bank and the Standing Committee of the Ho Chi Minh City party committee. It had the ability to overcome obstacles (*no co gia tri thao go*).[44]

Lo did not say who had signed for the party and to this day it remains something of a mystery.[45] According to the prosecution, Document 8 had been superseded by new regulations issued 28 days later by the then State Bank governor, Cao Sy Kiem. Called to give evidence, State Bank governor Chu Van Nguyen said that Vietcombank Ho Chi Minh City must have known about this. Lo, however, said that Document 8 continued to apply in Ho Chi Minh City even after the new regulations were issued.

At the end of the trial, the court handed out four death sentences to Phuoc, Hai, Vinh, and Canh. The other sixteen accused all received prison terms ranging from three years to life. Of the bankers, Lo and Linh were jailed for 15 years while De and Thuy received four and three year prison terms respectively. Le Thi Van and Pham Van Hoa were not convicted of anything. Truong My Hoa, who had served as party secretary in Tan Binh district during the late 1980s and early 1990s, was not even called to give evidence in the case.[46] On 7 January 1998, eight months after their appeals had been turned down, Phuoc, Vinh and Canh were executed by firing squad.[47] The fourth man sentenced to death, Le Minh Hai, had his sentence commuted to life imprisonment, saved on account of his father's heroic war service.[48] On 20 April 1999, Tamexco was declared bankrupt.[49]

Minh Phung–Epco

The first signs of what in time would come to be known as the Minh Phung–Epco case emerged just as the appeal in the Tamexco case was getting underway, with the arrest of Tang Minh Phung and Lien Khui Thin on 24 March 1997. (See Appendix A5.2 for chronology of key developments in the Minh Phung–Epco case.) They were originally charged with 'abusing confidence to appropriate socialist property', in connection with sale by Epco of commodities it had earlier lent to Minh Phung to use as collateral for a bank loan.[50] However, the scope of the investigation – like Tamexco led by the city police (*Co quan can sat dieu tra cong an thanh pho Ho Chi Minh*) – was soon widened, revealing a much more extensive pattern of indebtedness, mainly involving deferred-payment letters of credit taken out by a network of some 47 subsidiary companies controlled by Minh Phung and Epco. These companies were known locally as 'children' companies (*cong ty con*), or when they themselves spawned new satellite companies, 'grandchildren' companies (*cong ty con con*). Many of these were formed with the sole purpose of serving as a conduit through which Minh Phung and Epco could continue receiving bank credit even after they exceeded their credit limit.[51] The State Bank of Vietnam governor, Cao Sy Kiem, said on 23 April that commercial banks had guaranteed 44.02 million dollars worth of letters of credit to the two companies, of which 13.8 million dollars was overdue.[52] In the end, the combined debts of companies involved in the case would run to 357 million dollars.[53] Reflecting the widening of the investigation, the accusation against Phung and Thin was changed on 28 April 1997 to the more serious crime of 'fraud and embezzlement of state property' (*lua dao chim doat tai san xa hoi chu nghia*), for which the maximum sentence was death.[54]

In the following weeks, the investigation proceeded apace. On 15 May thirteen officials from Minh Phung were arrested.[55] On 31 May the deputy finance director of Minh Phung, Nguyen Van Ha, was found dead on the eleventh floor of the state-owned Incombank building on Ho Chi Minh City's Ham Nghi Street. He was reportedly found with a metal cord around his neck. In a macabre way, the development underlined just how the high the stakes were considered to be by those involved. As one newspaper headline read: 'Was the Minh Phung deputy director killed to prevent discovery of a clue?' (*Co phai giam doc cong ty Minh Phung bi giet bit dau moi?*).[56] Another led with 'Did the dead man talk before he died?' (*Mot cai chet da duoc bao truoc?*).[57] Before the investigation was complete another man had died in prison in

88 *Changing political economy of Vietnam*

Table 5.5 Key figures linked to the Minh Phung–Epco case

Tang Minh Phung	Director Minh Phung
Lien Khui Thin	Director Epco
Pham Nhat Hong	Deputy director Incombank
Nguyen Ngoc Bich	Deputy director Vietcombank
Nguyen Tuan Phuc	Epco management board chairman
Nguyen Xuan Phong	Director Grainco (Agriculture ministry firm)
Le Minh Xu	Director Dat Viet (Interior ministry firm)
Nguyen Hong Hai	Director Dat Thanh Limited Company
Tran Quang Hiep	Director Hiep Y Limited Company
Tran Binh Minh	Head credit department Incombank
Le Tot Nghiep	Deputy head credit department Incombank
Huynh Van Ut	Director Thai Tue Limited Company
Huynh Van Thanh	Chairman People's Committee District 3
Phan Tan Khoa	Deputy chairman People's Committee District 3

Sources: *Tuoi Tre* 23 December 1997; *Saigon Times Daily* 16 February 1998; *Thoi Bao Kinh te Saigon* 12 August 1999; *Vietnam Investment Review* 9–15 August 1999.

circumstances many believed were suspicious, while another reportedly had developed psychiatric problems (*bi benh tam than*).[58]

The Minh Phung–Epco investigation continued for the remainder of 1997 and into 1998. As with the Tamexco case, the investigation period also saw the removal from office of officials caught up in the case – on this occasion District 3 officials implicated on account of the district's controlling stake in Epco. Among officials removed in this way were District 3 People's Committee chairman, Huynh Van Thanh, who was relieved of his post on 18 December 1997 and the deputy People's Committee chairman in the district, Pham Tan Khoa, who relinquished his post on 16 February 1998.[59] Khoa was subsequently accused of 'intentionally doing wrong in economic management causing serious consequences'. Thanh was never formally accused of committing any crime. When questioned he said he was not aware of what Epco was doing. Nevertheless, in what might be regarded as an admission of guilt, Thanh was said in May 1998 to have used his own money to pay back the money taken from the District 3 budget to set up Epco. Commenting on how Thanh came to have such a large sum of money one journalist wrote cynically: '. . . one thing is clear. Thanh needed 500 months of his salary to accumulate such a huge amount of money if it really was his own money.'[60]

On 19 March permission was given for the investigation in the Minh Phung–Epco case to run a further four months until 24 July.[61] It then overran a second time before finally being completed on 21 October after a total of 19 months.[62] On 2 January 1999 the case file was transferred from the People's

Economic decentralisation: the Tamexco and Minh Phung–Epco cases 89

Court of Investigation to the People's Court in Ho Chi Minh City. The file's transfer was followed shortly afterwards by an announcement that the trial would commence at the 'beginning of May'.[63] By the time the trial began on 10 May the net had been widened to include a total of 77 people facing charges. Among those charged were Epco's management board chairman Nguyen Tuan Phuc, two deputy directors of Vietcombank and Incombank, Nguyen Ngoc Bich and Pham Nhat Hong, and Nguyen Xuan Phong, who was the director of a Ministry of Agriculture company called Grainco. In all, among the accused were 51 company directors and deputy directors, 18 banking officials, and one district People's Committee official.[64] In addition to those mentioned above, other companies and banks implicated in the case included the city party company, Saigon Petro, an Interior Ministry firm, Dat Viet, as well as five joint stock banks, including Exim Bank in which Minh Phung was at one stage a shareholder. All but two of those summoned to court were charged with 'fraud and embezzlement of state property'. The two exceptions were Phan Tan Khoa who, as we noted above, was charged with 'intentionally doing wrong in economic management causing serious consequences' and an official at Incombank, Pham Thanh Chau, who was charged with 'lacking responsibility resulting in serious losses to Socialist assets' (*thieu trach nhiem gay thiet hai nghiem trong den tai san xa hoi chu nghia*).

As with the Tamexco case, the investigation stage was also characterised by intense media interest. However, on this occasion, newspaper coverage was even more intensive. This was especially the case during the period October–December, which directly followed the investigation's completion. Tang Minh Phung, Lien Khui Thin, Pham Nhat Hong, Nguyen Ngoc Bich – or Phung–Thin–Hong–Bich as one newspaper put it – were very much depicted as the ringleaders who from the beginning had wilfully set out to defraud the system. Phung, Thin and Hong were alleged to have forged some kind of 'brotherhood' pact (*lam le an the ket nghia anh em*) in 1994.[65] Hong was said to have been instrumental in advising Phung and Thin to set up *cong ty con* and *con ty con con* subsidiary companies so that they were able to continue accessing bank credit.

Phung in particular appeared to receive harsh treatment in the press. He was now a man who 'lacked formal educational qualifications' and who 'used his own son in company advertisements'.[66] The atmosphere was almost one of gloating. As if to emphasise his fall from grace, there were humiliating pictures of him in the press. One featured an anxious-looking Phung standing before the arresting policeman in a comfortably furnished living room. In the background there was a large tropical fish tank, while on the table there were bouquets of flowers and cans of soft drinks as if the police had disturbed some kind of celebration.[67] Later, there were 'before' and 'after' shots. In the latter, Phung was no longer smiling and he looked as if he had put on weight. One article entitled 'Tang Minh Phung: the flamboyant prince's wings are broken' (*Tang Minh Phung: con phuong hoang gay canh*) sought to create the

90 *Changing political economy of Vietnam*

impression that Phung exercised total control. Nguyen Dinh Ha, a former deputy director at Minh Phung who was himself subsequently charged, was quoted as saying: 'On everything big or small *Anh Bay* [Tang Minh Phung] decided. Without his decision nothing moved forward.' In ridiculing tones, the article went on to relate how Phung had once even appointed his cook as a director of one of the *cong ty con*.[68]

When the trial got underway on 10 May intensive media coverage began all over again. Given the earlier coverage, there was a real sense of *déjà vu* about the proceedings. Reflecting the size of the case, the trial lasted nearly three months until 3 August. At its conclusion, six people were sentenced to death and six to life imprisonment. Among those sentenced to death were Phung and Thin, Incombank's Pham Nhat Hong, Vietcombank's Nguyen Ngoc Bich, Epco's management board chairman Nguyen Tuan Phuc, and Grainco's director Nguyen Xuan Phong. Those given life were all either company directors or bank officials.[69] Two of the death sentences – Bich's and Phong's – were later commuted to life by the Court of Appeal.[70] The remaining 65 people found guilty – all but five of the accused – received prison sentences ranging from 2–20 years. The former deputy People's Committee chairman in District 3 received a short prison sentence.

There was no great public surprise at the tough sentences. Speaking in March 1999 before the trial had even begun, one informant stated quite categorically that Tang Minh Phung knew he had a 99 per cent chance of being sentenced to death and a 1 per cent chance of getting life.[71] Another source said cynically how most people in Vietnam think that if you go to court you are dead already (*di ra toa chet roi*).[72] After an initial attempt to keep Minh Phung afloat given its large labour force, both Minh Phung and Epco were shut down.

Explaining Tamexco's and Minh Phung–Epco's fall

Both in official statements and in foreign accounts, the Tamexco and Minh Phung–Epco cases are usually depicted simply as the state getting tough on corruption. As the Tamexco trial got underway in January 1997, the Politburo member and National Assembly chairman, Nong Duc Manh, was quoted as saying that only by rooting out corruption could people's declining confidence in the state and the government be restored.[73] One foreign news report described the trial as a 'showcase for the government's determination to punish graft'.[74] When the Minh Phung–Epco case was first breaking, it was described as part of a 'concerted [party] campaign to crack down on private and public corruption'.[75] However, such a description does not adequately explain why these companies and the people associated with them were so thoroughly brought down. After all, much of the behaviour on which the trials centred, although by most definitions corrupt or involving rent-seeking, is fairly widespread: political involvement in credit allocations, for example; lending to companies even if they are in debt; setting up private companies as

Economic decentralisation: the Tamexco and Minh Phung–Epco cases 91

a way of siphoning off state assets (i.e. classic 'asset stripping'); using deferred payment letters of credit as a way of raising capital to speculate in land; re-mortgaging already mortgaged assets; setting up subsidiary companies to disguise one's activity; and operating multiple books. As was discussed in Chapter 2, this kind of activity is part and parcel of the political–business culture that had developed by the second half of the 1990s. There is also more to say about the role the Tamexco and Minh Phung–Epco cases played in diverting attention away from the real nature of Vietnam's political economy. Seeing the cases simply in terms of the authorities 'getting tough on corruption' does not allow for such an interpretation.

Others have sought to explain the fall of Tamexco and Minh Phung–Epco with reference to the fact that they ran up large debts.[76] However, again the existence of extensive debts is not in itself a satisfactory explanation, for many companies have debts.[77] Some have seen the fall of Minh Phung and Epco as symptomatic of an engrained official hostility to the private sector. However, this is simplistic. To begin with, it is not the label – private or state – that matters but what lies behind it. In the case of Epco, its credentials were solidly statist. Moreover, this type of explanation does not explain the fall of Tamexco given its formal status as a city party company. In the case of Minh Phung and Epco, it is noteworthy that both Tang Minh Phung and Lien Khui Thin are ethnic Chinese. Mistrust between Chinese business and the state is still current.[78] However, no one has suggested that their ethnicity was a factor in their fall and this interpretation is not considered further here.[79]

High-level political manoeuvring?

In relation to both Tamexco and Minh Phung–Epco, there were rumours of a high-level political dimension to the cases, with the suggestion being that this somehow lay behind their coming to a head. In the case of Tamexco, it was suggested that the company was a casualty of the fall of Politburo member Nguyen Ha Phan prior to the Eighth Party Congress in 1996.

The official foreign ministry statement at the time of Phan's expulsion from the party said that he had been expelled for 'abuse of power, authoritarianism and fanaticism'. In what was almost certainly a pretext, there was mention of the recent discovery of documents that implicated him in having revealed the names of comrades and locations of bases during the war after he had been arrested by the South Vietnamese government in 1959.[80] According to accounts linking Tamexco with Phan's fall, Tamexco director Pham Huy Phuoc was reportedly 'close' to Phan, who wanted to promote him to a higher position. However, when Phan was brought down in pre-Congress manoeuvring, Phuoc lost his umbrella and hence became vulnerable himself.[81] Certainly the timing is plausible: Phan's downfall was sealed at the Tenth Plenum of the Central Party Committee held from 12–20 April 1996, while news of Phuoc's difficulties first surfaced in early May. Prior to his fall, Phan was head of the central party's Economic Committee (*Ban kinh te trung*

92 *Changing political economy of Vietnam*

uong dang). One informant said that Phan was certainly the right person for Phuoc to know if he wanted promotion, given his position.[82]

However, there are also some potential inconsistencies. Accounts as to when Phuoc was arrested are not particularly precise and he may have been arrested in March shortly before Phan's fall at the tenth plenum. Although not necessarily inconsistent with a link between Tamexco and Phan, an article in August 1996 said that Tamexco had been under official investigation since October 1995.[83] In the Minh Phung–Epco case, there were rumours that the People's Committee chairman Vo Viet Thanh was in some way connected to Minh Phung.[84] One informant noted the way press coverage of the case spoke repeatedly of 'People's Committee responsibility'.

If such high-level connections existed in relation either to Tamexco or Minh Phung–Epco, these never came to light in either the investigation or the trial. Nevertheless, the idea that there was more to the cases than met the eye persisted to the end. Some of the newspaper headlines were tantalisingly provocative in this respect. 'Who stands behind Tamexco?' (*Ai dung sau lung Tamexco?*) one headline ran. 'Who saved Ming Phung?' (*Ai da nem phao cuu sinh cho Minh Phung?*) read another, asking why Minh Phung had been able to borrow money for so long despite its debts. In general, articles like these provided few answers, tending merely to skim the surface.

At the end of the Tamexco trial, the prosecutor, Tran Kim Tien, said that those still hiding in the shadows would be exposed (*toi tin chac rang nhung bong den con la se duoc dua ra anh sang*).[85] In the event, a few more people were called to give evidence at the Court of Appeal but there were no major revelations. There was also a suggestion that as Phuoc was led away to be executed he requested to make a statement but was not permitted to.[86] Asked why the likes of Phuoc or Phung did not blow the whistle in court given their certain knowledge that they were going to be sentenced to death, one informant said that they feared that if they did so that they would ruin what little chance their families and children had for a future.[87]

The loss of political backing?

In the absence of more evidence, this kind of 'high-level political' explanation for Tamexco or Minh Phung–Epco's fall must ultimately be treated with caution. Nevertheless, the idea of a loss of political backing as being a factor in the companies' downfall is less easily put to one side. The agglomeration of interests in Tan Binh district centred on Truong My Hoa and Le Thi Van certainly appear to be important in Tamexco's rise. Other sources have mentioned the former deputy People's Committee chairman, Nguyen Van Huan, as a one-time backer of Minh Phung.[88]

Another informant, while arguing that allegations of a link between Vo Viet Thanh and Minh Phung were not clear-cut, nevertheless suggested the evidence that Minh Phung once had the backing of the city People's Committee was compelling. The source cited three factors. First, the People's

Committee had reportedly allocated 20 ha of land to Minh Phung in return for the company doing minimal pavement repair work in District 1 and 3. Second, the source noted that at the time of Minh Phung's licensing by the People's Committee in 1993, there were irregularities relating to its declared registered capital that were not initially picked up.[89] Third, the informant said that Minh Phung's heavy involvement in the real estate business would have required People's Committee support. Other private companies, the source noted, were not so privileged. The same source also suggested that Epco's rise was in part the result of protection from the former party secretary in Ho Chi Minh City, Vo Tran Chi, who was said to particularly favour the brand of 'state capitalism' that Epco represented.[90]

Even if the evidence for the existence of these political umbrellas is in some cases quite good, the fact of their identification does not explain why these companies subsequently lost this support. One possibility is that they lost political backing on account of leadership change in Ho Chi Minh City, namely the retirement of party secretary Vo Tran Chi and his replacement with Truong Tan Sang in May 1996. Vo Tran Chi had been party secretary in the city for nearly ten years and it is possible that his departure precipitated some kind of 'cleaning out of the ranks'. Although the evidence is not strong, it is certainly plausible in the case of Epco, given the suggestions that the company enjoyed the support of Vo Tran Chi. However, the chronology is not quite right in relation to the Tamexco case, which was breaking shortly before Vo Tran Chi retired.

Something more intangible?

In the end, it is not possible to identify a single factor as lying behind the fall of these companies. More plausible is the idea that their downfall was the result of a combination of factors. Something that is discernible both in relation to Tamexco and Minh Phung–Epco is a sense of gathering momentum during the investigation stage. When news of the alleged misdemeanours involving the companies first broke, it was as if it was genuinely not clear – from the point of view of the investigators and more importantly their political masters higher up – how much was going to be made of the case, the nature of the charges, how wide the net was to be cast, and so on. This initial caution is reflected in the fairly muted press coverage to begin with. However, events have a habit of developing their own momentum. In relation to Tamexco, the charging of the bankers on 8 October 1996 clearly signalled a new stage. In the Minh Phung–Epco case there was a distinct sense in which the stakes had been upped when the charge against Phung and Thin was changed to a more serious crime on 28 April 1997. The arrest of 13 Minh Phung officials on 15 May was a further indication that the case was gathering momentum. Furthermore, in both Tamexco and Minh Phung–Epco the removal from political office of those implicated before their involvement became widely known also strongly gave the impression of

94 *Changing political economy of Vietnam*

people readying themselves for a wider storm. In addition, intensified coverage of the cases in the press carried with it a sense that a point of no return had been reached. Echoing this interpretation, one informant described how initially the aim was to keep the Tamexco case fairly low key but, according to the informant, as the case started to attract attention this was not possible and the Politburo felt a need to make an example of it.[91]

Why a case first breaks into the open and then gathers momentum may have to do with antagonistic institutions or political groupings seeking to use the case as a way of wrong-footing their rivals. The constant references to the 'responsibility of the People's Committee' in the Minh Phung–Epco case – yet another attempt to undermine Vo Viet Thanh – was commonly seen in this light.[92] In such a climate, emphasis on the extent of the debts run up by a company or the fact of an alleged playboy lifestyle are then used as justification for why the case must proceed.

The fact that the Minh Phung–Epco case followed so soon after Tamexco was attributed by one source to the climate of fear that had developed in the banking sector in its wake.[93] According to this source, the new director of Vietcombank was nervous that he would be blamed if further misdemeanours at the bank came to light. As a result he launched an investigation of Vietcombank's larger clients. When signs of wrongdoings involving Minh Phung–Epco came to light, he reportedly forwarded the details to the police, precipitating a wider investigation and the eventual arrest of Phung and Thin. In the case of Minh Phung–Epco, there is certainly a sense that the decision to mobilise the full weight of the judiciary against Phung and Thin was made within a matter of weeks of their arrest, notably with the amendment of the charges against them. This suggests that by the time Minh Phung–Epco surfaced a certain momentum in favour of these kinds of trials already existed following Tamexco. The speed with which Phung came to be vilified in the press – less than a month after he was arrested – also suggested that his fate was sealed early on. Phung's distinctly private credentials also arguably made him more vulnerable to abuse in the media than officials linked to Tamexco, the state-owned commercial banks, or to the more statist Epco.[94]

Proving guilt

Once a decision has been made to make an example of the accused, the investigation process then becomes more an exercise in assembling the necessary evidence to prove their guilt, and much less a search for the truth. Moreover, the trial is simply the culmination of that process, in which the outcome is never really in doubt. In this respect, it is striking how there is more than a passing resemblance in the way those connected to Tamexco and Minh Phung–Epco were brought down and the infamous show trials of the Soviet Union in the 1930s. Thus, despite the very different political and economic circumstances of 1990s Vietnam, it is noticeable how the state seems driven to respond in a recognisably traditional 'Stalinist' way.[95] It is in this context that the press coverage – creating the impression of guilt – is important. Thus, as we have seen, by the time the sentences are announced, the public is widely convinced of their guilt. The fact that the media coverage may paint a distorted picture is not so important. In the cases of both Phuoc and Phung there was a distinct discrepancy between the media picture and that offered by well-informed informants who had insights that went beyond those published in the press in the months after the men's arrest. One source described Phuoc as 'good businessman' but said that the responsibility – who was responsible when things went wrong – was not clear.[96] The bankers imprisoned in the Tamexco case had earlier been known as the 'four pillars' (*tu tru*) in recognition of their role in overseeing Vietcombank's transition from monobanking to a two-tier banking system. The same source described Vietcombank's Nguyen Duy Lo as a 'victim', saying he took responsibility but that it was not he who signed Document 8.[97] Another informant who had inside knowledge of Tang Minh Phung's character described him as someone who paid good salaries, was generous with bonuses and was frequently involved in charity work.[98]

This sense of a re-writing of the past comes across strongly elsewhere. In a 1997 directory of leading companies that had been compiled before the Minh Phung–Epco case broke but was still on sale afterwards, the entries for Minh Phung and Epco were blocked out, while two pages were glued together in an attempt to conceal a full-page advertisement for Epco.[99] Moreover, in court, awkward or uncomfortable details in the cases were simply glossed over or left out. In the Minh Phung–Epco trial, for instance, the issue of Nguyen Van Ha's murder was paid only the scantest attention while the death in custody of another suspect was attributed to his being ill.[100]

The politics of economic decentralisation

In this chapter I have concentrated on the Tamexco and Minh Phung–Epco cases. However, while major investigations and trials do not occur everyday, these two cases were by no means the only such events during the 1990s. In Ho Chi Minh City, Tamexco was preceded by the case of Gia Dinh joint stock bank, which following a trial in October 1996 resulted in one death sentence for the bank's deputy general director, two life sentences and four other jail terms ranging from three to 20 years in connection with embezzlement of the bank's assets.[101] Minh Phung–Epco was followed by another major court case in Ho Chi Minh City – the Tan Truong Sanh smuggling case, which came to light in October 1997. It revealed a smuggling network in which goods were imported by the container load with the connivance of the General Department of Customs in Ho Chi Minh City, Can Tho and Hue. So extensive was the smuggling network that when it was uncovered the price of electronic goods – in which the smugglers specialised – rose perceptibly in Ho Chi Minh City. When the trial ended, two more people had been sentenced to death and some 70 people given prison terms.[102] In southern Long An province another case of institutionalised smuggling came to light in 1998 involving key provincial officials, including the vice-chairman of the People's Committee, the director and deputy director of the Market Management Committee, the director of the provincial tax bureau, and the chief of the Frontier Post. Those involved collaborated to create a system whereby shipments were taxed at below official rates and smugglers were allowed to operate as long as they paid token 'fines'.[103]

Moreover, cases such as these were not just a southern phenomenon during the late 1990s. In 1996–7 a major drug smuggling ring involving Interior Ministry officials was uncovered in the north, resulting in a court case in which eight people were sentenced to death and 14 given jail terms.[104] There was also the 'corruption' trial involving the once revered Nam Dinh textile company in Hanoi.[105] Furthermore, earlier in the 1990s, there were the cases of the Bamboo Garden rotating credit scheme (*hui vuon tre*) (1993) and Legamex (1994).[106] Compared with the previous decade, this type of case appears to be becoming more common during the 1990s. From a survey of the secondary literature, it is certainly hard to find so many equivalent episodes for the 1980s.

With reference to Tamexco and Minh Phung–Epco, the seeming increase in these kinds of trials would appear to reflect the decentralisation of He Chi Mirth City's political economy that has occurred particularly since the late 1980s. As economic power has become decentralised – and the kind of activity on which the cases centred has become more common – it is as if the higher levels periodically feel the need to discipline the lower levels. However, given that similar kinds of trials can be observed up and down the country, this is clearly not a Ho Chi Minh City phenomenon or even just a southern phenomenon.

In the case of both Tamexco and Minh Phung–Epco the investigation and trial process was conducted at the city level – by the city police and in the city courts. However, these institutions are linked vertically and directly to the centre (*nganh doc*). Moreover, it is inconceivable, given that many of those involved were being tried on charges that carried capital offences, that the process was not being controlled at the very top. There are not many explicit references to this, although speaking just after the conclusion of the Tamexco trial the prosecutor, Tran Kim Tien, said that the aim was to wrap up the trial as quickly as possible as 'instructed by Prime Minister [and Politburo member] Vo Van Kiet'.[107] I also noted earlier the comment of one informant that it was the Politburo that felt the need to proceed with the Tamexco case once it had attracted a certain level of attention.

While in a more decentralised environment there may be a greater need for the higher levels periodically to discipline the lower levels, it is important to ask what purpose the cases serve beyond simply keeping the lower levels in line. Who is actually punished is revealing in this respect. In the Tamexco and Minh Phung–Epco cases, it is the businessmen and bankers who bore the brunt of the sentencing, including receiving the death penalties. District politicians, although in some cases implicated, removed from office and summoned to give evidence, were rarely charged with anything and as a result get off relatively lightly.[108] To the extent that they were involved, politicians higher up were rarely implicated at all. As a result, rather than the cases simply being an undifferentiated clampdown on corruption, the message becomes more mixed. In terms of the public at large, the main goal of creating the impression that justice has been done would however seem to be achieved.

Businessmen and bankers, meanwhile, are shown to be vulnerable in the event of such cases developing, for their one-time political backers will drop them if it is expedient to do so. Politicians, on the other hand, appear to have a good chance of getting off, including lower level ones. Furthermore, by creating the impression that cases such as Tamexco and Minh Phung–Epco involve 'exceptional acts by a handful of fallen officials' (*can bo thoai hoa*), they serve the purpose of diverting attention away from the real nature of the country's political economy, which can continue largely uninterrupted. Moreover, in an era that has placed great emphasis on developing the 'rule of law', the way the judicial process is being deployed to deliver a highly political message is striking.

6 Rethinking reform: property rights and the dynamics of change

Introduction

Ho Chi Minh City's political economy in the late 1990s was, as we have seen, characterised by a significant amount of what we might describe as fairly unreformed behaviour: anti-competitive practices, a tendency for credit constraints to be soft, rent-seeking, and corruption. In keeping with the prognosis of one section of the academic literature on reforming state socialist countries – although in stark contrast to the typical image of Ho Chi Minh City as a bastion of reformism – Vietnam's second city would thus appear to be a prime example of the pitfalls of partial reform: a key candidate for economic stagnation and decline as officials seek to obstruct or block reforms that threaten these interests.[1] And yet, it is clearly more complicated than this.

First, Ho Chi Minh City's economy has not stagnated. Economic growth rates in the city over the last decade have been more than respectable and above the national average.[2] Second, while formal reforms have undoubtedly encountered opposition and advanced slowly at best, it is certainly not the case that no change has taken place at all. On the contrary, one senses that rather significant change has occurred: Ho Chi Minh City's political economy is now clearly far removed from any pre-reform state-socialist blueprint.

So what has changed? This concluding chapter seeks to pin this down. It argues that change has to do with a largely spontaneous process involving changes in property rights governing control over state-owned enterprises or state assets. The issue of property rights was first tackled earlier in Chapter 3. This chapter seeks to extend the analysis of this issue. In particular, it seeks to explain why the property rights regime has evolved the way it has in Ho Chi Minh City. Most importantly, I shall look at the dynamics that have underpinned changes in property rights, pointing out that they differ substantially from those commonly highlighted in mainstream discussions of reform and change, notably in the literature on Vietnam and Ho Chi Minh City. I also consider what bearing this has on how we conceive of reform and ask what, if any, is the link between the process of change I have described and reform.

Opposition to reform?

Those who have argued against partial reform do so on the grounds that continued state intervention in the economy and the rent-seeking associated with it leads to vested interests, which in turn can be expected to resist reform. This position, which is sometimes classified under the umbrella of neo-liberalism or referred to as the 'new political economy', has been summarised by scholars writing on China as follows:

> Strong critiques of partial reform are founded on the conviction that the behaviour of socialist bureaucrats is decisively influenced by the rents that they receive from their interference in, or predation upon, profit-generating enterprises. . . . Partial reform is therefore seen as an invitation to obstruction, as bureaucrats seek to maintain their hold over the economic assets on which their traditional privileges rest, and to a stagnant economy, as needed reforms are blocked.[3]

Tracing its roots from neo-classical economics and strongly influenced by Janos Kornai's writings on the failed reforms in Hungary in the late 1960s and 1970s, such thinking continues to be influential today.[4] Advocates of big-bang reforms may have been chastened by some spectacular setbacks, notably in Russia but the essential point – that officials have vested interests that make them likely to try to block reforms – is still widely heard.[5]

That such views continue to be heard is perhaps not surprising. In many respects, such ideas make a lot of sense. In the findings presented in this book, the image of different institutions in Ho Chi Minh City strongly resisting outside encroachment, very often in defence of 'gate-keeping' activity such as licensing, inspection powers or business interests of affiliated companies, comes across strongly. Moreover, the defence of such activity can also be seen to have a debilitating effect on reforms. The case of the Road Vehicle Inspection stations (Chapter 4) asserting their view that the Ho Chi Minh City People's Committee had no right to suggest that they should be put forward for equitisation provides a good example. Foot-dragging on the part of Ho Chi Minh City's departments in relation to the 'one stop, one stamp' administrative reform programme, also considered in Chapter 4, is another. As the advocates of the 'new political economy' have suggested, the defence of rent-seeking activity clearly does result in opposition to reform.

Can we not be more precise as to what is being opposed and what is not? Ho Chi Minh City may exhibit some of the characteristics warned of by critics of partial reform, while officially sanctioned reforms may also not have advanced very fast. However, it is certainly not just a picture of stagnation. Aside from impressive city growth rates, many city firms recorded spectacular rates of expansion from the late 1980s and during the 1990s, as we saw with the companies profiled in Chapter 2.[6] Moreover, such performances seem to have been accompanied by genuine shifts in business practice. Companies dominated by state business interests such as Saigon Tourist, Saigon Jewellery Company or even Epco and Tamexco appear fully at home in competitive markets, whether it be the real estate market, foreign exchange dealing or international trade. Moreover, they produce real products and provide real services, which people are prepared to pay for. Furthermore, they – and other firms like them – appear constantly to be pushing out the boundaries with new ways of doing business, often involving innovative ways of raising capital.[7] There is thus no opposition to reform here.

And yet at the same time, the very fact that these firms are able to do these things and that they have been successful rests to a large extent on a political economy that is skewed in their favour, whether it be through barriers to entry that limit the competition they face or through privileged access to land, often rooted in a process of confiscation and reallocation that occurred in the period immediately after 1975. Furthermore, as we saw in Chapter 2, these same companies are quick to exploit advantages derived from the fact that more often than not their owners hold political office. Such advantages might include preferential access to contracts, or to credit through the state-dominated banking system.[8] As we saw in relation to Tamexco, Minh Phung and Epco, the credit constraint had a tendency during the 1990s to be distinctly soft. Advantages might also include the opportunity to engage in distinctly illegal acts, such as smuggling, where a company's political standing afforded a certain level of protection against being 'found out'. Thus, while companies are engaging in rent-seeking activity and happy to operate in an environment of limited competition, they are in other respects embracing the market. That companies are behaving in this way would appear to suggest a modification of the idea of the 'entrepreneurial state' put forward by Ducker insofar as based on the Ho Chi Minh City case, reform or the market is supported selectively.[9]

Changes in property rights

Underpinning the changes in company behaviour highlighted earlier have been changes in property rights, as discussed in Chapter 3. In Vietnam's case, including Ho Chi Minh City, the dominant formal arrangement has been the reformed state enterprise where from the late 1970s onwards companies were given greater responsibility for production decisions as well as extended rights over generated income compared with the 'traditional state firm' under planning.[10] However, while formal reforms have not gone much further than those changes detailed in relation to the reformed state enterprise, property arrangements have continued to evolve informally.[11] As we saw in Chapter 2, two forms are particularly common in Ho Chi Minh City: first, local elite privatisation, whereby those running state enterprises gradually assume greater control over company assets, with the result that they eventually exercise a much fuller set of rights than is consistent with the property regime pertaining to the reformed state enterprise; and second, the siphoning off of public funds or assets into newly established enterprises, which operate as private firms.

Government-centred property rights

It is possible, however, to advance our discussion of property rights a stage further. Literature on China also distinguishes between government-centred and entrepreneur-centred property regimes. Ho Chi Minh City seems to lean towards the former, with control generally in the hands of officials linked to the original controlling institution.[12] Where the property regime is government-centred, managers tend to be paid employees rather than owners. This can be seen in Ho Chi Minh City in the movement of managers between different institutions in ways that cut across our understanding of ownership. For example, new managers are sometimes brought on board as a 'safe pair of hands' in the event of a crisis.[13]

However, it is not always so clear-cut or straightforward. Sometimes it is possible to distinguish between owners and managers, but sometimes it is not. In some cases, managers appear to be owners as well.[14] Moreover, in the same way that officials linked to a company's formal controlling institution can gradually appropriate control over an enterprise in a way inappropriate to its status as a reformed state enterprise, it appears that managers can also garner greater authority, particularly if they hold office for a long time. The case of Nguyen Huu Dinh and Saigon Jewellery Company is illustrative in this respect. Here, there are hints of possible conflict between the company's would-be owners and its manager, namely Dinh. A former District 10 official, Dinh was made the director of Saigon Jewellery Company at its founding in 1988. He was still serving until his death from cancer over a decade later.[15] The company's controlling institution was the Department of Trade, although many informants were of the opinion that Dinh was the dominant influence at the firm – a controller of capital in his own right.[16] Certainly, after problems arose in the late 1990s linked to Saigon Jewellery Company's incorporation in the Department of Trade dominated Saigon Trading Corporation (Satra), as described in Chapter 4, one interpretation was that Dinh was happy to see the company removed from Satra influence. However, even here Dinh seems more like the company employee – if a rather influential one – with rival government institutions wrestling for control of a lucrative asset. Thus, in the final analysis, property arrangements at Saigon Jewellery Company would appear to be more government-centred than entrepreneur-centred.[17]

Enforcing property rights

Scholars on China have also sought to address issues surrounding the security and enforcement of property rights, arguing that enforcement can work in a variety of ways, ranging from the application of law to social custom.[18] In Ho Chi Minh City, the security of the property rights regime that emerged over the 1980s and 1990s rests primarily on the ability of company owners, or the institutions to which they are linked, to resist outside encroachment. There is nothing institutionalised about this. Rather it rests fundamentally on the application of power. However, as we saw in Chapter 4, institutional particularism is well-developed in Ho Chi Minh City, and hence for much of the time companies are able to enjoy a rather extensive range of property rights.[19]

At the same time, because existing property arrangements emerged informally – often involving plainly illegal or corrupt acts – they are also characterised by a degree of vulnerability. Companies have to walk a difficult tightrope. As they interact with other institutions on an official basis, they have to maintain the pretence that they are compliant reformed state enterprises while at the same time defending their property rights. To protect their property rights, managers or would-be owners have to conduct much of their activity on a covert basis, concealing their business plans or the true size of their profits. As companies get larger, this is not easy. It is in this context that paying for foreign trips for officials, funding the cost of overseas study for their children, or buying them cars – as we saw in the Tamexco and Minh Phung–Epco cases – can make the difference as to whether or not a company is successful in maintaining its control over the assets it has appropriated for itself.

The reorganisation of Satra, as detailed in Chapter 4 and mentioned above, in which a number of particularly lucrative companies were wrested from the hands of one owner to be placed under the control of another in the name of 'organisational efficiency', would appear to be a prime example of the relative lack of security associated with existing property arrangements. This is not to say that this kind of process is easy to execute – it is not and the fact that it involved the powerful Department of Trade makes it all the more stunning – but it can happen. Furthermore, even if we reject an interpretation of the Tamexco and Minh Phung–Epco cases that sees them as undifferentiated clampdowns on corruption, as articulated in Chapter 5, it remains the case that the people brought down in these cases were vulnerable because of the way they had embezzled public assets. With its origins in the informal way property arrangements have evolved in Ho Chi Minh City, this vulnerability was something that was evident throughout the city.

Ho Chi Minh City's property arrangements explained

Research on rural industry in China has sought to explain differences between government-centred and entrepreneur-centred property regimes by referring to differing resource endowments and access to capital.[20] In areas where property arrangements have been government-centred, existing enterprises, capital, and to some extent business expertise, tended to be in the hands of local officials when reforms began.[21] When reforms got under way, officials in such areas generally sought to retain control of these enterprises and indeed often expand their interest in them. Managers were employed to run the enterprises but more liberal property arrangements, such as leasing and contracting, were generally shunned. In government-centred property regimes, officials have tended to enjoy preferential access to capital, whether through the budget or the banking system. In areas where property regimes are entrepreneur-centred, scholars on China have suggested that there was often no industrial base worth speaking of when reforms began. Moreover, entrepreneur-centred property regimes were generally characterised by more diverse sources of credit, notably in the form of overseas remittances from Chinese communities in South East Asia. In such an environment of little or no industrial base and access to capital from overseas Chinese, officials tended much more towards encouraging private entrepreneurship, working with entrepreneurs and in the process benefiting from the collaboration.[22] Entrepreneur-centred property regimes have found to be common in coastal areas in South East China.

These findings on China offer helpful pointers to explaining the dominant property arrangements found in Ho Chi Minh City. Notwithstanding the pre-1975 legacy in the south of greater experience of the market compared with the north, the nature of the Communist take-over was such that control over the commanding heights of the economy was largely wrested from the hands of the old elite and placed in the hands of party and government officials by the time reforms began.[23] Moreover, Ho Chi Minh City's longstanding position as an economic centre of repute underlined the fact that the city possessed an industrial and commercial base that was worth holding on to and developing.[24] The desire to protect this legacy offers an explanation for the relative hostility to the private sector in the 1980s and 1990s, in turn favouring covert local-elite privatisation and a government-centred private sector (i.e. officials channelling public resources into private companies). There is also the suspicion that the heavy presence of centrally managed companies in Ho Chi Minh City – themselves a legacy of the way the former Saigon was taken over – may have added to this unfavourable environment for an entrepreneur-centred private sector.

With respect to capital, the importance attributed to preferential access to credit on the part of officials in government-centred property regimes fits my findings on Ho Chi Minh City, where access to credit through the banking system seems to ensure that the credit constraint tended to be soft. Furthermore, although Ho Chi Minh City is a port city with large numbers of former inhabitants and their descendants living abroad (the Viet Kieu) – which would suggest it has something in common with some of China's coastal provinces in its access to overseas remittances – the reality is that overseas Vietnamese have never been a really significant source of capital inflows. In large part, this is because the events of 1975 and the continuing exodus of so-called 'boat people' into the 1980s are just too recent to instil any sense of confidence among potential investors.[25] This, one suspects, contrasts with China's coastal provinces where the links with overseas Chinese are often the result of migration which goes back much further, generally pre-dating the Communist victory in 1949. As a result, relations with one's 'native land' tend to be much less emotionally and ideologically charged.[26]

Ho Chi Minh City's pre-1975 legacy should also have left a solid body of expertise in the hands of non-party people, which might have been expected to have contributed to the creation of a more entrepreneur-centred property regime. However, many of the very people with such expertise fled the country, have been prevented from applying their knowledge, or are now past working age. Pre-1975 expertise, whether it be in banking or law, can be seen in individual cases in Ho Chi Minh City but it very often seems to have been gained by people who were loyal or sympathetic to the party, and were subsequently employed as company or bank managers in the 1980s and 1990s.[27]

What has changed?

Returning to the question posed earlier regarding what has changed, the central point is that the most substantive change in Ho Chi Minh City during the 1980s and 1990s involved an informal process, whereby property arrangements evolved far from the officially sanctioned reformed state enterprise. As we have noted, this evolution has gone in two principal directions: local-elite privatisation, whereby those in charge of state assets gradually, by an informal process, assume greater and greater control over these assets so that in the end they are effectively running them as a privatised firm; and a process whereby public funds or assets are siphoned off to be used in the establishment and/or operation of a private, or nominally private, firm. What is most striking is that 'reform', understood as a set of formally sanctioned policies, has played very little part in this process. Early enterprise reforms may be partly significant in contributing to a rather ambiguous situation in which enterprise managers could gradually assume control of state assets and become owners. However, in many respects, this process of change has had a momentum largely divorced from formal reforms.

What is the momentum of change?

Writing on China, a number of scholars have also downplayed the significance of policy. They emphasise instead the economic logic of change. Barry Naughton, for example, argues that the 'pattern of reform was shaped more by economic conditions and the interaction between economics and politics than it was by ideology and politics'. He also suggests that what actually happened – as opposed to policy choices — depended largely on the 'nature of the underlying economic conditions'.[28] Similarly, Jean Oi and Andrew Walder place the emphasis on competitive markets as the determinant of change:

Whatever officials' initial preferences may have been, once local enterprises begin to participate in competitive markets whose boundaries are far beyond local political jurisdictions, officials, like managers and entrepreneurs, must respond to competitive market pressures or suffer the financial consequences.[29]

As well as downplaying the importance of policy, these authors also place little emphasis on the role of individual leaders. Naughton is clearest on this point. Rejecting an interpretation that places heavy emphasis on China's leadership, he writes:

> Needless to say, the most energetic purveyors of this view are in the Chinese propaganda apparatus. In this semi-official view, Chinese leaders adopted cautious, experimental reforms. Policies were tried out first in local experiments, and policies that worked were spread nationwide. Reforms began in rural areas, and achieved great success. As a result, a second stage of urban reforms was attempted and, although this was harder, it also eventually achieved success. Reforms succeeded because Chinese leaders were flexible and pragmatic. This is a highly sanitised account of the reform process, sufficiently misleading to count as misinformation: It distracts us from the real dynamics of the reform process in favour of an oversimplified morality tale.[30]

Naughton also rejects interpretations that place heavy emphasis on the growth of the non-state or private sector, which he also says tend to go hand in hand with a view of state enterprises as remaining 'stubbornly unreformed'.[31]

In my findings on Ho Chi Minh City, there is much that supports the relative weight given to the different dynamics of change by these authors. I have already drawn attention to the relative unimportance of policy reforms in the evolution of property rights. However, I would also downplay the importance of leaders in their role as purveyors of policy in this largely spontaneous process of change. Arguments about the relative importance of economic factors, and in particular pressures imposed by competitive markets, are also attractive. Although I have made reference to the limits to competition in Ho Chi Minh City, there is a strong sense in which competition is sufficient – if only between rival 'state' capital – to drive changes in property rights.

The meaning of reform

At this point, it seems appropriate to take stock of what is to be understood by 'reform' in light of the findings on Ho Chi Minh City presented here. In this respect, it seems appropriate to distinguish between 'reform as a set of policies' and 'reform' as a convenient shorthand for a period of time embodying both formal reform policies and a much more spontaneous process of change only very loosely connected to 'reform as a set of policies'. Despite my emphasis on the spontaneous, I can agree with Naughton that there is something real and substantive that can be called reform. However, it was not something clearly foreseen or designed in advance – there was no blueprint – but it is marked by substantial *ex post* coherence.[32] Nevertheless, reform as a set of policies is but one factor and often a rather insignificant one in a wider process of change that has taken place during the 'reform years'.

Furthermore, while the changes in property arrangements or business practice I have outlined are undoubtedly far-reaching, both in their own right and in their potential long-term political and economic consequences, there is also a sense in which the conception of the reform years purely in terms of change needs to be qualified. Clearly, there has been change. However, there is also a sense in which this period has been a time of incorporation.[33] One of the most prominent themes of the reform years has been the development of businesses with strong roots in the state sector whose growth has involved the hollowing out of public assets. This may have set in train a process that will ultimately lead to the emergence of a new elite but in the story so far the existing elite has been conspicuous among the beneficiaries of the so-called process of reform.[34] It is worth also recalling that the state in Ho Chi Minh City, rather than contracting, actually expanded during the 1990s.[35] Thus, beneath the veneer of reform with its emphasis on marketisation, it can be seen that the heavy hand of the state is still crucial. Moreover, instead of classic privatisation as envisaged by the multilateral institutions such as the World Bank, we see a different kind of 'privatisation' by the elite. Furthermore, instead of politicians fighting over policies on ideological grounds, we see rent-seeking and the use of policy instruments and so-called corruption cases as part of power struggles to defend such commercial interests. What also comes across strongly in some findings is the manner ruling elites continue to respond in some areas in ways that seem to have much in common with long-standing Leninist practice. A good illustration of this is the trials of Tamexco and Minh Phung–Epco detailed in Chapter 5, which had the distinct feel of a 'show trial' to them.

Critiquing the Vietnam literature

Vietnam

The Vietnam literature generally does not distinguish between 'reform as a set of policies' and as a 'wider process of change in which policy plays only a marginal role'.[36] In most accounts, the abiding focus is on reform as policy. Any sense of a much more spontaneous process of change, which lies at the heart of the research in this book, is often absent or is paid lip-service to and does not inform the account as a whole.[37] Moreover, in the literature on explaining change, the focus is again on reform. In fact, the terms 'reform' and 'change' are very often used interchangeably.[38] For many, change is synonymous with reform, while reform is what has driven change. As I have sought to show, this is mistaken: so much of what I regard as the really significant changes of the last two decades have had very little to do with reform as a set of policies, while what has driven this process is largely unconnected with reform.

Earlier I noted that the dynamics of this wider process of change have more to do with economics and politics and the interaction between them than with policy. This wider process of change has, I argued, much less to do with ideology or the role of individual leaders. And yet, with its overly narrow focus on change as reform, the Vietnam literature tends to highlight these very factors as being the key to understanding what has driven the process. It is this stance that lies behind the two main preoccupations of the literature, namely on debates over policy and an overly keen interest in the stance of individual leaders. Emphasising the importance of policy debates, Gareth Porter writes:

> Throughout most of the 1980s, debate continued within the VCP Political Bureau between those who believed that the state violated objective economic laws by maintaining tight controls over production and trade, and those who were primarily concerned with the supremacy of the state sector in the economy.[39]

More recently, Mark Sidel has seen the Eighth Party Congress in 1996 as being the product of 'conflict over policy', while Zachary Abuza asserts that there is 'still no consensus within the elite Politburo over the pace and scope of reform'.[40] In all these accounts, it is either implicit or explicit that the outcome of these debates is viewed as a key determinant behind change or the pace of reform.

A tendency to personalise the reform process – and hence see change as a product of actions by individual leaders – is also widespread in the Vietnam literature. The leader who has most commonly received such treatment is Nguyen Van Linh (party general-secretary 1986–91), although he is not the only one. Carlyle Thayer has written:

> The person most identified with Vietnam's new economic policies is Nguyen Van Linh, the new party general-secretary. . . . Already Linh has spoken out, urging reconciliation between the Party and Vietnam's ethnic Chinese, Catholics, and former members of the Saigon regime.[41]

Writing in the aftermath of the Eighth Congress, Abuza quoted comments by the party general-secretary Le Kha Phieu that the country must 'persist and push ahead with the renovation cause', suggesting that this provided 'some reasons to be hopeful' that reform would move forward.[42] Again,

108 *Changing political economy of Vietnam*

implicit or explicit in such accounts is the idea that what these leaders say or do matters greatly in relation to the course of change. One of the consequences of this combined focus on policy debates and individual leaders is a tendency to try to identify ever more subtle differences in the policy stances of politicians, and then extrapolate from them in ways that are often scarcely plausible.[43]

Ho Chi Minh City

The literature's tendency to depict Ho Chi Minh City as a bastion of reformism ultimately represents a similar type of analysis. Viewing the city as reformist the literature tends to see it as a source of reformist policies or as falling on the reformist side of the continuum in terms of the national 'policy debate'. Moreover, it is the city's post-1975 leadership that is closely identified in the literature with reformist policy positions. Turley and Womack, for example, attribute significant weight to Ho Chi Minh City's 'reformist' leaders in influencing the direction of change:

> Formal recognition of Ho Chi Minh City's special character came with the rise of the city's own leaders to national power. This occurred after a conservative retrenchment in the early 1980s provoked southern leaders to develop a comprehensive program whose basis elements foreshadowed Doi Moi.
> ... local leaders could not spur growth or even govern effectively while remaining faithful to national policy. Non-compliance with central diktat was more in congruence with local conditions and could not be prevented, so local leaders ultimately had to choose between failure or disobedience.[44]

Ultimately, their account is not very far removed from the official one, which emphasises experimental reforms pursued locally before later being applied nationally. As I noted above, this is a sanitised account, which attributes far too much influence to the city's leaders and not enough to the spontaneous nature of change over which leaders – if they were not a part of it – had little influence.[45]

There is also a tendency in the Vietnam literature to overemphasise the importance of the private sector in explaining change. Thayer refers to an 'explosion of private sector activity'. However, such a description seems out of step with the findings of this book, where the development of state business interests has been emphasised. Writing in 1993, the World Bank asserted that the private sector already accounted for two thirds of GDP. In my view, this afforded the private sector with greater importance than it merited in the 1990s. Moreover, analysis as to what constitutes the private sector, as was explored in Chapter 2, is generally lacking.[46] Ho Chi Minh City is very often seen as epitomising such trends.[47]

Spontaneous change and reform

In nearly all respects, this traditional image of Ho Chi Minh City represents a poor fit with the findings of this book. Here, very little evidence of 'policy debates' in the city was found. Indeed, in my view, officials were interested in 'policy' only when it threatened to upset existing practices, whether it be prevailing regulatory powers or the way state enterprises were being operated. The knee-jerk 'southerner therefore reformer' tendency of the literature looks distinctly lame given the very great diversity of people – nearly all 'southerners' – who have dominated this account. Moreover, the sectoral school's blanket classification of provincial party secretaries, economic specialists and technocrats as 'secondary party and state officials' is similarly unsatisfactory insofar as it suggests a commonality of purpose that, based on the findings of this research, does not stand up to close scrutiny.[48] Finally, this book has stressed the importance of state institutions much less the private sector as conventionally understood in terms of the changing nature of Ho Chi Minh City's political economy.

In the end, it is not that formal processes, policy making or leadership change do not matter or are not a legitimate area for study at all. However, they represent a fairly narrow focus, which in trying to understand the dynamics of change in its totality is rather unsatisfactory. In the Vietnam literature to date, there has not been sufficient recognition of this fact. Moreover, it seems that one way speeches and the set-piece political events might be better studied is to try to understand their relationship to the kind of informal processes that have been at the heart of this research. For example, if a so-called policy speech is not really about the niceties and nuances of policy, what purpose does it serve? Moreover, what role do formal political processes serve in facilitating and protecting gate-keeping and political-business interests?[49]

In this concluding chapter, I have emphasised the importance of distinguishing between a spontaneous process of change that is only very loosely connected to reform and reform as policy. However, the two are clearly related. A more authentic account of reform would emphasise the way reform as policy very often emerged as a response to changes which had already taken place but had not been officially sanctioned. Thus, I suspect that the so-called reform 'experiments' that have now entered the official lexicon as being *officially approved* more often than not emerged *spontaneously* at the lower levels of the state apparatus and in state companies. Nevertheless, there is often a substantial lag between what emerges informally and changes in official policy. Equitisation, for example, can hardly be said to have been influenced by the reality of actual property arrangements governing Vietnam's state enterprises, which as I have previously emphasised offers an explanation of why the process has advanced slowly. Ultimately though, I suspect that formal reforms will catch up.

Appendix

Table A1.1 Ho Chi Minh City key economic statistics in 1998
Table A1.2 Ho Chi Minh City's population 1975–98
Table A1.3 GDP growth in Ho Chi Minh City and nationwide 1976–98
Table A1.4 Ho Chi Minh City's share of nationwide output 1990–8
Table A1.5 Ho Chi Minh City's share of nationwide industrial output 1989–98
Table A1.6 Transfers from state enterprises as a share of total revenue 1986–98
Table A1.7 State sector employment in Ho Chi Minh City 1990–8
Table A2.1 Share of GDP in Ho Chi Minh City, by type of ownership 1994–8
Table A2.2 Share of industrial output in Ho Chi Minh City, by type of ownership 1994–8
Table A2.3 Numbers of industrial enterprises in Ho Chi Minh City, by ownership: 1994 and 1998 compared
Table A2.4 Numbers of companies in Ho Chi Minh City's industrial sector, by management type (including labour force) 1994–8
Table A2.5 Top 100 companies and banks in Ho Chi Minh City, by turnover in 1995: type of ownership (%)
Table A2.6 Shareholding structure of Ho Chi Minh City's joint stock banks
Table A3.1 Biographical data on prominent Ho Chi Minh City politicians
Table A3.2 Ho Chi Minh City politicians with identifiable business connections
Table A5.1 Key developments in the Tamexco case
Table A5.2 Key developments in the Minh Phung–Epco case

Table A1.1 Ho Chi Minh City key economic statistics in 1998

Population (m)	5.1
GDP (bn dong)	45,760
GDP per capita (US$)	103[a]
Breakdown of GDP (%)	
Agriculture	2.4
Industry	41.8
Services	55.8
Share of nationwide industrial output (%)	27.0
Share of nationwide external trade (%)	36.2
Share of labour force employed in Agriculture (%)	0.01

a = 1996 figure

Sources: *Nien Giam Thong Ke Thanh Pho Ho Chi Minh 1998* [Ho Chi Minh City Statistical Yearbook 1998], *Cuc Thong Ke Thanh Pho Ho Chi Minh* [Ho Chi Minh City Statistical Office], 1998, pp. 17–21, p. 24 and p. 34; World Bank, *Vietnam: Economic Report on Industrialisation and Industrial Policy*, Report No. 14645-VN, 17 October 1995; Economist Intelligence Unit, *Vietnam Country Report*, fourth quarter 1999, p. 5; *Nien Giam Thong Ke 1998* [Statistical Yearbook 1998], *Ha Noi: Nha Xuat Ban Thong Ke* [Hanoi: Statistical Publishing House], 1999, p. 11; *Saigon Times Daily* 12 February 1997.

Table A1.2 Ho Chi Minh City's population 1975–98

	1975[e]	1976	1979	1984	1985	1989	1990	1991	1992	1993	1994	1995	1998
Population (m)	4.5	3.5	3.4	3.2	3.3	3.9	4.1	4.3	4.4	4.5	4.7	4.8	5.1
Growth rate (%)	n/a	−22.2	−1.0	−1.2	3.1	4.6	5.1	4.9	2.3	2.3	4.4	2.1	2.1

[e] = estimate for 30 April 1975 by Thrift and Forbes 1986.

Sources: *Thanh Pho Ho Chi Minh* [Ho Chi Minh City], Ho Chi Minh City Publishing House, 1983, pp. 12–13; Dean Forbes and Nigel Thrift, eds, *The Socialist Third World: Urban Development and Territorial Planning*, Oxford: Basil Blackwell, 1987, pp. 114–19 and pp. 121–6; Tran Khanh, *The Ethnic Chinese and Economic Development in Vietnam*, Indochina Unit, Institute of Southeast Asian Studies, 1993, pp. 26–7; Nigel Thrift and Dean Forbes, *The Price of War: Urbanization in Vietnam 1954–1985*, London: Allen and Unwin, 1986, p. 126; Nguyen Dinh Dau, *From Saigon to Ho Chi Minh City: 300 Year History*, Ho Chi Minh City: Land Service, Science and Technics Publishing House, 1998, p. 178.

Table A1.3 GDP growth in Ho Chi Minh City and nationwide 1976–98

	Ho Chi Minh City growth (annualised %)	Nationwide growth (annualised %)
1976–80	2.1	n/a
1980–85	9.8	n/a
1985–90	4.6	5.5 (1986–90)
1990–94	14.3	7.3
1994–98	13.2	8.3
1994	14.6	8.8
1995	15.3	9.5
1996	14.6	9.3
1997	12.1	8.2
1998	9.2	5.8

Sources: *Ban Thuong Vu Thanh Uy Dang Cong San Viet Nam Thanh Pho Ho Chi Minh* [Standing Committee of the Ho Chi Minh City Communist Party], *Thanh Pho Ho Chi Minh Hai Muoi Nam (1975–1995)* [Ho Chi Minh City: Twenty Years (1975–1995)], *Nha Xuat Ban Thanh Pho Ho Chi Minh* [Ho Chi Minh City Publishing House], 1996; Vu Tuan Anh, *Development in Vietnam: Policy Reforms and Economic Growth*, Indochina Unit, Institute of Southeast Asian Studies, 1994; *Nien Giam Thong Ke Thanh Pho Ho Chi Minh 1997* [Ho Chi Minh City Statistical Yearbook 1997], *Cuc Thong Ke Thanh Pho Ho Chi Minh* [Ho Chi Minh City Statistical office], 1997; *Nien Giam Thong Ke Thanh Pho Ho Chi Minh 1998* [Ho Chi Minh City Statistical Year Book 1998], *Cuc Thong Ke Thanh Pho Ho Chi Minh* [Ho Chi Minh City Statistical Office], 1998. Nationwide GDP data is available only from 1986. The Ho Chi Minh City Statistical Department has estimated GDP data from 1976, which is what is cited here.

Table A1.4 Ho Chi Minh City's share of nationwide output 1990–8

	Ho Chi Minh City GDP (bn dong)	National GDP (bn dong)	Ho Chi Minh City share of national GDP (%)
1990	4,475	29,526	15.2
1991	4,816	31,286	15.4
1992	5,170	33,991	15.2
1993	5,600	36,735	15.2
1994	6,681	39,982	16.7
1995	32,596	195,566	16.7
1996	37,380	213,832	17.5
1997	41,900	231,262	18.1
1998	45,760	244,740	18.7

Sources: *Nien Giam Thong Ke Thanh Pho Ho Chi Minh 1998* [Ho Chi Minh City Statistical Yearbook 1998], *Cuc Thong Ke Thanh Pho Ho Chi Minh* [Ho Chi Minh City Statistical Office], 1998; World Bank, *Vietnam: Economic Report on Industrialisation and Industrial Policy*, Report No. 14645-VN, 17 October 1995. Two data series are used here: 1990–4 is at constant prices for 1989; 1995–98 is at constant prices for 1994.

114 Appendix

Table A1.5 Ho Chi Minh City's share of nationwide industrial output 1989–98

	Ho Chi Minh City industrial output (bn dong)	National industrial output (bn dong)	Ho Chi Minh City share of national industrial output (%)
1989	3,922	13,583	28.9
1990	3,886	14,011	27.7
1991	4,299	15,471	27.8
1992	4,954	18,117	27.3
1993	6,282	20,412	30.8
1994	6,539	23,214	28.2
1995	29,602	103,375	28.6
1996	33,721	118,097	28.6
1997	37,255	134,420	27.7
1998	40,653	150,685	27.0

Sources: *Nien Giam Thong Ke 1995* [Statistical Yearbook 1995]; *Ha Noi: Nha Xuat Ban Thong Ke* [Hanoi: Statistical Publishing House], 1996; *Nien Giam Thong Ke 1998* [Statistical Yearbook 1998]; *Ha Noi: Nha Xuat Ban Thong Ke* [Hanoi: Statistical Publishing House], 1999; World Bank, *Vietnam: Economic Report on Industrialisation and Industrial Policy*, Report No. 14645-VN, 17 October 1995. Two data series are used here: 1990–4 is at constant prices for 1989; 1995–8 is at constant prices for 1994.

Table A1.6 Transfers from state enterprises as a share of total revenue 1986–98

	State enterprise transfers (bn current dong)	Total revenue (bn current dong)	State enterprise transfers as a share of total revenue (%)
1986	60	84	71.4
1987	385	379	75.2
1988	1,110	1,740	63.8
1989	2,244	3,899	57.5
1990	3,620	6,153	58.8
1991	6,189	10,353	59.8
1992	11,913	21,023	56.7
1993	15,322	30,696	49.9
1994	20,557	42,125	48.8
1995	21,938	53,370	41.1
1996	25,887	62,387	41.5
1997	27,549	66,252	41.6
1998	27,267	68,600	39.7

Sources: World Bank, *Vietnam: Economic Report on Industrialisation and Industrial Policy*, Report No. 14645-VN, 17 October 1995; World Bank, *Vietnam: Deepening Reform for Growth: An Economic Report*, Report No. 17031-VN, 31 October 1997; World Bank, *Vietnam: Preparing for Take-off? How Vietnam Can Participate Fully in the East Asian Recovery*, an Informal Report of the World Bank Consultative Meeting for Vietnam, Hanoi, 14–15 December 1999.

Table A1.7 State sector employment in Ho Chi Minh City 1990–8

	1990	1991	1992	1993	1994	1995	1996	1997	1998
Total (000)					372.8	419.8	422.5	439.3	420.3
By central management					175.7	221.6	221.8	222.2	213.2
By local management	178.3	174.5	171.5	186.6	194.7	194.8	207.1	211.3	207.1
By kind of activities									
Industry					102.9	114.9	115.2	115.1	111.6
Education and training					73.1	76.6	98.3	101.1	103.5
Trade, hotel, restaurant					93.7	111.7	84.4	94.4	80.7
Public health and social affairs					32.7	35.6	37.3	34.5	34.9
Construction					21.4	26.0	30.4	32.1	33.0
State management, party, national defence					14.9	19.1	22.5	22.9	21.7
Transport, storage, communications					12.7	14.4	12.1	15.5	14.1
Agriculture, forestry, fishery					8.8	8.1	8.5	10.0	8.1

Sources: *Nien Giam Thong Ke 1995* [Statistical Yearbook 1995], Ha Noi: Nha Xuat Ban Thong Ke [Hanoi: Statistical Publishing House], 1996; *Nien Giam Thong Ke 1998* [Statistical Yearbook 1998], Ha Noi: Nha Xuat Ban Thong Ke [Hanoi: Statistical Publishing House], 1999; *Nien Giam Thong Ke Thanh Pho Ho Chi Minh 1997* [Ho Chi Minh City Statistical Yearbook 1997], Cuc Thong Ke Thanh Pho Ho Chi Minh [Ho Chi Minh City Statistical Office], 1997; *Nien Giam Thong Ke Thanh Pho Ho Chi Minh 1998* [Ho Chi Minh City Statistical Yearbook 1998], Cuc Thong Ke Thanh Pho Ho Chi Minh [Ho Chi Minh City Statistical Office], 1998.

Appendix

Table A2.1 Share of GDP in Ho Chi Minh City, by type of ownership 1994–8

	1994	1995	1996	1997	1998
Central state	30.1	29.1	28.8	27.7	27.7
Local state	21.1	20.1	19.0	19.4	18.8
Non-state	40.5	39.7	38.1	37.4	36.4
Foreign	8.2	11.1	14.0	15.6	17.0

Sources: *Nien Giam Thong Ke Thanh Pho Ho Chi Minh 1997* [Ho Chi Minh City Statistical Yearbook 1997], *Cuc Thong Ke Thanh Pho Ho Chi Minh* [Ho Chi Minh City Statistical Office], 1997; *Nien Giam Thong Ke Thanh Pho Ho Chi Minh 1998* [Ho Chi Minh City Statistical Yearbook 1998], *Cuc Thong Ke Thanh Pho Ho Chi Minh* [Ho Chi Minh City Statistical Office], 1998.

Table A2.2 Share of industrial output in Ho Chi Minh City, by type of ownership 1994–8 (%)

	1994	1995	1996	1997	1998
Central state	46.0	44.1	42.5	37.9	37.7
Local state	17.3	15.9	14.8	15.1	14.0
Non-state	25.1	23.8	23.3	25.1	24.3
Foreign	11.6	16.2	19.4	21.9	24.0

Sources: *Nien Giam Thong Ke Thanh Pho Ho Chi Minh 1997* [Ho Chi Minh City Statistical Yearbook 1997], *Cuc Thong Ke Thanh Pho Ho Chi Minh* [Ho Chi Minh City Statistical Office], 1997; *Nien Giam Thong Ke Thanh Pho Ho Chi Minh 1998* [Ho Chi Minh City Statistical Yearbook 1998], *Cuc Thong Ke Thanh Pho Ho Chi Minh* [Ho Chi Minh City Statistical Office], 1998.

Table A2.3 Numbers of industrial enterprises in Ho Chi Minh City, by ownership: 1994 and 1998 compared

	1994	1998
Central state	139	120
Local state (city)	145	129
Local state (district)	63	35
Cooperatives	107	71
Joint stock, limited liability, private	581	704
Family firms	22,421	23,028
Foreign	145	312

Sources: *Nien Giam Thong Ke Thanh Pho Ho Chi Minh 1997* [Ho Chi Minh City Statistical Yearbook 1997], *Cuc Thong Ke Thanh Pho Ho Chi Minh* [Ho Chi Minh City Statistical Office], 1997; *Nien Giam Thong Ke Thanh Pho Ho Chi Minh 1998* [Ho Chi Minh City Statistical Yearbook 1998], *Cuc Thong Ke Thanh Pho Ho Chi Minh* [Ho Chi Minh City Statistical Office], 1998.

Table A2.4 Numbers of companies in Ho Chi Minh City's industrial sector, by management type (including labour force) 1994–8

	1994	1995	1996	1997	1998
Central state	139	128	122	122	120
	(96,797)	(104,841)	(97,570)	(103,769)	(107,248)
Local state	231	209	181	167	164
	(60,084)	(69,816)	(54,562)	(50,478)	(50,341)
Stock, limited, private	581	699	827	816	704
	(59,051)	(69,198)	(86,130)	(89,472)	(91,844)
Family firms	22,421	31,355	29,840	23,703	23,028
	(92,156)	(119,101)	(116,522)	(100,519)	(143,274)
Foreign	145	183	200	287	312
	(26,632)	(39,486)	(45,557)	(83,294)	(93,796)

Sources: *Nien Giam Thong Ke Thanh Pho Ho Chi Minh 1997* [Ho Chi Minh City Statistical Yearbook 1997], *Cuc Thong Ke Thanh Pho Ho Chi Minh* [Ho Chi Minh City Statistical Office], 1997; *Nien Giam Thong Ke Thanh Pho Ho Chi Minh 1998* [Ho Chi Minh City Statistical Yearbook 1998], *Cuc Thong Ke Thanh Pho Ho Chi Minh* [Ho Chi Minh City Statistical Office], 1998.

118   *Appendix*

Table A2.5 Top 100 companies and banks in Ho Chi Minh City, by turnover in 1995: type of ownership (%)

1	Petrolimex Saigon	Central state
2	Petec	Central state
3	Geruco	Central state
4	Saigon Beer Company	Central state
5	Saigon Cigarette Factory	Central state
6	Vinamilk	Central state
7	Ha Tien 1 Cement Company	Central state
8	Minh Phung	Private limited liability, local Chinese
9	Vietnam Brewery	Central state
10	Sugar Cane 2 General Corporation	Central state
11	Saigon Jewellery Company	Local state
12	Southern Steel Company	Central state
13	Sagimexco	Local state
14	Vinametal Company Ho Chi Minh City	Central state
15	Vietnam Food General Corporation	Central state
16	Food Technology Company	Local state
17	Saigon Tourist	Local state
18	APT Co	Local state
19	Sapharco	Local state
20	Seprotimex	Local state
21	Yteco	Local state
22	APM Saigon Shipping Company	Foreign joint venture
23	Tenimex	Local state
24	Seaspimex	Central state
25	International Beverages Company	Local state
26	Viet Tien Garment Import–Export Company	Central state
27	T Citex	Central state
28	Vocarimex	Central state
29	Saigon Port	Central state
30	Gemartrans Company	Foreign joint venture
31	Saigon Inn Hotel	Foreign joint venture
32	Higimex	Central state
33	Vifon	Central state
34	Gemexim	Local state
35	Southern Fertilise Company	Central state
36	Fosco	Local state
37	Viettronimex	Central state
38	Ho Chi Minh City Water Company	Local state
39	Phong Phu Textile Company	Central state
40	Tan Thuan Construction	Local state
41	Vicotex	Central state
42	Power Construction Company No. 2	Central state
43	Golden Hope Nha Be Company	Foreign joint venture
44	Saigon Fire Company	Local state
45	Vipesco	Central state
46	Cadivi	Central state
47	Vitexim	Central state
48	Vitranschart	Central state
49	Exim Bank	Local state

Table A2.5 (cont.)

50	Vafaco	Local state
51	A-I International Corporation	Foreign joint venture
52	Vitaco	Central state
53	Bao Minh	Central state
54	Seaco	Local state
55	Pinaco	Central state
56	Vigecam III	Central state
57	Tan Binh Viettronics Company	Local state
58	Viet Hoa Bank	Local Chinese
59	Binh Tay Processing Company	Local state
60	Rang Dong Plastics	Central state
61	Lixco	Central state
62	Casumina	Central state
63	Triumph International (Vietnam)	Foreign joint venture
64	Thu Duc Electronics Company (VTD)	Central state
65	Fahasa	Local state
66	Biti's	Private limited liability/local Chinese
67	Tribeco	Private limited liability/local state
68	Epco	Private limited liability/local state/local Chinese
69	Wrapping Production and Export Company	Central state
70	Saigon Bank for Industry and Commerce	Local state
71	Embassy Hotel Company	Foreign joint venture
72	Sacombank	Local state
73	Lac Ty Company	Foreign joint venture
74	Saigon Railway Company	Central state
75	Tapack	Central state
76	Asia Commercial Bank	Local state
77	First Vina Bank	Foreign joint venture
78	Huy Hoang	Local state
79	International Burotel Company	Foreign joint venture
80	Phu Tho Tourist	Local state
81	East Asia Bank	Local state
82	Indovina Bank	Foreign joint venture
83	Hoa Viet Company	Foreign joint venture
84	Tacombank	Local state
85	Construction Company 3	Local state
86	Caesar Hotel Company	Foreign joint venture
87	Vicotrade Company	Foreign joint venture
88	Century Saigon Hotel	Foreign joint venture
89	Foreign Service Office	Foreign joing venture
90	Tan Binh Housing Development Company	Local state
91	Norfolk Hotel	Foreign joint venture
92	Buildebank	Local state
93	Navifico Factory	Local state
94	Nam A Bank	Local state
95	Phuong Nam Bank	Local state
96	Saigon Star Hotel	Foreign joint venture
97	Saigon Petro	Local state

Table A2.5 (cont.)

98	Vinh Thinh Wool Company	Central state
99	Shangrila	Foreign joint venture
100	Tecasin	Local state

Sources: *Chan Dung Nhung Doanh Nghiep Thanh Dat* [A Portrait of Business on the March], *Nha Xuat Ban Thanh Pho Ho Chi Minh* [Ho Chi Minh City Publishing House], Saigon Times Group, VAPEC, 1997; *Danh Muc Co Quan Xi Nghiep Tai Thanh Pho Ho Chi Minh* [List of Commercial Organisations in Ho Chi Minh City], *Cuc Thong Ke Thanh Pho Ho Chi Min*h [Ho Chi Minh City Statistical Office], 1 January 1996; interview 20 September 2000. An attempt has been made to censor this latter source. The data extracted from it and used here is that which existed before the censor sought to delete references to certain companies. All this means is that it includes references to two limited companies that subsequently fell from grace, namely Minh Phung and Epco.

Table A2.6 Shareholding structure of Ho Chi Minh City's joint stock banks

Name	Year founded	Leading shareholders	Management board chairman, key personalities
Asia Commercial Bank	1993	Saigon Jewellery Company; 30% foreign shareholders	Nguyen Mong Hung (management board chairman); Lam Hoang Loc (management board deputy chairman); Pham Trung Cang (general director)
Asia-Pacific Bank	1994	Huy Hoang Limited Company	Le Van Kiem (management board chairman)
Buildebank	1989	Began under Department of Housing and Land; came under influence of local state Ho Chi Minh City Urban Investment Development Fund in 1997	Le Thanh Hai (management board chairman, late 1980s); Vu Van Thanh (general director)
Dai Nam Bank	1992 (absorbed by Phuong Nam Bank in 1999)	Formed by merger of credit cooperatives in District 3, with Malaysian/Australian Viet Kieu investment	Dang Hong Chau (management board chairman); Foreign investor Nguyen Trung Truc and his wife (Truc, who represented Peregrine in Vietnam, later jailed for alleged tax evasion)
East Asia Bank	1992	Phu Nhuan Jewellery Company; Phu Nhuan Construction and Housing Business Company; city party Financial Management Committee absorbed Long Xuyen Bank	Cao Thi Ngoc Dung (founder and management board chairman); Ngo Dinh Ngon (founder, general director until c. 1998), replaced by Tran Phuong Binh
Exim Bank	1989	Saigon Jewellery Company; Vietcombank; Huy Hoang Limited Company; Minh Phung Limited Company (c. 1994)	Nguyen Huu Dinh (management board chairman); Nguyen Nhat Hong (general director); Do Hoang Hai (member management board early 1990s)
Ficombank	1993	Local Chinese	Huynh Van Cao (management board chairman c. 1994)

Table A2.6 (cont.)

Name	Year founded	Leading shareholders	Management board chairman, key personalities
Gia Dinh Bank	1992	Formed by merger of credit cooperatives in Binh Thanh District; Vietcombank became lead shareholder from c. 1994	Thai Kim Lieng (management board chairman pre-1994) (deputy director Nguyen Van Son executed for alleged fraud; other bank employees jailed, c. 1996)
Mekong Bank	1994 (closed 1999)	Credit cooperative merger	Nguyen Van Tu (management board chairman); Nguyen Chan Hung (general director)
Nam A Bank	1992	Benh Thanh focus; possibly some local Chinese investment	Tran Van Sanh (management board chairman); Bach Xuan Giai (general director) (fraud allegations; deputy director Ngo Quy Triet on the run c. 1997)
Nam Do Bank	1994 (expected to be closed)	Merger of credit cooperative in District 11; local Chinese	Ha Ngoc Thac (management board chairman until c. 1998); Tran Van Phuoc (general director); Lam Dao Thao (management board chairman from 1998) (embroiled in fraud allegations in 1998–99)
Oricom Bank	1996	Saigon Tourist; Vietcombank; Sunimex; Fimexco	Do Van Hoang (management board chairman); Nguyen An Chuyen (general director)
Phuong Nam Bank	1993	Credit cooperative merger; absorbed Dai Nam and Dong Thap Banks	Lam Truoc (management board chairman); Hoang Van Toan (general director)
Que Do Bank	1992	Local Chinese	Ta Hong (management board chairman); Bao Lan (general director)

Saigon Industrial and Commercial Bank	1987	Vietcombank: Saigon Tourist; city party Financial management committee	Nguyen Ngoc An (management board chairman): Duong Xuan Minh (general director)
Sacombank	1991	Credit cooperative merger in Go Vap District	Tran Kiem Khai (management board chairman), replaced by Dang Van Thanh; Tran Van Phuoc (general director), replaced by Ho Van Ho
Tacombank	1992	Tamexco: Tanimex; Vietcombank (following Tamexco case)	Pham Huy Phuoc (management board chairman), replaced by Luong Van Yen; Le Tran Ba (general director) (Pham Huy Phuoc executed following Tamexco case in 1998)
Techombank	1994	Cotec limited company: capital generated from doing business in the former Soviet Union	Hoang Quang Vinh (management board chairman); Dang Trong Cuong (general director); son of former party general secretary Le Duan
Viet Hoa Bank	1992	Local Chinese: merger of five credit cooperatives in District 5; memorandum of understanding signed with Germany's Kreiss Bank to take a 33% share	Tran Tuan Tai (management board chairman; died 1997), replaced by Diep Vi Nam; Vu Ngoc Nhung (general director), replaced by Lam Tan Loi
VP Bank	1993	Northern shareholders, including Huy Hoang limited company: capital generated from doing business in Eastern Europe: 30% foreign shareholders: Incombank took a share in the bank in 1997	Hoang Minh Thang (chairman management board); Le Van Kiem (management board deputy chairman); Tran Ba Tuoc (chairman Ho Chi Minh City branch), replaced by Huynh Ba Tuoc in 1997; Nguyen Tien Minh (deputy general director)

Sources: Vietnamese press 1987–99; interviews 8 May 1997; 11 February 1998; 7 May 1999; 26 May 1999; 8 June 1999. Individual joint stock banks often have hundreds of shareholders, most of whom are small-scale individual investors. Assertions in this table regarding who are the dominant shareholders are based on information about the institutional affiliations of those in key bank positions, such as chairmen of the management board (*chu tich hoi dong quan tri*) or board members.

Table A3.1 Biographical data on prominent Ho Chi Minh City politicians (in alphabetical order)

Nguyen Ngoc An	Member of Ho Chi Minh City party Standing Committee 1983, 1986 and 1991; Head of city party Economics Committee (c. 1991); Management board chairman Saigon Industrial and Commercial Bank (c. 1994)
Le Minh Chau (*Ba Chau*)	Born in Can Tho in 1935. Joined the party in 1959. Member of the Standing Committee of party organisation in Saigon-Gia Dinh during the war. Arrested and imprisoned on Poulo Condore in 1965. After the war held appointment at Trade Union Federation in Ho Chi Minh City before becoming party secretary in District 6. Director of Department of Industry and Trade 1992. Director of Department of Trade 1994. People's Committee deputy chairman until 1996. Management board chairman Saigon Trading Corporation 1995–present. Married to Truong My Hoa's sister (see entry below).
Nguyen Van Chi	Born in Cu Chi in 1939. Chairman of Fatherland Front after the war. General director of Imexco. Director of Department of Labour, War Invalids and Social Affairs 1991–6. Member of city party Executive Committee 1991 and 1996. Deputy People's Committee chairman 1996–9.
Vo Tran Chi (*Hai Chi*)	Born in Long An in c. 1930s. Served as a provincial militia leader in Long An during the war. Appointed party secretary in Ho Chi Minh City's District 5 in 1975 before going to study in the Soviet Union. On his return, he became head of the agricultural section of Ho Chi Minh City party committee. Member of city party Standing Committee 1983, 1986 and 1991. Party secretary in Ho Chi Minh City 1986–96. Appointed member of party Central Committee in 1986. Politburo member 1991–6. In retirement in Ho Chi Minh City 1996–present.
Tran Ngoc Con	Born in Ben Tre in 1941. Deputy director and then Director Industry Department 1991–9. Member city party Executive Committee 1991 and 1996. People's Committee deputy chairman 1999–present.
Do Hoang Hai (*Nam Khoa*)	Born in Ben Tre in 1941. Member of the party organisation in Saigon-Gia Dinh during the war. Imprisoned on Poulo Condore. After the war held an appointment at the Trade Union Federation before becoming deputy director Housing and Land Department. Deputy party secretary at District 6 c. 1981 and later secretary. Acting deputy general director of Imexco 1985–9. Director of Fideco 1989. Member of Management Board of Exim Bank and of Inspection Board of Saigon Finance Company ('early 1990s'). Member of party Executive Committee 1991 and 1996. General director of Saigon Trading Corporation 1995–8. Head of the Economics Committee 1998–present. Married to Truong My Hoa (see entry below).

Le Thanh Hai *(Hai Nhut)*	Born in 1950 in Tien Chang. Head of Youth Volunteer Force after the war. Director Housing and Land Department and management board chairman Buildebank 1989. Member city party Executive Committee 1986 and 1991. Party secretary District 5 c. 1991–4. Director Department Planning and Investment 1995. People's Committee deputy chairman 1996–present. Member city party Standing Committee 1996.
(Ba) Truong My Hoa *(Bay Thu)*	Born in 1945 in Tien Chang. Joined the party in 1962. Member of party organisation in Saigon-Gia Dinh during the war. Imprisoned on Poulo Condore 1964–75. Deputy party secretary in District 10 after the war. Party deputy secretary and later secretary (1986–1991) in Tan Binh district. Alternate member of the party Central Committee and member of the city party Standing Committee 1986. Member of Central Committee and party Secretariat following Seventh Congress in 1991. Chairman of the Women's Union 1992. Secretary Central Party 1994. Re-elected member of Central Committee in 1996. National Assembly vice-president 1997–present. Married to Do Hoang Hai (see entry above).
Do Van Hoang	People's Committee chairman District 1 c. 1996–97. General-director Saigon Tourist 1996. Management board chairman Oricom Bank 1996–present. Management board chairman Saigon Tourist General Corporation 1999–present.
Phan Van Khai	Born in Cu Chi in 1933. Re-grouped to the north in 1954. Studied economics in Moscow 1960–5. Conducted research on the southern economy 1972–5. Deputy head of the Planning Committee in Ho Chi Minh City 1976–8. Deputy chairman Ho Chi Minh City People's Committee 1979. Member of city party Standing Committee 1983 and 1986. Appointed full member of party Central Committee in 1984. Ho Chi Minh City People's Committee chairman 1985–9. Chairman of State Planning Committee 1989–91. Politburo member 1991–present. Deputy prime minister 1992–7. Prime minister 1997–present.
Vo Van Kiet *(Sau Dan)*	Born in Vinh Long in 1922. Secretary of Kien Chang provincial party committee in the 1940s. Political commissar of the Saigon-Gia Dinh Military Zone in 1958. Appointed to the party Central Committee in 1960. In charge of the 'Front Command 2' attack on Saigon during the Tet Offensive of 1968. Secretary and political commissar Western Nam Bo Military Zone 1971–3. On the staff of the Central Office for South Vietnam 1973–5. Deputy chairman of the Military Management Committee 1975–6. Alternate Politburo member 1976–82. Party Secretary Ho Chi Minh City 1976–82. Member of city party Standing Committee 1977 and 1980. Full Politburo member 1982–97. Chairman of the State Planning Committee 1982–9. Prime minister 1992–7. Party adviser 1997–present.

Table A3.1 (cont.)

Nguyen Van Linh (*Muoi Cuc*)	Born in Hung Yen in 1915. Imprisoned on Poulo Condore 1930–36 and 1941–45. Assigned to party work in Saigon in 1939. Held key positions in the south from 1945. Appointed to the party Central Committee in 1960. Deputy secretary of the Central Office for South Vietnam 1960–75. Politburo member 1976–82. Party secretary in Ho Chi Minh City 1976. Held various central positions 1976–81. Party secretary in Ho Chi Minh City 1982–85. Member of city party Standing Committee 1983. Re-elected to the Politburo 1985. Party general-secretary, 1986–91. Party adviser 1991–98. Died 1998.
Tran Thanh Long	Born in Ben Tre in 1940. Studied in Soviet Union and East Germany. University positions in Hanoi and Ho Chi Minh City. Member party Standing Committee 1996. People's Committee deputy chairman 1995–99. Chairman of Fatherland Front in Ho Chi Minh City 1999–present.
Le Van Nam	Born in 1938 in Dong Thap. Relocated to the north in 1954. Studied in Russia, China and Poland. Head of Planning Institute 1986. Director Construction Department 1991. General director Saigon Export Processing Zone 1991. Member of party Executive Committee 1991 and 1996. Chief Architect 1993–present.
Nguyen Thien Nhan	Born in 1953 in Tra Vinh. Holds an associate professorship in economics, a Ph.D. in cybernetics and a M.A. in public administration. Director Department of Science, Technology and the Environment. Deputy People's Committee deputy chairman 1999–present.
Nguyen Vinh Nghiep (*Sau Tuong*)	Member of Ho Chi Minh City party Standing Committee 1977, 1986 and 1991. Deputy chairman city People's Committee 1986–89. People's Committee chairman 1989–92. Stepped down on grounds of ill-health. In retirement in Ho Chi Minh City 1992–present.
Truong Tan Sang (*Tu Sang*)	Born in Long An in 1949. Secretary of the Youth Union of guerrilla force in Long An 1971. Imprisoned 1971–73. Cadre in department of Central Reunification Committee 1973–75. Various appointments in Youth Volunteer Force and director of Forestry Department in Ho Chi Minh City 1975–86. Party secretary in city's Binh Chanh district 1986–88. Member of party Standing Committee 1986, 1991 and 1996. Studied at Nguyen Ai Quoc Institute in Hanoi 1989. Director of city's Agriculture Department 1990–91. Appointed member of party Central Committee 1991. Chairman of Ho Chi Minh City People's Committee 1992–96. Party secretary in Ho Chi Minh City 1996–2000. Politburo member 1996–present.
Vo Viet Thanh	Born in 1943 in Ben Tre. Served in military intelligence in the south during the war. Various positions in the Communist Youth League and Youth Volunteer Force after 1975. Graduated in law in the Soviet Union 1984. On return became deputy director and in turn director of Police in Ho Chi Minh City. Member of city party Standing

	Committee 1986, 1991 and 1996. Deputy interior minister 1987–91. Member of party Central Committee 1986–91. Ho Chi Minh City People's Committee deputy chairman 1992–96. People's Committee chairman 1996–present.
(Ba) Pham Phung Thao	Born in 1952. Secretary national Youth Union 1986. Deputy head Ho Chi Minh City party Ideology and Culture Committee. Member city party Executive Committee 1996. People's Committee deputy chairman 1996–present.
Mai Chi Tho	Born in the north c. 1920s. Younger brother of Le Duc Tho. Politically active in Tien Chang in 1940s. Remained south in 1954. Ended the war as chief of security in T4 (incorporating Saigon-Gia Dinh and a number of other southern provinces). Chief of police in Ho Chi Minh City 1975. Ho Chi Minh City People's Committee chairman 1976–85. Member of city party Standing Committee 1977, 1980 and 1983. Appointed member of party Central Committee in 1976. Interior minister 1987–90. Politburo member 1986–91. In retirement in Ho Chi Minh City 1991–present.
Le Van Triet	Born in 1930 in Tien Chang. Politically active from 1946. Deputy minister Ministry of Mechanical Engineering and Metallurgy 1979. Member Central Committee at Fifth Congress in 1982. Ho Chi Minh City People's Committee deputy chairman 1982. Member city party Standing Committee 1983 and 1986. Deputy minister in Foreign Economic Relation Ministry 1988. First deputy minister in Ministry of Trade and Industry. Member Central Committee 1991 and 1996. Minister of Trade 1992–98.
Nguyen Minh Triet	Born Binh Duong (former Song Be) in 1942. Politically active from 1960. Labour union work in the south 1963–75. Appointment in Ho Chi Minh Communist Youth League 1976–87. Party secretary Song Be province 1991–97. Permanent vice-secretary of Ho Chi Minh City party committee 1997–98. Appointed to the Politburo 1997. Head of central party Mobilisation Committee 1998–2000. Ho Chi Minh City party secretary 2000–present.
Pham Chanh Truc (Nam Nghi)	Born in 1939 in Tien Chang. Politically active in Saigon during the war. Imprisoned in 1960s. Secretary Communist Youth League 1977. Party secretary District 5. Member Ho Chi Minh City party Standing Committee 1983, 1986, 1991 and 1996. Deputy People's Committee chairman 1991. People's Council chairman 1996. Permanent vice-secretary city party committee 1997. Deputy head central party Economics Committee 1998–present.
(Ba) Le Thi Van	Born in 1942 in Cu Chi. People's Committee chairman Tan Binh district 1986–94. Member of Ho Chi Minh City party Executive Committee 1991. People's Committee deputy chairman 1994–6. Censured by city party Standing Committee for her part in the Tamexco case 1997.
Vu Hung Viet	Born in 1947 in Minh Hai. Director Ho Chi Minh City Construction department. Member city party Executive Committee 1996. People's Committee deputy chairman 1996–present.

Sources: Vietnamese press reports 1977–2000. Interviews 18 February 1998, 26 May and 5 July 1999.

Table A3.2 Ho Chi Minh City politicians with identifiable business connections

	Early career	Business position	Held simultaneously with political office	Subsequent political posts
Nguyen Cong Ai	Member Ho Chi Minh City party Standing Committee 1986; People's Committee deputy chairman 1991	Deputy head of the Management Committee of Tan Thuan Export Processing Zone	Yes	No
Nguyen Ngoc An	Member Ho Chi Minh City party Standing Committee 1983, 1986 and 1991	Chairman Management Board Saigon Bank for Industry and Commerce first half of 1990s	Yes Head of city party's Economic Committee	No
Le Minh Chau	Born Can Tho 1935; politically active from 1953; member of the Standing Committee of the Saigon-Gia Dinh party group; imprisoned on Con Dao 1967–75; after the war held positions at Trade Union Federation; Party secretary in District 6 (c. 1980s); Director Department of Trade and Industry	Chairman Management Board Saigon Trading Corporation since 1995	Yes Deputy People's Committee chairman (until 1996)	No
Nguyen Van Chi	Born Cu Chi 1939; chairman of Fatherland Front in Ho Chi Minh City	General director of Imexco (Department of Trade company); probably in 1980s	No	Director of Department of Labour, War Invalids and Social Affairs; Deputy chairman People's Committee

Duong Van Day	Born Can Tho 1944; underground activist in Saigon during war; after 1975 deputy secretary of the Youth League; general secretary of the Fatherland Front in Ho Chi Minh City	Director of Saigon Tourist 1991–6	Yes Chairman of People's Committee in District 1	No, died July 1996
Do Hoang Hai	Born Ben Tre 1941; imprisoned on Poulo Condore during war; served on Standing Committee of Trade Union Federation; Deputy director of Department of Land and Housing; Deputy party secretary and later secretary District 6	General-director of Imexco (Department of Trade company); Director of Fideco and Saigon Frozen Food Company; Member of Management Board of Exim Bank and of Inspection Board of Saigon Finance Company; chairman management board of Tomsaca and Cofidec (latter is Department of Trade firm); General-director of Saigon Trading Corporation; spans 1985–97	Only from 1996 Member of city party Executive Committee	Head of city party Economics Committee
Le Thanh Hai	Born Tien Giang 1950; Commander of Youth Volunteer Force after 1975	Chairman of Management Board of Buildebank late 1980s/early 1990s	Yes Director Department Housing and Land	Party secretary District 5; Director of Planning and Investment Department; Deputy chairman People's Committee

Table A3.2 (cont.)

	Early career	Business position	Held simultaneously with political office	Subsequent political posts
Do Van Hoang	People's Committee chairman District 1	Chairman of Management Board of Oricom Bank; General director Saigon Tourist; chairman Management Board Saigon Tourist General Corporation since 1996	No	No
Pham Hao Hon	Deputy director and director Department of Trade	General director Saigon Trading Corporation since 1997	No	No
Le Van Nam	Born Dong Thap 1938; went north in 1954; studied in Russia, Poland and China; Head of Planning Institute in Ho Chi Minh City mid 1980s	General director Saigon Export Processing Zone early 1990s	Yes Director Construction Department	Chief Architect in Ho Chi Minh City

Sources: Vietnamese press 1983–99.

Table A5.1 Key developments in the Tamexco case

Date	Event
6–12 May 1996	English-language *Vietnam Investment Review* reports arrest of Tamexco director Pham Huy Phuoc in March/April in connection with losses at Tamexco and a run on Tacombank.
27 May 1996	*Sai Gon Giai Phong* reports personnel changes in Tan Binh district, including departure of the People's Committee chairman, Phan Van Hoa.
5–11 August 1996	Deputy People's Committee chairman (*Ba*) Le Thi Van resigns on 'health grounds'.
8 October 1996	The security and investigation office of the Ho Chi Minh City Police (*phong an ninh dieu tra Cong an thanh pho Ho Chi Minh*) sign a decree charging Vietcombank directors Nguyen Van De and Nguyen Duy Lo with 'lacking responsibility with serious consequences'.
24 October 1996	A press advertisement announces a proposed increase in Tacombank's registered capital (*von dieu le*) to 60 billion dong based on an official letter of the State Bank of Vietnam dated 23 April 1996. New management at Tacombank is in place.
26 October 1996	The security and investigation office of the Ho Chi Minh City Police transfer the Tamexco file to the People's Court of Investigation in Ho Chi Minh City (*vien kiem sat nhan dan thanh pho Ho Chi Minh*) proposing that in the light of their investigation 19 people be brought to court.
29 October 1996	In an interview with *Tuoi Tre* a senior court official reveals various details about what Pham Huy Phuoc is said to have done but says that the investigation process is not yet completely finished.
5 November 1996	The People's Court of Investigation transfer the Tamexco file back to the investigating organ to clarify a number of matters.
26 November 1996	Two more officials are implicated, including acting general director of Vietcombank Nguyen Manh Thuy. The charges against the other official are later dropped because of a lack of evidence.
12 December 1996	The Tamexco file is transferred in its entirety from the People's Court of Investigation to the People's Court in Ho Chi Minh City (*toa an nhan dan thanh pho Ho Chi Minh*). The plan is to settle the case by the end of January.
23 January 1997	Trial opens.
31 January 1997	Trial ends.
24 March 1997	The appeal against the verdicts begins.
31 March 1997	Appeal turned down.

Table A5.1 (cont.)

19–25 June 1997	The Standing Committee of the Ho Chi Minh City party censures seven cadres for their connections to the Tamexco case. They are exclusively from Tan Binh district and the Financial Management department of the city party committee (*ban tai chinh quan tri thanh uy*), and include Le Thi Van, Phan Van Hoa and Pham Ngoc Suong.
22–8 September 1997	The death sentence of Le Minh Hai is commuted to life imprisonment on account of his father's war record.
7 January 1998	Three executions are carried out.
20 April 1999	Tamexco is declared bankrupt.

Source: Vietnamese press reports.

Table A5.2 Key developments in the Minh Phong–Epco case

Date	Event
24 March 1997	Minh Phung and Epco directors, Tang Minh Phung and Lien Khui Thin, are arrested accused of 'abusing confidence to appropriate socialist property'; arrest warrants issued by the Ho Chi Minh City municipal procuracy office.
4 April 1997	Ho Chi Minh City People's Committee intervening to try to keep Minh Phung operating normally.
28 April 1997	Charge against Tang Minh Phung and Lien Khui Thien changed to 'fraud and embezzlement of state property'.
15 May 1997	Thirteen officials from Minh Phung arrested.
31 May 1997	Deputy finance director of Minh Phung, Nguyen Van Ha, found dead on the roof of Incombank, Ham Nghi Street in Ho Chi Minh City's District 1.
23 December 1997	People's Committee chairman in District 3, Huynh Van Thanh, relieved of his post because of the district's association with the Minh Phung–Epco case.
16 February 1998	People's Committee deputy chairman, Pham Tan Khoa, relieved of his post because of his involvement in the Minh Phung–Epco case (later charged with 'intentionally doing wrong').
19 March 1998	Permission granted for the investigation to run a further four months, until 24 July.
2 May 1998	Three more Minh Phung deputy directors arrested.
5 May 1998	Ex-People's Committee chairman in District 3 reportedly repays 500 million to the district budget that he had earlier improperly loaned to Epco.
1 June 1998	Order is passed permitting accused to be kept in custody.
10 June 1998	Two further people charged in connection with case.
15 June 1998	Charge against the 12 bankers implicated in the case changed to 'fraudulently appropriating socialist assets' from 'intentionally disobeying state regulations in economic management'.
21 August 1998	Investigation again extended.
21 October 1998	Investigation completed.
26 October 1998	Ho Chi Minh City People's Committee issues a decision formally discharging Huynh Van Thanh of his responsibilities as District 3 chairman.
19 November 1998	Domestic banks move to try and settle Minh Phung–Epco debts.

Table A5.2 (cont.)

2 January 1999	Case file transferred from the People's Court of Investigation in Ho Chi Minh City (*vien kiem sat nhan dan thanh pho Ho Chi Minh*) to the People's Court in Ho Chi Minh City (*toa an nhan dan thanh pho Ho Chi Minh*).
11 February 1999	'Beginning of May' date for trial announced.
10 May 1999	Trial begins.
3 August 1999	Trial ends.
1 December 1999	Appeal begins.
13 January 2000	Death sentences upheld for Tang Minh Phung, Lien Khui Thin, Pham Nhat Hong, Nguyen Tuan Phuc, and commuted to life for Nguyen Ngoc Bich and Nguyen Xuan Phong.

Source: Vietnamese press reports.

Notes

1 From plan to market: the logic of decentralisation

1 The term 'local government' is being used as a shorthand for the party-state at the sub-national level. It therefore includes both party and government institutions. A similar duality applies to the use of the term 'the state'.
2 For a discussion of commonalities and distinguishing features of transitional economies see Dean Forbes and Nigel Thrift (eds), *The Socialist Third World: Urban Development and Territorial Planning*, Oxford: Basil Blackwell, 1987, pp. 1–5 and Barrett L. McCormick, 'Political Change in China and Vietnam: Coping with the Consequences of Economic Reform', *The China Journal*, no. 40 (July 1998): pp. 121–6.
3 Vivienne Shue, *The Reach of the State: Sketches of the Chinese Body Politic*, Stanford, CA.: Stanford University Press, 1988.
4 Nee, Victor, 'A Theory of Market Transition: From Redistribution to Markets in State Socialism', *American Sociological Review*, no. 54 (October 1989), pp. 663–81.
5 On the growth in studies of local politics in China see Avery Goldstein, 'Trends in the Study of Political Elites and Institutions in the PRC', *China Quarterly*, no. 139 (September 1994), p. 718. By placing the emphasis on decentralisation and an increase in local government power, the intention is not to dismiss entirely these earlier contrasting views, for in certain respects they remain important. As the subsequent discussion will make clear, it is important to get the balance right when discussing issues of centralisation versus decentralisation because pressures are almost certainly at work in both directions at the same time.
6 The view that the local state would withdraw or abstain derives from neoclassical economics. See Jane Duckett, *The Entrepreneurial State in China*, Routledge: London and New York, 1998, p. 10.
7 McCormick, 'Political Change', p. 127.
8 Christopher Earle Nevitt, 'Private Business Associations in China: Evidence of Civil Society or Local State Power?', *The China Journal*, no. 36 (July 1996), p. 37.
9 Douglas Pike, 'Vietnam: Its Durability and Its Direction', a paper presented to a conference on 'The Durability and Direction of the Four Remaining Socialist Countries: China, Vietnam, Cuba and North Korea', the Korean Association of International Studies and the Research Institute for National Unification, 27–8 May, Seoul 1994, p. 4. Note there are in fact five 'remaining Socialist countries'. Laos had been forgotten.
10 Adam Fforde and Stefan de Vylder, *From Plan to Market: The Economic Transition in Vietnam*. Boulder, CO.: Westview Press, 1996, pp. 49–50.
11 The so-called March South (*nam tien*) from the twelfth century through to the early nineteenth century saw settlers encountering and, it is argued, being

changed over the course of generations by the differing cultural heritage of the Indianised-Champa or Khmer kingdoms and the distinctive ecological environment of the Mekong River Delta. See Michael G. Cotter, 'Towards a Social History of the Vietnamese Southward Movement', *Journal of Southeast Asian History*, no. 9 (March 1968); Terry Rambo, 'A Comparison of Peasant Social Systems of Northern and Southern Viet-Nam: A Study of Ecological Adaption, Social Succession and Cultural Evolution', Ph.D. diss., University of Hawaii, 1972; Gareth Porter, *Vietnam: The Politics of Bureaucratic Socialism*. Ithaca, NY: Cornell University Press, 1993, pp. 2–4 and p. 163; and Pierre Brocheux, *The Mekong Delta: Ecology, Economy and Revolution, 1860–1960*, University of Wisconsin-Madison: Center for Southeast Asian Studies, Monograph no. 12, 1995, pp. xv–xix and pp. 1–15. It is important not to overstate the contemporary significance of southern settlement patterns. Gareth Porter would appear to do this when he writes: 'The contrast between a southern population that is relatively unafraid to assert its political interests and northern and central Vietnamese populations that remain politically more timid is striking testimony to the divergence of social structures in the south from the longer-settled north and centre.' I am not sure that the southern population has been more assertive of its political interests since 1975.

12 Melanie Beresford and Bruce McFarlane, 'Regional Inequality and Regionalism in Vietnam and China', *Journal of Contemporary Asia*, vol. 25, no. 1 (1995), pp. 53–4. This article also explores other determinants of regionalism in Vietnam, including the war and central planning.

13 Fforde and de Vylder, *From Plan to Market*, p. 84; Adam Fforde, 'The Vietnamese Economy in 1996 – Events and Trends – The Limits of Doi Moi?', in *Ten Years after the 1986 Party Congress*, edited by Fforde. Political and Social Change Monograph 24, The Australian National University, Canberra, 1997, p. 149. See also William S. Turley, 'Vietnam: Ordeals of Transition', in *Asian Contagion: The Causes and Consequences of Asia's Financial Crisis*, edited by Karl D. Jackson, Boulder, CO.: Westview Press, 1999, p. 8. The constitution was revised in 1980 and again in 1992 but the structural tension highlighted above with reference to the 1960 Constitution remained. See *The Constitution of Vietnam: 1946–1959–1980–1992*, Hanoi: The Gioi Publishers, 1995.

14 World Bank, *Vietnam: Transition to the Market*, Country Operations Division, Country Department I, East Asia and Pacific Region, September 1993; Porter, *Vietnam*, pp. 140–5; Fforde and de Vylder, *From Plan to Market*, pp. 125–37; Thaveeporn Vasavakul, 'Sectoral Politics and Strategies for State and Party Building from the VII to the VIII Congress of the Vietnam Communist Party (1991–96)', in *Ten Years after the 1986 Party Congress*, edited by Adam Fforde, Political and Social Change Monograph 24, The Australian National University, Canberra, 1997, pp. 89–90. Fforde and de Vylder have emphasised the spontaneous nature of the process. The major liberalisation of price controls occurred in 1989. Limited decision-making responsibility was first formally devolved to enterprises at the Sixth Plenum of the Party Central Committee in August 1979. The equivalent formal decentralising move in agriculture occurred with Directive 100 in 1981.

15 Carlyle A. Thayer, 'The Regularization of Politics: Continuity and Change in the Party's Central Committee, 1951–86', in *Postwar Vietnam: Dilemmas in Socialist Development*, edited by David G. Marr and Christine P. White, Ithaca, NY: Southeast Asian Program, Cornell University, 1988, pp. 177–93; Carlyle A. Thayer, 'The Regularization of Politics Revisited: Continuity and Change in the Party's Central Committee, 1976–96', a paper presented to a panel on 'Vietnamese Politics in Transition: New Conceptions and Inter-Disciplinary Approaches, Part 2' at the 49th Annual Meeting of the Association

for Asian Studies, Chicago, 13–16 March 1997; and Vasavakul, 'Sectoral Politics'.
16 Fforde and de Vylder, *From Plan to Market*, pp. 132–3 and Adam Fforde, *Vietnam: Economic Commentary and Analysis*, no. 7. Canberra: ADUKI, November 1995, pp. 18–30.
17 Thayer, 'The Regularization of Politics'; Thayer, 'The Regularization of Politics Revisited'; and Vasavakul, 'Sectoral Politics'.
18 *Nien Giam Thong Ke Thanh Pho Ho Chi Minh 1998* [Ho Chi Minh City Statistical Yearbook 1998]; *Cuc Thong Ke Thanh Pho Ho Chi Minh* [Ho Chi Minh City Statistical Office], 1998, pp. 17–21. Unofficial estimates put the city's actual population at nearer 7.5 million in the late 1990s. For a discussion of how official population statistics significantly underestimate Ho Chi Minh City's true population owing to rural to urban migration see *Vietnam Business Journal*, October 1998. For national population figures see World Bank, *Vietnam: Preparing for Take-off? How Vietnam Can Participate Fully in the East Asian Recovery*, an Informal Economic Report of the World Bank Consultative Meeting for Vietnam. Hanoi, 14–15 December 1999.
19 *Nien Giam Thong Ke Thanh Pho Ho Chi Minh 1998*, p. 31; World Bank, *Vietnam: Economic Report on Industrialization and Industrial Policy*. Report No. 14645-VN, 17 October 1995.
20 For literature that deals with the early political and economic development of Saigon see Norman G. Owen. 'The Rice Industry of Mainland Southeast Asia 1850–1914', *The Journal of the Siam Society*, vol. 59, part 2 (July 1971), pp. 75–143; Vietnamese Studies, *Saigon From the Beginnings To 1945*, no. 45, 1977, pp. 5–16; Melanie Beresford, *National Unification and Economic Development in Vietnam*, New York: St Martin's Press, 1989, pp. 16–46; Gwendolyn Wright, *The Politics of Design in French Colonial Urbanism*, The University of Chicago Press, Chicago, 1991, pp. 161–178; Martin J. Murray, 'White Gold or White Blood? The Rubber Plantations of Colonial Indochina, 1910–40', *Journal of Peasant Studies*, vol. 19, no. 3/4 (April–July 1992); Tran Khanh, *The Ethnic Chinese and Economic Development in Vietnam*. Indochina Unit, Institute of Southeast Asian Studies, 1993, Chapter 1; Brocheux, *The Mekong Delta*, pp. 51–90.
21 Economist Intelligence Unit, *Vietnam Country Forecast*, first quarter 2000, pp. 30–31; Business Monitor International, *Vietnam 1998*, pp. 30–1.
22 *Nien Giam Thong Ke Thanh Pho Ho Chi Minh 1998*, p. 34.
23 Economist Intelligence Unit, *Vietnam Country Report*, fourth quarter 1999, p. 5.
24 *Nien Giam Thong Ke Thanh Pho Ho Chi Mirth 1998*, p. 24; *Nien Giam Thong Ke 1998* [Statistical Yearbook 1998], Ha Noi: Nha Xuat Ban Thong Ke [Hanoi: Statistical Publishing House], 1999, p. 11.
25 The others are Hanoi and Haiphong.
26 Nguyen Dinh Dau, *From Saigon to Ho Chi Minh City: 300 Year History*, Ho Chi Minh City: Land Service, Science and Technics Publishing House, 1998; *Saigon Times Weekly* 7–13 June 1997.
27 In 1977, 1980, 1983, 1986, 1991, and 1996 the city party Executive Committee has numbered 53, 51, 56, 58, 51, and 51 respectively. In 1983, 1986, 1991, and 1996 the city party Standing Committee has numbered 15, 18, 16, and 13 respectively. See *Ban Thuong Vu Thanh Uy Dang Cong San Viet Nam Thanh Pho Ho Chi Minh* [Standing Committee of the Ho Chi Minh City Communist Party], *Thanh Pho Ho Chi Minh Hai Muoi Nam (1975–1995)* [Ho Chi Minh City: Twenty Years (1975–1995)], Nha Xuat Ban Thanh Pho Ho Chi Minh [Ho Chi Minh City Publishing House], 1996, p. 536; *Sai Gon Giai Phong* 19 November 1983, 6 November 1986, 1 November 1991, and 15 May 1996; *Saigon Times Weekly* 18–24 May 1996.

138 *Notes*

28 The departments are sometimes referred to as 'services'.
29 Based on the principle of democratic centralism, the lower levels elect the higher ones at party Congresses. However, this is a formality and does not detract from the fact that each level is formally subordinate to the level above. These issues are discussed further in Chapter 3.
30 This way of thinking can be traced to writings by Marx, Engels and Mao, if sometimes rather loosely. E. Mingione talks about the creation of 'undivided, polyvalent productive entities', including the development of uninhabited regions and industrialisation of the countryside. 'Polyvalent' refers to the idea of drawing on both urban and rural but being neither one nor the other in terms of what this means for capitalist production relations. Quoted in Forbes and Thrift, *The Socialist Third World*, pp. 7–10.
31 In April 1983, Nhan Dan articulated the issue as follows. 'Before liberation day, Ho Chi Minh City . . . was notorious for the consumption, spending and debauchery of the US-oriented neo-colonialist regime. . . . During the past eight years . . . the city Party organisation and people have carried out many tasks to turn the life of Ho Chi Minh City from that of a big city . . . into that of a city with a new, socialist system; transform it from a consumer into a productive city.' See British Broadcasting Corporation, Summary of World Broadcasts (BBC SWB) FE/7348/B/4–5 1 June 1983 and also FE/7934/B/2–3 25 April 1985, FE/8404/B/2 31 October 1986.
32 There are thus a number of common strands linking Ho Chi Minh City's experience as a city under planning after 1975 with that of Shanghai, Tianjin or Guangzhou after 1949. See Barry Naughton, 'Cities in the Chinese Economic System: Changing Roles and Conditions for Autonomy', in *Urban Spaces in Contemporary China: The Potential for Autonomy and Community In Post-Mao China*, edited by Deborah S. Davis, Richard Kraus, Barry Naughton, and Elizabeth J. Perry, Woodrow Wilson Center Press and Cambridge University Press, 1995, pp. 61–7; and Forbes and Thrift, *The Socialist Third World*, pp. 5–18.
33 The term comes from Naughton, 'Cities in the Chinese Economic System', p. 61.
34 Quoted in Nigel Thrift and Dean Forbes, *The Price of War: Urbanization in Vietnam 1954–1985*, London: Allen and Unwin, 1986, p. 129.
35 Beresford and McFarlane, 'Regional Inequality', p. 52; see also Jayne Werner, 'The Problem of the District in Vietnam's Development Policy', in *Postwar Vietnam: Dilemmas in Socialist Development*, edited by David G. Marr and Christine P. White, Ithaca: Southeast Asian Program, Cornell University, 1988, pp. 147–62.
36 According to Thrift and Forbes, the plan was to move 370,000 Ho Chi Minh City residents to New Economic Zones (NEZs) during 1976–80. For the south as a whole, they estimate that 'less than one million' urban residents were actually moved during these years. Another source suggests there were 750,000 people in the NEZs by the end of 1977. Conditions in the New Economic Zones were tough and the enforced movement was naturally unpopular. See Thrift and Forbes, *The Price of War*, pp. 130–2 and Duiker, *Vietnam*, p. 45.
37 Ho Chi Minh City's population was estimated at 4.5 million in 1975. By 1976 it had fallen to 3.5 million and by 1984 to 3.2 million, according to official figures. See *Thanh Pho Ho Chi Minh* [Ho Chi Minh City], Ho Chi Minh City Publishing House, 1983, pp. 12–13; Forbes and Thrift, *The Socialist Third World*, pp. 114–19 and pp. 121–6; Tran Khanh, *The Ethnic Chinese*, pp. 26–7; Thrift and Forbes, *The Price of War*, p. 126; Nguyen Dinh Dau, *From Saigon to Ho Chi Minh City*, p. 178. On the pre-1975 South Vietnamese economy see Douglas C. Dacy, *Foreign Aid, War and Economic Development: South Vietnam 1955–75*, Cambridge University Press, 1986.

Notes 139

38 Some 600,000 people moved from north to south during 1976–80 (Thrift and Forbes, *The Price of War*, p. 132). While this was primarily about placing loyalists throughout the new administration, the fact that it was necessary to bring people down from the north reflects the very high casualty rate suffered by the party in the south during the Tet offensive in 1968 and following the introduction of the US-sponsored Phoenix programme, which targeted cadres for assassination. See Duiker, *Vietnam*, p. 10 and Porter, *Vietnam*, pp. 24–5.

39 Inevitably some rural to urban migration did occur. However, in an era of food rationing and given the close surveillance of urban populations during these years, it was significantly more difficult to move to the cities in the late 1970s and the first half of the 1980s compared with later in the 1980s and during the 1990s. According to one source, some 30 per cent of those moved to the New Economic Zones returned to the cities. See Thrift and Forbes, *The Price of War*, p. 132.

40 Writing on China, Barry Naughton has referred to cities as 'cash cows' (Naughton, 'Cities in the Chinese Economic System', p. 67).

41 As late as 1987, state enterprises were the source of around 75 per cent of total revenue collected nationwide. See Vu Tuan Anh, *Development in Vietnam: Policy Reforms and Economic Growth*, Indochina Unit, Institute of Southeast Asian Studies, 1994, p. 29, and World Bank, *Vietnam: Economic Report on Industrialization and Industrial Policy*, Report No. 14645-VN, 17 October 1995, Statistical Appendix (Table 5.1).

42 In Vietnam, some 51 per cent of total industrial output was concentrated in just five cities in 1991. See *Nien Giam Thong Ke 1995* [Statistical Yearbook 1995]. *Ha Noi: Nha Xuat Ban Thong Ke* [Hanoi: Statistical Publishing House], 1996, pp. 175–6.

43 State enterprises in Vietnam are formally classified as either centrally managed (*trung uong*) or locally managed (*dia phuong*). The importance of Ho Chi Minh City to the budget is emphasised in a report of a meeting of the Ho Chi Minh City party Executive Committee held in August 1984 in response to a resolution of the party Central Committee which called for the city authorities to reorganise production in some key sectors, which were described as 'injecting great percentages of revenue into the budget'. See BBC SWB FE/7729/B/2–4 23 August 1984.

44 Evidence of this can be seen across Vietnam, where in quite small towns one encounters disproportionately wide avenues, extensive and large administrative buildings and public spaces dominated by Socialist realist monuments, usually in a state of decay. These are mostly post-1975 creations that reflect the investment priorities of the early planning period. A southern example would be Phan Thiet. Given the paucity of data, it is not possible to show shifts in investment in statistical terms.

45 Naughton also makes the important point that it was only their façades that had not changed, underlining the fact that during these years major changes were taking place beneath the surface. See Naughton, 'Cities in the Chinese Economic System', p. 70.

46 These observations are derived from my first visit to Ho Chi Minh City in 1990. A Vietnam News Agency broadcast in the same year entitled 'Saigon, 15 years after Liberation' similarly recalls the downturn that occurred in the city after 1975, noting how 'fashionable boulevards like Dong Khoi, Nguyen Hue, Le Loi suddenly became mute and dormant after most of the popular private restaurants and hotels had been taken over by the state restaurant service'. See SWB FE/0755 B/8 4 May 1990.

47 Turley and Womack, 'Asian Socialism's Open Door', pp. 101–2.

48 Comparing Ho Chi Minh City's growth rate in the 1970s and 1980s with either the pre-1975 period or with that of the country as a whole is difficult because of inadequate or problematic data. The tendency is to assume that growth in the city

140 *Notes*

slowed after 1975 following the loss of aid, imports and the end of the war. For a qualitative assessment see Thrift and Forbes, *The Price of War*, pp. 122–41 and pp. 152–63. Prior to 1986 Vietnam produced only national income data, which includes value added only in material production, not gross domestic product (GDP) data, which includes valued added in all economic activities, including services. The Ho Chi Minh City Statistical Department has produced adjusted GDP statistics for the city for the period 1976–95. This shows the city averaging annual GDP growth of 5.5 per cent during 1976–90. National income figures suggest that nationwide growth averaged 3.5 per cent annually between 1976–90. Strictly speaking a comparison between these figures is not possible. However, if it is assumed that GDP data tends to exaggerate growth compared with national income data, then it can be argued that the data suggests economic growth in Ho Chi Minh City was faster but not much faster than nationwide growth during this period. In the 1985–90 period, there is GDP data that suggests Ho Chi Minh City may have been growing more slowly than the nationwide average. In the reform era, economic growth in Ho Chi Minh City has been significantly faster than nationwide growth. For pre-1990 economic data see *Ban Thuong Vu Thanh Uy Dang Cong San Viet Nam Thanh Pho Ho Chi Minh* and Vu Tuan Anh, *Development in Vietnam: Policy Reforms and Economic Growth*, Indochina Unit, Institute of Southeast Asian Studies, 1994, p. 51. For further data on Ho Chi Minh City's post-1975 economic growth rates see Appendix Table A1.3.

49 Ho Chi Minh City's share of nationwide GDP was estimated at 15.2 per cent in 1990. By 1998, this figure had risen to 18.7 per cent. See *Nien Giam Thong Ke Thanh Pho Ho Chi Minh 1998* [Ho Chi Minh City Statistical Yearbook 1998], *Cuc Thong Ke Thanh Pho Ho Chi Minh* [Ho Chi Minh City Statistical Office], 1998; World Bank, *Report on Industrialization*. See also Appendix Table A1.4.

50 Forbes and Thrift, *The Socialist Third World*, p. 116. People were still being sent to the New Economic Zones in 1985. See Thrift and Forbes, *The Price of War*, p. 132.

51 In 1985, Ho Chi Minh City's population was 3.3 million, up from a low of 3.2 million in 1984. By 1998, it was officially estimated to be 5.1 million, significantly higher than in 1975. See note 37 for references.

52 For a general discussion of off-plan business activities by state companies see Fforde and de Vylder, *From Plan to Market* and Porter, 'Politics of Renovation', p. 73. Fforde and de Vylder refer to the now well-known concept of 'fence-breaking', which is a translation from the Vietnamese *pha rao*. Porter notes the involvement of all types of state agencies (i.e. not just state enterprises) in activities that exploited the two price system. For references to off-plan activities specifically in Ho Chi Minh City during the 1980s see BBC SWB FE/7197/B/2–5 1 December 1982; FE/7334/B/2 16 May 1983; FE/7348/B/4–5 1 June 1983; FE/7729/B2–4 23 August 1984; FE/7825/B/4–6 13 December 1984; FE/8068/B/6–7 28 September 1985. Often these sources refer simply to the activities of 'speculators and smugglers' without revealing who these people are. However, despite the inhibited nature of the official media, the participation of state institutions comes across frequently enough. For example, in an article in October 1985 former Ho Chi Minh City party secretary Vo Van Kiet, then chairman of the State Planning Committee, called for 'stern punishment' to be meted out in Ho Chi Minh City to 'party cadres and members who engage in under-the-counter deals, work hand in glove with speculators and smugglers, and lend a hand to economic saboteurs'. The article also says: 'Speculation . . . is usually connected with encroachers of state prosperity and property embezzlers in agencies and enterprises. They siphon off commodities and channel them to speculators . . . causing market disruption'. See BBC SWB FE/8078/B/5–6 10 October 1985. My assertion that such activities began to occur almost from

liberation is based on references to cadres exploiting their public position for private gain as early as September 1975. This was in the context of the replacement of the old southern piaster with a new currency. See BBC SWB FE/5004/B3–5 11 September 1975. The granting of increased autonomy to state enterprises goes back to August 1979. However, various reforms and adjustment affecting enterprises continued throughout the 1980s. For details see Fforde and de Vylder, *From Plan to Market*.

53 This is not to say that there were not important grounds for the centre to continue exercising control over Ho Chi Minh City. However, it is a question of degree. This issue is discussed further later in this chapter.

54 The turning point in the reliance on state enterprises as a revenue source occurred in 1988 when transfers from state enterprises fell to 64 per cent of total revenue from 75 per cent the previous year. The decline continued through the 1990s so that by 1998 revenue from state enterprises fell to below 40 per cent of the total for the first time. The government introduced fiscal reforms from 1989. See David Dollar, 'Macroeconomic Management and the Transition to the Market in Vietnam', *Journal of Comparative Economics* 18 (1994), pp. 361–2 and pp. 365–7.

55 In the mid 1980s, the economic potential of Ho Chi Minh City was beginning to be recognised but it is often qualified. A Vietnam News Agency report in 1985, while noting the city's potential in terms of industrial production, nonetheless expressed concern about the city's 'capitalist class', which, it suggested, had the ability to 'manipulate the entire region's economy'. In the second half of the 1980s, the tone towards Ho Chi Minh City changed substantially. The city's importance as an economic and commercial hub, both in the context of the national economy and regionally, was more clearly stated. Moreover, in light of experimentation with different ownership and management forms in the city, it was increasingly seen as a potential model for the rest of the country. Another aspect of the change in language was the recognition that the city had been performing well below its potential and for this to change it needed to be allowed to exploit its economic comparative advantage. By the second half of the 1990s, references to the city's recognised position as being at the forefront of *doi moi* (*di tien phong trong cong cuoc Doi Moi*) are standard. See BBC SWB FE/7934/B/2–4 25 April 1985; FE/8404) B/2–16 31 October 1986; FE/8450/C1/5–8; FE/8493/B/4–5 16 February 1987; FE/0755/B/8 4 May 1990; FE/W0127/A/7 9 May 1990; *Thanh Pho Ho Chi Minh Hai Muoi Nam*, pp. 29–38 and pp. 511–31; *Dau Tu* 1 January 1998; *Saigon Giai Phong* 25 August 1998.

56 For references in the secondary literature to 'reform experiments' in Ho Chi Minh City in the 1980s, such as the 'Ba Thi model' or new state–private trading companies, see Melanie Beresford, *National Unification and Economic Development in Vietnam*, New York: St Martin's Press, 1989, p. 207; Beresford and McFarlane, 'Regional Inequality', p. 58; Duiker, *Vietnam*, pp. 95–6; Kolko, *Vietnam*, p. 25; Porter, *Vietnam*, p. 125; Stern, 'The Overseas Chinese', pp. 532–4; Thrift and Forbes, *The Price of War*, p. 159.

57 See Adam Fforde and Steve Seneque, 'The Economy and the Countryside: The Relevance of Rural Development Policies,' pp. 124–8 and Doug J. Porter, 'Economic Liberalization, Marginality, and the Local State', in *Vietnam's Rural Transformation*, edited by Benedict J. Tria Kerkvliet and Doug J. Porter, Boulder, CO.: Westview Press, 1995, pp. 233–43. See also the Law on Foreign Investment in Vietnam, November 1996 (Article 55) and *Vietnam Investment Review*, 20–6 March 2000.

58 Local state sector employment in Ho Chi Minh City, which includes public administration and state business, fell in 1990–2 but rose from 1993–7. This is no different from the pattern observed in state sector employment in other localities, although employment growth in Ho Chi Minh City began a year

earlier than most other provinces and cities. *Nien Giam Thong Ke 1995* [Statistical Yearbook 1995], *Ha Noi: Nha Xuat Ban Thong Ke* [Hanoi: Statistical Publishing House], 1996; *Nien Giam Thong Ke 1998*; *Nien Giam Thong Ke Thanh Pho Ho Chi Minh 1997*; *Nien Giam Thong Ke Thanh Pho Ho Chi Minh 1998*. By 'gatekeeping', I am referring to the licensing, inspection and other regulatory powers of state institutions. This will be discussed in more detail in Chapter 2.

59 See Fforde and Seneque, 'The Economy and the Countryside' and Porter, 'Economic Liberalisation'.

60 During 1994–8, annual average GDP growth in Ho Chi Minh City was 13.2 per cent compared with 8.5 per cent nationally. See *Nien Giam Thong Ke TPHCM 1997* and *1998*, pp. 31–2 and pp. 31–2.

61 In 1998, Ho Chi Minh City's share of nationwide GDP was 18.7 per cent compared with 15.2 per cent in 1990. One might have expected the city's share of nationwide industrial production to have risen, though the data suggests it fell slightly between 1989 and 1998. See *Nien Giam Thong Ke TPHCM 1998*; World Bank, *Economic Report on Industrialization*; *Nien Giam Thong Ke 1995* and *1998*.

62 Carlyle A. Thayer, 'Mono-organizational Socialism and the State', in Kerkvliet and Porter (eds), *Vietnam's Rural Transformation*, p. 55. Thayer's point is clear but it is of course erroneous to suggest that political and economic power was ever exclusively located in Hanoi.

63 Fforde and de Vylder, *From Plan to Market*, p. 163 and note 17. Vo Van Kiet went on to be prime minister and remained on the Politburo until 1997 when he formally retired. See Appendix A3.1 for full biographical details.

64 Turley and Womack, 'Asian Socialism's Open Doors', pp. 95–6 and 108–15. Nguyen Van Linh retired in 1991 and died in 1998. For full biographical details see Appendix A3.1. The argument that Ho Chi Minh City has been influential in the direction 'reform' has taken, although widely accepted, has not in my view been adequately researched. However, this is a subject that would require different research from that conducted here and hence is not addressed directly in this book.

65 For references to Ho Chi Minh City leaders as 'reformers' see Zachary Abuza, 'Leadership Transition in Vietnam Since the Eighth Party Congress: The Unfinished Congress', *Asian Survey*, vol. 38, no. 12 (December 1998), p. 1110; Ronald Cima, 'Vietnam in 1988: The Brink of Renewal', *Asian Survey* 29, no. 1 (January 1989), pp. 64–5; William J. Duiker, *Vietnam Since the Fall of Saigon*, updated edition, Monographs in International Studies, Southeast Asia Series, no. 56A, Athens, Ohio: OH University, 1989, pp. 244–5 and p. 256; John H. Esterline, 'Vietnam in 1987: Steps towards Rejuvenation', *Asian Survey* 28, no. 1 (January 1988), p. 89; Gabriel Kolko, *Vietnam: Anatomy of a Peace*, Routledge: London and New York, 1997, p. 125; Gareth Porter, 'The Politics of "Renovation" in Vietnam', *Problems of Communism*, vol. 39 (May–June 1990), p. 85; Porter, *Vietnam*, pp. 108–10 and p. 141; Riedel and Turley, *Vietnam*, p. 33; Mark Sidel, 'Generational and Institutional Transition in the Vietnamese Communist Party: The 1996 Congress and Beyond', *Asian Survey* 37, no. 5 (May 1997), p. 483; Neil Sheehan, *Two Cities: Hanoi and Saigon*, London: Picador and Jonathan Cape, 1992, pp. 77–81; Lewis M. Stern, 'The Overseas Chinese in the Socialist Republic of Vietnam, 1979–82', *Asian Survey* 25, no. 5 (May 1985), pp. 533–4; Lewis M. Stern, *Renovating the Vietnamese Communist Party: Nguyen Van Linh and the Programme for Organisational Reform, 1987–91*, Singapore: Institute of Southeast Asian Studies, 1993, p. 1; Thayer, 'Regularisation of Politics', pp. 190–1; Thayer, 'Mono-organisational Socialism', pp. 48–9; Thayer, 'Regularization of Politics Revisited', p. 12; Turley and Womack, 'Asian Socialism's Open Door', pp. 102–4 and p. 111. Ho Chi Minh City's leadership is discussed at length in Chapter 3. See Appendix A3.1 for biographical data.

Notes 143

66 For expressions of unease regarding the terms 'reformer' and 'conservative', see Dang Phong, 'Viewing the Decade 1976–1986 in Vietnam Vertically and Horizontally', in Researching the Vietnamese Economic Reforms: 1979–86, Australia–Vietnam Research Project, Monograph Series no. 1, School of Economic and Financial Studies, Macquarie University, Sydney, January 1995, p. 21; David W. P. Elliott, 'Dilemmas of Reform in Vietnam', in *The Challenge of Reform in Indochina*, edited by Borje Ljunggren, Cambridge, MA.: Harvard Institute for International Development, 1993, p. 80; Sidel, 'Generational and Institutional Transition', p. 483.
67 Thayer, 'The Regularisation of Politics'; Thayer, 'The Regularisation of Politics Revisited'; and Vasavakul, 'Sectoral Politics'.
68 David Elliott describes Ho Chi Minh City as 'impervious to control from Hanoi'. However, in my view, this is to overstate the case. See Elliott, 'Dilemmas of Reform', p. 88.
69 Melanie Beresford has suggested that the planned economy was always an 'ideological fiction', insofar as planning was never all-encompassing. See Melanie Beresford, 'Interpretation of the Vietnamese Economic Reforms 1979–85', in Researching the Vietnamese Economic Reforms: 1979–86, Australia–Vietnam Research Project, Monograph Series no. 1, School of Economic and Financial Studies, Macquarie University, Sydney, January 1995, p. 4.
70 See note 56 and also Thrift and Forbes, *The Price of War*, Chapter 7 for insights into the limits of state control over the market. For details of attempts to stop both inter-provincial trade and trade with regional markets see *Ban Thuong Vu Thanh Uy Dang Cong San Viet Nam Thanh Pho He Chi Minh*, pp. 31–2 and p. 515.
71 For analogous literature on China that draws attention to attempted centralisation under reform see John P. Burns, 'Strengthening Central CPP Control of Leadership Selection: The 1990 Nomenklatura', *The China Quarterly*, no. 138 (June 1994), pp. 458–91; Yasheng Huang 'Central–Local Relations in China During the Reform Era: The Economic and Institutional Dimensions', *World Development*, vol. 24, no. 4 (1996), pp. 655–72; Linda Chelan Li, 'Provincial Discretion and National Power: Investment Policy in Guangdong and Shanghai, 1978–93', *The China Quarterly*, no. 152 (December 1997), pp. 778–804; and Dorothy Solinger, 'Despite Decentralisation: Disadvantages, Dependence and Ongoing Central Power in the Inland – the Case of Wuhan', *The China Quarterly*, no. 145 (March 1996), pp. 1–34. On Vietnam see also Turley and Womack, 'Asian Socialism's Open Door', p. 114 and p. 116. Turley and Womack emphasise the limits to autonomy granted to Ho Chi Minh City compared with Guangzhou, which they attribute to the fact that the former was significantly more important to the national economy compared with the latter.
72 The conventional interpretation is that Ho Chi Minh City's constitutional position enhances its power. See Turley and Womack, 'Asian Socialism's Open Door', pp. 118–19. A similar argument in terms of 'central control versus local influence' can be made with reference to the fact that it is now customary for Ho Chi Minh City's party secretary to be a Politburo member. This is discussed further in Chapter 3.
73 Turley and Womack, 'Asian Socialism's Open Door', p. 116.
74 The literature makes frequent passing reference to the existence of alleged friction between Ho Chi Minh City and the centre in fiscal relations. See Kolko, *Vietnam*, p. 48 and Turley and Womack, 'Asian Socialism's Open Door', pp. 114–15. Nevertheless, the subject is complex and under-researched. For literature that discusses fiscal issues in Vietnam, see World Bank, *Vietnam: Poverty Assessment and Strategy*, Report no. 13442-VN, 23 January 1995; World Bank, *Vietnam: Fiscal Decentralisation and the Delivery of Rural Services: An Economic Report*, Report no. 15745-VN, 31 October 1996; and International Monetary Fund and

World Bank, *Vietnam: Towards Fiscal Transparency*, June 1999. For analogous literature on China see Michel Oksenberg and James Tong, 'The Evolution of Central–Provincial Fiscal Relations in China, 1971–84: the Formal System', *The China Quarterly*, no. 125 (March 1991), pp. 1–32; Christine P. W. Wong, 'Central–Local Relations in an Era of Fiscal Decline: The Paradox of Fiscal Decentralisation in Post-Mao China', *The China Quarterly*, no. 128 (1991), pp. 691–714; and Le-Yin Zhang, 'Chinese Central–Provincial Fiscal Relationships, Budgetary Decline and the Impact of the 1994 Fiscal Reform: An Evaluation', *The China Quarterly*, no. 157 (March 1999), pp. 115–41. With regard to arguments about declining central control over the local economy in Ho Chi Minh City, it is worth emphasising that locally managed state enterprises were considerably less important sources of tax revenue than their centrally managed counterparts during the 1990s. This potentially has important ramifications for the degree to which the centre may have acquiesced to such enterprises becoming more autonomous during the 1980s and 1990s.
75 Gordon White, *Riding the Tiger: The Politics of Economic Reform in Post-Mao China*, Macmillan 1993, pp. 4–6; Marc J. Blecher, 'Developmental State, Entrepreneurial State: the Political Economy of Socialist Reform in Xinji Municipality and Guanghan county', in *The Chinese State In the Era of Economic Reform: The Road to Crisis*, edited by Gordon White, London, Macmillan, 1991, pp. 265–94; Marc J. Blecher and Vivienne Shue, *Tethered Deer: Government and Economy in a Chinese County*, Stanford: Stanford University Press, 1996.
76 Jonathan Unger and Anita Chan, 'China, Corporatism, and the East Asian Model', *The Australian Journal of Chinese Affairs*, no. 33 (January 1995), pp. 29–53. Drawing on the work of Philippe Schmitter, Unger and Chan conceive corporatism as the state deciding which social organisations are legitimate and then seeking to incorporate them in the decision-making structure of the state. Corporatism is thus government through a limited number of interest groups. See also Jonathan R. Stromseth, 'Reform and Response in Vietnam: State-Society Relations and the Changing Political Economy', Ph.D. diss., University of Columbia, 1998, pp. 31–44.
77 Jean Oi, 'Fiscal Reform and the Economic Foundations of Local State Corporatism in China', *World Politics* (October 1992), pp. 99–126. Note that Oi distinguishes between 'local state corporatism' and the normal way corporatism is understood. By local state corporatism, she is referring to the workings of a local government. She is not concerned with 'the role of the central state in the vertical interests of society as a whole'. See pp. 100–1.
78 Ibid. p. 121.
79 Ibid. p. 110.
80 Ibid. p. 114.
81 Ibid. p. 118. Andrew Walder makes a similar point when he argues that the way the tax system is structured seems to work against predatory behaviour by local governments. See Andrew Walder, 'Local Bargaining Relationships and Urban Industrial Finance', in *Bureaucracy, Politics and Decision Making in Post-Mao China*, edited by Kenneth G. Lieberthal and David M. Lampton, Berkeley: University of California Press, 1992, pp. 308–33.
82 This has been particularly developed by Jane Duckett. See Duckett, *The Entrepreneurial State*.
83 Ibid. pp. 13–15.
84 Ibid. pp. 11–13. Lam Tao-Chiu also argues that entrepreneurial and developmentalist activity can exist side by side. See Lam Tao-Chiu, review of 'Tethered Deer: Government and Economy in a Chinese Country', by Marc Blecher and Vivienne Shue, *The China Journal*, no. 38 (July 1997), pp. 179–81.
85 McCormick, 'Political Change'.

86 Yia-Ling Liu, 'Reform from Below: The Private Economy and Local Politics in Rural Industrialisation', *The China Quarterly*, no. 130 (June 1992), pp. 293–316. Liu's 'sporadic totalitarianism' is similar to Lieberthal and Oksenberg's 'fragmented authoritarian regime'. See Kenneth Lieberthal and Michael Oksenberg, *Policy Making in China: Leaders, Structures, and Processes*, Princeton: Princeton University Press, 1988.
87 See also Shu-Yan Ma, 'The Role of Spontaneity and State Initiative in China's Shareholding System Reform', *Communist and Post-Communist Studies* 32 (1999), p. 335. Some of Jean Oi's earlier writing seems to take a less flattering view of the state. See Jean C. Oi, 'Market Reforms and Corruption in Rural China', *Studies in Comparative Communism*, vol. 22 (Summer/Autumn 1989).
88 See note 65.
89 Fforde and Seneque, 'The Economy and the Countryside', p. 130. Similar arguments are also implicit in writing by Ari Kokko and Fredrik Sjoholm. See Ari Kokko and Fredrik Sjoholm, *Small, Medium, or Large? Some Scenarios for the Role of the State in the Era of Industrialisation and Modernisation in Vietnam*, Swedish International Development Cooperation Agency, 1997.
90 Jane Duckett also emphasises the importance of breaking the state down into its constituent parts. See Duckett, *The Entrepreneurial State*, p. 14. Jean Oi makes similar claims, although in my view she does not really follow it through in her analysis. See Oi, 'Fiscal Reform', p. 110.
91 Elizabeth J. Perry, 'Trends in the Study of Chinese Politics: State–Society Relations', *The China Quarterly*, no. 139 (September 1994), pp. 705 and 707. Note that the point being made here is not about the merits or otherwise of the state–society approach to studying politics *per se*, which will be dealt with shortly. Here, the point is simply that to talk about 'the state' is too imprecise.
92 Nevitt, 'Private Business', especially pp. 37–41.
93 Ibid. p. 38.
94 Like Ho Chi Minh City, Tianjin is a city with status of a province so there is no intervening level of administration between it and the centre as there is for most cities.
95 With reference to China, other scholars who highlight conflict between state institutions include David L. Wank, 'Private Business, Bureaucracy, and Political Alliances in a Chinese City', *Australian Journal of Chinese Affairs*, no. 33 (January 1995), pp. 55–71; and Ellen Hertz, *The Trading Crowd: An Ethnography of the Shanghai Stock Market*, Cambridge and New York: Cambridge University Press, 1998.
96 Apart from the buying, selling and leasing of land to a far greater extent than had ever occurred under planning, I am also thinking of the use of land and property as collateral to secure bank credit.
97 Of the 23,028 so-called non-state companies in Ho Chi Minh City in 1998 over 97 per cent were either family firms or cooperatives. Only 704 or less than 3 per cent constituted a private corporate sector comprising mainly limited liability companies. Figures for the contribution to total industrial output in Ho Chi Minh City of the private corporate sector are not available but the non-state sector as a whole was responsible for 24.3 per cent of the total in 1998 compared with 51.7 per cent for state companies (both centrally and locally managed) and 24 per cent for foreign-invested enterprises. See *Nien Giam Thong Ke TPHCM 1998*. It is also the case that some of the so-called private sector is only nominally so, incorporating as it does state capital, assets and management. Writing on Vietnam's private sector generally fails to do this issue justice, partly I suspect because it is politically sensitive. The rather statist nature of sections of the private sector is addressed more fully in Chapter 2 and Chapter 6. For literature on the private sector in Vietnam see World Bank *Vietnam: Public Sector*

146 *Notes*

> *Management and Private Sector Incentives: An Economic Report*, Report no. 13143-VN, 26 September 1994; James Riedel and Chuong S. Tran, *The Emerging Private Sector and Industrialisation in Vietnam. Report on the Project: Vietnam's Emerging Private Sector and Promising Private Companies*, James Riedel Associates, Inc., April 1997; Nguyen Dinh Cung, John Bentley, Le Viet Thai, Hoang Xuan Thanh and Phan Nguyen Toan, *Research Report on Improving Macroeconomic Policy and Reforming Administrative Procedures To Promote Development of Small and Medium Enterprises in Vietnam*, United Nations Industrial Development Organisation and Ministry of Planning and Investment, Hanoi, January 1999; Leila Webster and Markus Taussig, *Vietnam's Under-Sized Engine: A Survey of 95 Larger Private Manufacturers*, Mekong Project Development Facility, 4 June 1999; Leila Webster, *SMEs in Vietnam: On the Road to Prosperity*, Private Sector Discussions no. 10, Mekong Project Development Facility.

98 My rejection of the state–society approach to studying politics in Vietnam can be explained in one of two ways. The first is that societal forces are still weak. Alternatively and more importantly, one can argue that it sets up a false dichotomy. Drawing on writing by Timothy Mitchell, Adam Fforde and Doug Porter argue that the distinction between the state and civil society is not best understood as a boundary between two distinct entities but instead focus on 'zones of contest' (Mitchell talks in terms of 'lines of contest') that develop internally within the network of institutional mechanisms through which social and economic order is maintained. Mitchell's principal point is that the elusiveness of the boundary between state and society provides a clue to the nature of the state. See Adam Fforde and Doug Porter, 'Public Goods, the State, Civil Society and Development Assistance in Vietnam: Opportunities and Prospects', a paper presented to Doi Moi, the State and Civil Society: Vietnam Update 1994 Conference, Canberra 10–11 November 1994. For an example of the use of the state-society approach in the Vietnam case see Benedict J. Tria Kerkvliet, 'Village–State Relations in Vietnam: The Effect of Everyday Politics on Decollectivisation', *The Journal of Asian Studies* 54, no. 2 (May 1995), pp. 396–418.

2 In business: the hollowing out of the state sector

1 These companies have been chosen because they offer an unrivalled window onto local politics. They are also among the most substantial firms in Ho Chi Minh City. It is not intended to suggest that these companies have been any more successful than companies controlled by other state institutions.
2 The fall of these companies is addressed in Chapter 5.
3 There is almost certainly considerable overlap between the factors that lie behind the success of companies linked to local institutions and that of business interests linked to central institutions or the military or police.
4 James Riedel and Chuong S. Tran, *The Emerging Private Sector and Industrialisation in Vietnam*, report on the Project: Vietnam's Emerging Private Sector and Promising Private Companies, James Riedel Associates, Inc., April 1997, p. 22.
5 In Vietnamese it is common to say that the enterprise belongs (*thuoc*) to the controlling institution. However, the precise relationship between a controlling institution and its companies is complex and under-researched. Reference to a company's controlling institution may be only a preliminary guide to the interests that prevail in the company. For example, companies with the same controlling institution will often be controlled by different interests. What is meant by 'control' obviously leads into a discussion of the nature of the property rights regime in state enterprises. This will be addressed later in this chapter and in Chapter 6.

6 In 1998, foreign-invested companies contributed 24 per cent to total industrial output in Ho Chi Minh City, up from 11.6 per cent in 1994. See *Nien Giam Thong Ke Thanh Pho Ho Chi Minh 1997* [Ho Chi Minh City Statistical Yearbook 1997], *Cuc Thong Ke Thanh Pho Ho Chi Minh* [Ho Chi Minh City Statistical Office], 1997; *Nien Giam Thong Ke Thanh Pho Ho Chi Minh 1998* [Ho Chi Minh City Statistical Yearbook 1998], *Cuc Thong Ke Thanh Pho Ho Chi Minh* [Ho Chi Minh City Statistical Office], 1998.
7 *Thoi Bao Kinh te Saigon* 12–18 December 1991 and *Thoi Bao Kinh te Viet Nam* 18 March 1998; *Far Eastern Economic Review* 29 February 1996.
8 *Thoi Bao Kinh te Saigon* 21 January–3 February 1993; *Tuoi Tre* 20 May 1997; Murray Hiebert, *Chasing the Tigers: A Portrait of the New Vietnam*, Kodansha International, 1996, pp. 7–8.
9 *Vietnam Investment Review* 29 May–4 June 1995. For additional literature on local Chinese in Vietnam, including relevant academic literature, see Alexander Woodside, 'Nationalism and Poverty in the Breakdown of Sino–Vietnamese Relations', *Pacific Affairs* 52 (Fall 1979), pp. 381–409; Lewis M. Stern, 'The Overseas Chinese in the Socialist Republic of Vietnam, 1979–82', *Asian Survey* 25, no. 5 (May 1985), pp. 521–36; E. S. Ungar, 'The Struggle Over the Chinese Community in Vietnam, 1946–84', *Pacific Affairs* 60, no. 4 (Winter 1987–88), pp. 596–614; Tran Khanh, *The Ethnic Chinese and Economic Development in Vietnam*, Indochina Unit, Institute of Southeast Asian Studies, 1993; East Asia Analytical Unit Department of Foreign Affairs and Trade, 'Vietnam', in *Overseas Chinese Business Networks in Asia*, Commonwealth of Australia, 1995, pp. 80–5; Hiebert. *Chasing the Tigers*, pp. 81–85; *Vietnam Economic Times*, June 1997.
10 See *Danh Muc Co Quan Xi Nghiep Tai Thanh Pho Ho Chi Minh* [List of Commercial Organisations in Ho Chi Minh City], *Cuc Thong Ke Thanh Pho Pho Chi Minh* [Ho Chi Minh City Statistical Office], 1 January 1996.
11 For references to military involvement in business especially involving companies in Military Zone 7 covering Ho Chi Minh City see *Thoi Bao Kinh te Saigon* 22–28 December 1994; *Vietnam Investment Review* 4–10 August and 10–16 November 1997, 12–18 January; *Vietnam Business Journal* April and August 1998; *Saigon Newsreader* 3 November 1998; *South China Post* 11 June 1998.
12 *Thoi Bao Kinh te Saigon* 7–13 May 1992, 7–13 October 1993 and 4–10 May 1995.
13 Ibid. 15–21 May 1997; *Vietnam Investment Review* 10–16 November 1997; personal communication from Kate Lloyd.
14 Interview 23 June 1999.
15 *Thoi Bao kinh te Saigon* 31 August–6 September 1999.
16 A good example is the Trade Department company, Imexco, which was founded in 1983. During the early 1990s it frequently ran advertisements in *Thoi Bao kinh te Saigon* but later in the decade it was far less prominent. See *Thoi Bao kinh te Saigon* 10–16 October 1991 and 30 December 1991–5 January 1992.
17 Until 1998 the Cadastral, Land and Housing Department was two separate departments: the Cadastral Department and the Land and Housing Department. See *Sai Gon Giai Phong* 30 May 1998.
18 An example of a company affiliated to the Health Department is Yteco, which ranks 21 in Ho Chi Minh City in terms of turnover. It is involved in the pharmaceutical business. A company linked to the Culture and Information Department is Fahasa, which is involved in book retailing and publishing. It ranks 65 out of the top 100. See *Danh Muc Co Quan Xi Nghiep Tai Thanh Pho Ho Chi Minh*.
19 *Thoi Bao Kinh te Saigon* 17–23 October 1991 and 3–9 October 1996.
20 *Tuoi Tre* 25 March 1997.
21 Although a party company, Phu Nhuan Jewellery Company began life as Cong ty Vang Bac-My Nghe-Kieu Hoi. While its roots are clearly in Phu Nhuan district,

how it came to be a party company is less obvious. What emerges more clearly is its links with Cao Thi Ngoc Dung and Ngo Dinh Ngon, who have been the dominant influences at the company since its founding. See *Sai Gon Giai Phong* 24 June 1992; *Thoi Bao Kinh te Saigon* 27 April–3 May 1995; *Saigon Times Daily* 6 May 1998.

22 City party companies formally come under the Financial Management Department of the Ho Chi Minh City party committee. See *Nguoi Lao Dong* 10 February 1999.

23 Adam Fforde and Stefan de Vylder have argued that deep antagonism towards the private sector did not really abate until after 1986. See Adam Fforde and Stefan de Vylder, *From Plan to Market: The Economic Transition in Vietnam*, Boulder, CO.: Westview Press, 1996, p. 69.

24 *Thoi Bao Kinh te Saigon* 8–14 December 1994.

25 Interview 26 September 2000.

26 *Far Eastern Economic Review* 29 February 1996; *Financial Times* 13 January 1997; *Reuters* 14 April 1997. Huy Hoang possibly represents an example of central state business interests operating under a private label. Certainly, it is his central credentials that have been emphasised. See note 77 for the relevant references.

27 See *Dieu Le Dang Cong San Viet Nam* [Communist Party of Vietnam Statutes], Ha Noi: Nha Xuat Ban Chinh Tri Quoc Gia [Hanoi: National Political Publishing House], 1996. The point about party members not being allowed to engage in exploitation is contained in Article 1.

28 In 1997 then party secretary in Ho Chi Minh City, Truong Tan Sang, oversaw the introduction of a decree that forbade party members in the city from running private businesses. Similar measures were not announced in other parts of the country and the word at the time was that Sang came under a lot of criticism for his efforts in this area, which in any event came to nothing. One source suggested Sang may have been lured into trying to clamp down on private business by party members 'by way of a trap'. See *Thoi Bao Kinh te Saigon* 7–13 August 1997 and interviews 6 December 1997 and 7 January 1998. The difficulties of reining in the private business activity of officials also came across clearly in the debates in the National Assembly about the draft Business Law (*Luat doanh nghiep*) in 1999. One delegate noted that while the draft law would prevent him using the name of his father, mother, wife, husband or children to establish a company it said nothing about his son-in-law or a close friend. See *Sai Gon Giai Phong* 25 May 1999 and *Nguoi Lao Dong* 28 May 1999. The new Business Law includes articles that seek to limit the private business activities of serving officials and their relatives in the sector where they specifically have state management responsibilities. However, as anticipated, this has yet to lead to a sudden change in practice.

29 In 1994–6 services growth in Ho Chi Minh City was 13.5 per cent but the trade, hotels and banking expanded at 18.1 per cent, 16.8 per cent and 14.3 per cent respectively. Manufacturing grew by 18.5 per cent and construction by 15.3 per cent. One sector that showed surprisingly low growth during this period is property and consulting, which according to official statistics rose by just 2.3 per cent in 1994–6. This may have to do with the informal way much real estate business was being conducted at this time. See *Nien Giam Thong Ke Thanh Pho Ho Chi Minh* 1997, p. 32 and 1998, pp. 32 and 246.

30 For background on the emergence of the land market see Adam Fforde, *Vietnam Economic Commentary and Analysis*, no. 6. Canberra: ADUKI, April 1995; International Monetary Fund, *Vietnam: Recent Economic Developments*, IMF Staff Country Report no. 96/145 1996.

31 *Saigon Times Weekly* 11 March 2000.

32 See *Danh Muc Co Quan Xi Nghiep Tai Thanh Pho Ho Chi Minh*.

33 Ibid. The Youth Volunteer Force is a political organisation for young adults. It has historically been involved in relief and educational work. After 1975, members of the Youth Volunteer Force were involved in land clearance for the New Economic Zones. The organisation has in the past frequently acted as a conduit for up-and-coming leaders in Ho Chi Minh City, although its importance had declined by the 1990s.
34 *Thoi Bao Kinh te Saigon* 4–10 May 1995; *Saigon Times Weekly* 12 June 1999.
35 *Thoi Bao Kinh te Saigon* 5–12 December 1996 and 15–21 May 1997.
36 For background on changes in the banking sector see World Bank. *Transforming a State Owned Financial System: A Financial Sector Study of Vietnam*, Report No. 9223-VN, 15 April 1991; World Bank, *Vietnam Financial Sector Review: An Agenda for Financial Sector Development*, Report No. 13135-VN, 1 March 1995.
37 *Thoi Bao Kinh te Saigon* 7–13 November 1991; 3–9 October 1996; *Vietnam Investment Review* 7–13 October 1996; interview 7 May 1999. The other main shareholder in Exim Bank is Vietcombank. Asia Commercial Bank also has four foreign shareholders.
38 *Ngan Hang* 94, 3 December 1993; *Thoi Bao Kinh te Saigon* 6–12 June 1996; *Vietnam Investment Review* 26 August–1 September 1996; *Vietnam News* 23 May 1997. VP Bank and Asia-Pacific Bank were founded in Hanoi but both have branches and a sizeable portion of their business in Ho Chi Minh City. Since 1997 Vietcombank and Incombank have been *de facto* shareholders in VP Bank following a cash injection after the bank got into financial difficulty over a letter of credit. See *Saigon Times Daily* 24 April 1997 and *Thoi Bao Kinh te Saigon* 24–30 July 1997.
39 *Thoi Bao Kinh te Saigon* 6–12 June 1996; 3–9 October 1996; and *Saigon Times Weekly* 12 June 1999.
40 *Thoi Bao Kinh te Saigon* 26 May–1 June 1994 and unpublished material provided by Dong A Bank officials during interview 5 December 1997. Apart from Phu Nhuan Jewellery Company the other main shareholders are Phu Nhuan District Construction and Housing Company and the Financial Management Department of the city party committee.
41 *Nien Giam Thong Ke Thanh Pho Ho Chi Minh 1998*, p. 180.
42 *Thoi Bao Kinh te Saigon* 12–18 December 1991.
43 On the gold market see Nguyen Huu Dinh, *Kinh Doanh Vang Tai Thanh Pho Ho Chi Minh: Chinh Sach Va Giai Phap* [The Gold Business in Ho Chi Minh City: Policy and Solutions], Nha Xuat Ban Thanh Pho Ho Chi Minh [Ho Chi Minh City Publishing House], Saigon Times Group, Vapec, 1996; *Saigon Times Weekly* 19–15 October 1996; *Saigon Times Daily* 4 June 1997; *Vietnam News* 2 February 1998.
44 This was with Decree 63/CP dated 24 September 1994 (*Vietnam Investment Review* 27 January–2 February 1997). Despite the formal absence of gold ownership rights until 1994, gold remained a popular savings medium throughout the 1980s.
45 Interview 6 December 1997.
46 It is also a popular place for black market foreign exchange dealers. Middle-aged women with small black leather bags loiter on the pavement ready to exchange money for passing customers, who do not even have to get off their motorbikes to complete a transaction.
47 The video business is almost entirely comprised of pirated films.
48 *Vietnam News* 11 April 1998; *Saigon Times Daily* 8 February 1999.
49 Economist Intelligence Unit, *Vietnam: Country Profile 1996–97*, p. 55; Business Monitor International, *Vietnam 1998*, p. 108.
50 *Saigon Times Weekly* 12 June 1999.

51 From 1994 many state enterprises both in Ho Chi Minh City and nationally were organised in general corporations (*tong tong ty*). These grouped companies in similar or diverse fields with the stated aim of creating internationally competitive conglomerates. However, the nascent business groups I have identified in this chapter are *different* from these formal creations, which have often sought to impose unity between capital where there is none. As a result they have tended to be rather unsuccessful. These issues will be discussed further in Chapter 4. For literature on the general corporations see Anne Jerneck, *The Role of the State in a Newly Transitionary Economy: The Case of Vietnam's General Corporations*, a report prepared as part of a collaboration between Sida, Stockholm, the Department of Economic History at Lund University, and the Embassy of Sweden in Hanoi, Vietnam, September 1997; Anne Jerneck and Nguyen Thanh Ha, 'The Role of the Enterprise Unions in the Shift from Central Planning to Market Orientation', in *Vietnam In a Changing World*, edited by Irene Norlund, Carolyn L. Gates and Vu Cao Dam, London: Curzon Press, 1995, pp. 159–80; Adam Fforde, *Vietnam: Economic Commentary and Analysis*, no. 7. Canberra: ADUKI, November 1995, pp. 50–6.
52 *Chan Dung Nhung Doanh Nghiep Thanh Dat*, p. 16.
53 Ibid. and *Thoi Bao Kinh te Saigon* 7–13 October 1993.
54 *Saigon Times Daily* 4 June 1997.
55 *Thoi Bao Kinh te Saigon* 4–10 May 1995.
56 Before their fall both Tamexco and Epco had all the hallmarks of nascent, diversified business corporations. See Tables 5.1 and 5.3 in Chapter 5.
57 The issue of enforcement is addressed in Chapter 6, as is the question of whether Ho Chi Minh City's property regime is government or entrepreneur centred.
58 Jean Oi and Andrew Walder (eds), *Property Rights and Economic Reform in China*, Stanford: Stanford University Press, 1999, pp. 4–5.
59 Ibid. pp. 7–10.
60 For discussion of the 1979 changes see Irene Norland, 'The Role of Industry in Vietnam's Development Strategy', *Journal of Contemporary Asia*, vol. 14, no. 1, 1984, pp. 94–107; Chris Nyland, 'Vietnam, the Plan/Market Contradiction and the Transition to Socialism', *Journal of Contemporary Asia*, vol. 11, no. 4, 1981, pp. 426–49; and Max Spoor, 'Reforming State Finance in Post-1975 Vietnam', *Journal of Development Studies*, vol. 24, no. 4 (July 1988), pp. 102–14.
61 Privatisation (*tu nhan hoa*) has been shunned in favour of the more limited equitisation (*co phan hoa*). Here the state retains a significant stake in the company while the tendency in practice has been for shares to be sold to existing management and those connected to them. During the 1990s the equitisation programme advanced only slowly. Other property forms such as contracting and leasing have not been widely applied.
62 In press reports, it was stated clearly that Tan Truong Sanh had bought the rights to the eight companies (*mua phap nhan cua tam doanh nghiep nha nuoc. thuong do la cac don vi kinh te Dang, kinh te cong an*). Four of the eight companies were named. They were Cong ty thuong nghiep mien nui Thua Thien-Hue; Cong ty xuat nhap khau Hue; Cong ty thuong mai Ben Tre; Cong ty Thai Hoa; and a company based in Can Tho called Cataco. See *Tuoi Tre* 3 November 1998
63 For press articles that discuss the problems encountered in advancing the equitisation process, including difficulties relating to the valuation of enterprise assets see *Thoi Bao Kinh te Vietnam* 22 November 1997, 6 June and 5 September 1998; *Tuoi Tre* 6 June 1998; *Thoi Bao Kinh te Saigon* 13–19 August and 1–6 October 1998 and *Sai Gon Giai Phong* 23 October 1998.
64 Walder and Oi 'Introduction' in Oi and Walder, *Property Rights*, pp. 17–19.
65 Jean Oi and Andrew Walder argue that small initial changes or theoretically suboptimal solutions can have a large impact on behaviour. Ibid. p. 24.

66 *Sai Gon Giai Phong* 27 April 1998. The article is entitled 'It takes a hard tree to stand a strong wind' (*co tung moi dung dau gio*).
67 Ibid.
68 For examples of the problems that can arise either with tax inspectors or the police see *Tuoi Tre* 14 May 1998; *Nguoi Lao Dong* 18 May 1998.
69 This has been a key factor in the relative success in business of the children of the political elite. In Ho Chi Minh City, children of political leaders commonly mentioned as having diverse business interests include the daughter of Vo Van Kiet and the son of Phan Van Khai. A son of Le Duan is also prominent in Techombank, which is one of the city's joint stock commercial banks. Interview 8 March 1999.
70 'Social evils' is the official term for prostitution, drug-taking and other unhealthy social practices sometimes regarded as having increased with the 'open door'.
71 This is slightly to pre-empt issues that will be dealt with in more depth in Chapter 3. However, suffice it to say at this stage that a prominent figure associated with business interests at the Department of Trade is married to a senior politician at the centre (interview 5 July 1999).
72 Interview 23 June 1999.
73 The pattern is that the number of permits or pieces of paper required tends to multiply as one moves down the administrative hierarchy. Examples of the number of licences required to do quite simple things, such as register a motorbike, are legion. In the case of one set of regulations on setting up a business, it was specified that just one or two licences were required. At the city level, this had risen to three or four while by the time the decree was being implemented at the district level the number of licences required ranged from seven to seventeen. See *Than Nien* 15 May 1998.
74 The others are Asia Commercial Bank, Dai Nam Bank, Than Tai in District 5, and a centrally managed company, Vietnam Jewellery Corporation. See *Saigon Times Daily* 21 May 1997. Note that Saigon Jewellery Company is a key shareholder in Asia Commercial Bank. Dai Nam Bank was taken over by Phuong Nam Bank in 1999 (*Saigon Times Daily* 5 May 1999).
75 Dorothy Solinger, for example, sees 'a stratum of people exclusively pursuing business who are inextricably entangled with cadredom and an official class increasingly corroded by commercialism'. Both, she says, are entrepreneurs. As a result, exchanges such as the issuing of licences or contracts, which are often depicted as occurring between distinct groups, in fact take place 'within a single, blended class'. Jean Oi also notes that it is not always easy to distinguish between the regulators and the regulated because the latter are often the 'former colleagues and friends and relatives of the regulators'. In such a climate traditional patron–client type analyses become more harder to sustain. See Dorothy J. Solinger, 'Urban Entrepreneurs and the State: The Merger of State and Society', in *State and Society in China: The Consequences of Reform*, edited by Arthur Lewis Rosenbaum. Boulder, CO.: Westview Press, 1992, pp. 123–4; and Jean C. Oi, 'Market Reforms and Corruption in Rural China', *Studies in Comparative Communism*, vol. 22 (Summer/Autumn 1989), p. 232.
76 The company is called Tocontap and belongs to the Ministry of Commerce. During the 1990s there was also a direct link with Ho Chi Minh City within the Ministry of Commerce insofar as the Commerce Minister was Le Van Triet, who had previously served as People's Committee vice-chairman in the city (interview 23 June 1999).
77 *Sai Gon Giai Phong* 16 October 1998 and *Thoi Bao Kinh Te Viet Nam* 21 October 1998.
78 World Bank, *Vietnam: Transition to the Market*, Country Operations Division, Country Department I, East Asia and Pacific Region, September 1993, p. iii;

Gareth Porter, *Vietnam: The Politics of Bureaucratic Socialism*, Ithaca, NY: Cornell University Press, 1993, pp. 132–3 and 150–1.
79 A similar distinction between a hard budget constraint and a soft credit constraint via the banking system is made by scholars writing on China. See Gabriella Montinola, Yingyi Qian, and Barry R. Weingast, 'Federalism, Chinese Style: The Political Basis for Economic Success in China', *World Politics* 48 (October 1995), p. 66. This is not to say that the credit constraint was always or uniformly soft. Looking at the 1990s as a whole and compared with the previous decade, the trend was probably towards it becoming harder.
80 An interesting question is whether by the late 1990s lending practices had been significantly altered by the spectacle of the Tamexco and Minh Phung–Epco trial. This requires further research, although preliminary enquiries suggest they had not. One banking source said that political-style lending had not disappeared but the trials had just made people more cautious. Interview 28 March 1998.
81 *Tuoi Tre* 28 January 1997.
82 *Reuters* 23 April 1997 and *Agence France Press* 4 August 1999.
83 See BBC SWB FE/5014/B/4–6 23 September 1975 and FE/5015/B/2–4 24 September 1975.
84 Sometimes a nominal fee was charged, although land or property distributed in this way was often acquired for free. In some cases, it was seen as compensation for loss of state housing or other state-sector privileges. It was also conceived of as by way of a supplement to pension for long service. Such assets effectively became private property. See Fforde, *Vietnam: Economic Commentary and Analysis*, no. 7, pp. 74–5.
85 *Far Eastern Economic Review* 29 February 1996.
86 There were also signs that the process had become institutionalised in the case of the Tan Truong Sanh smuggling ring. Officials investigating the company's activities claimed it had paid bribes totalling VND9.11 billion and US$44,000 to customs officials in Ho Chi Minh City, Can Tho and Thue Thien-Hue. They said they were able to estimate the amount paid quite accurately because customs officials kept detailed records in order to ensure that the money was divided up fairly. See *Saigon Newsreader* 6–7 November 1998.
87 *Sai Gon Giai Phong* 30 March 1999.
88 Ibid.
89 *Vietnam Investment Review* 29 December 1997–4 January 1998.
90 Until 1999 the exchange rate was fixed by the State Bank of Vietnam on a daily basis. From 1994 commercial banks were permitted to buy and sell currency within a narrow band either side of the official rate (the so-called 'managed float'). In 1999 the official rate was abolished and replaced with what has been referred to locally as a 'crawling peg'. The exchange rate is now permitted to fluctuate in a narrow band either side of the previous day's closing interbank market rate. See Martin Gainsborough, 'The Politics of the Greenback: The Interaction Between the Formal and Black Markets in Ho Chi Minh City', in Lisa Drummond, Thuy Pham and Mandy Thomas (eds), *Urban Tiger*, London: Curzon Press 2002; Business Monitor International, *Vietnam 2000*, p. 39.
91 *Thoi Bao Kinh te Saigon* 29 October 1998. Sources I spoke to claimed that the State Bank in Ho Chi Minh City was also overcharging for dollars. In one case a prominent local state company wishing to purchase $1m was offered a price by the State Bank which was 500 dong per dollar over and above the official rate. Interview 4 February 1998.
92 *Vietnam Investment Review* 26 April–3 May 1999.
93 *Tuoi Tre* 9 December 1997.
94 *Thoi Bao Kinh te Saigon* 11 November 1998.
95 *Saigon Newsreader* 23–4 October 1998.

96 *Tuoi Tre* 8 October 1998. Note the delay between the devaluation and when the journalist wrote about it, reflecting the fact that some of the article's assertions are potentially sensitive.
97 Such an interpretation has also been borne out in conversation with local informants.
98 *Nguoi Lao Dong* 3 March 1999.
99 Ibid.
100 Interview 7 April 1998.
101 Interview 25 January 1999.
102 *Nguoi Lao Dong* 28 March 1995. This is discussed in more detail in Chapter 4.
103 *Nguoi Lao Dong* 5 March 1999. The three limited companies were Van Thong, An Dong and Van Tham.
104 See *Vietnam Business Journal*, December 1998.
105 *Nhan Dan* 29 October 1997 in BBC SWB FE/3069 B/7–8 6 November 1997.
106 *Nguoi Lao Dong* 27 May 1998
107 In conversation it was said that this explained the heavy involvement of military and police interests in smuggling.
108 In the south, the main international crossing point for smugglers is the south-western border with Cambodia. The south-western provinces of An Giang, Dong Thap, Long An and Tay Ninh are all within easy reach of Ho Chi Minh City. Ho Chi Minh City's Cho Lon (District 5) is well-known for having markets specialising in particular types of smuggled goods. An Duong Vuong market, for instance, specialises in electronic goods while Hoc Loc market is well-known for dealing in smuggled cigarettes. One newspaper reported that most days between 8 and 9 a.m. and 4 and 5 p.m., cigarette smugglers resembling 'robots on bicycles' (*nhu ro bo chay xe dap*) can be seen making their way to the market. See *Nguoi Lao Dong* 27 May 1998.
109 *Saigon Times Daily* 9 January 1997; *Vietnam News* 2 February 1998. In 1997, a single jewellery shop owner said his company was processing at least 50–60 kg of smuggled gold daily. There is a familiar pattern to gold smuggling in Ho Chi Minh City: whenever the world gold price falls below the Vietnamese gold price, smuggling picks up. This is commonly followed by a rise in the US dollar price on the black market as gold smugglers scour the market for hard currency to pay for the gold. See *Tuoi Tre* 15 April 1999.
110 According to the State Bank of Vietnam, the re-introduction of quotas would lead to a fall in the gold price and the risk of deflation. This also highlights the way the absence of quotas is designed to keep the gold price up, which is clearly of benefit to the companies involved in the gold trade. See *Vietnam Investment Review* 17–23 March 1997.
111 *Thoi Bao Kinh te Saigon* 2 February 1999.
112 *Vietnam Investment Review* 26 May–1 June 1997.
113 *Phu Nu* 24 April 1997. I put a similar question to a Saigon Jewellery Company official about where the company gets its gold in the absence of an import quota. The response was equally non-committal but tellingly good-humoured (interview 12 December 1997).
114 Duckett, *The Entrepreneurial State*, pp. 13–15.

3 Patterns of circulation: democratic centralism under strain

1 Tom Bottomore, Laurence Harris, V. G. Kiernan and Ralph Miliband (eds), *A Dictionary of Marxist Thought*, second edition, Oxford: Blackwell 1991, pp. 134–7.
2 Ibid.
3 Ibid.

154 Notes

4. Ibid.
5. For a discussion of People's Council elections see Gareth Porter, *Vietnam: The Politics of Bureaucratic Socialism*, Ithaca, NY: Cornell University Press, 1993, pp. 15–16 and pp. 79–80.
6. People have been dismissed. See Carlyle A. Thayer, 'Mono-organizational Socialism and the State', in *Vietnam's Rural Transformation*, edited by Benedict J. Tria Kerkvliet and Doug J. Porter, Boulder, CO.: Westview Press, 1995, p. 55.
7. John P. Burns, 'Strengthening Central CPP Control of Leadership Selection: The 1990 Nomenklatura', *China Quarterly*, no. 138 (June 1994), p. 458 and p. 472.
8. Andrew Walder, *Communist Neo-Traditionalism, Work and Authority in Chinese Industry*, Berkeley and Los Angeles: University of California Press, 1986; Yia-Ling Liu, 'Reform from Below: The Private Economy and Local Politics in Rural Industrialisation', *The China Quarterly*, no. 130 (June 1992), pp. 293–316.
9. Jean Oi, 'Market Reforms and Corruption in Rural China', *Studies in Comparative Communism*, vol. 22 (Summer/Autumn 1989), p. 224.
10. *Nhan Dan* web site, Hanoi, in Vietnamese 13 January 2000, BBC SWB FE/3738 B/6 15 January 2000.
11. *Tuoi Tre* 27 December 1997; *Sai Gon Giai Phong* 20 June 1999.
12. *Thoi Bao Kinh te Sai Gon* 3–9 September 1992 and 27 June–3 July 1996.
13. *Sai Gon Giai Phong* 24 March 1998; *Tuoi Tre* 1 June 1999.
14. See Article 4 of the 1992 Constitution. *The Constitution of Vietnam: 1946–1959–1980–1992*, Hanoi: The Gioi Publishers, 1995.
15. Interview 8 March 1999. When questioned about what would happen if the People's Council disagreed with the party's choice, the same source said this had never happened and anyway 'they are the same people'.
16. Interview 5 July 1999.
17. A good example concerns the appointment of Vo Viet Thanh as People's Committee chairman. His appointment was clearly controversial, as indicated by the fact that he held the post in an acting capacity for over a year before the People's Council voted on the matter. However, when it voted, it was unanimous in backing Thanh. See *Thoi Bao Kinh te Sai Gon* 27 August–3 September 1997. Thanh's appointment is discussed further later in the chapter.
18. This issue is considered at greater length in Chapter 4.
19. *The Constitution of Vietnam*, p. 203. According to press coverage of the National Assembly debate on the issue, some Ho Chi Minh City delegates favoured giving greater power to the prime minister in the appointment of People's Committee chairmen, on the grounds that it would lead to greater 'individual responsibility' on the part of incumbents. See *Sai Gon Giai Phong* 11 April 1992.
20. The argument is that by seeking to create a better balance between party and government – and rein in the worst excesses of the party – political reforms have led to greater assertiveness on the part of government institutions. For discussion of this in the Vietnam literature see Carlyle A. Thayer, 'Political Reform in Vietnam: Doi Moi and the Emergence of Civil Society', in *The Developments of Civil Society In Communist Systems*, edited by Robert F. Miller, London: Allen and Unwin 1992, pp. 112–15; Porter, *Vietnam*, pp. 84–6.
21. *Thoi Bao Kinh te Sai Gon* 20–6 August 1992; 22–8 April 1993; 27 June–3 July 1996; and 27 August–3 September 1997.
22. Interviews 4 February 1998; 30 June 1998; and 26 May 1999.
23. One possibility is differences between the then party general-secretary, Do Muoi, and the prime minister, Vo Van Kiet. According to some sources, Sang is close to Do Muoi and Thanh to Kiet (interview 5 July 1999). However, this view is not unanimous and overall the evidence linking problems about appointments in Ho Chi Minh City and national politics is thin.

24 The People's Committee chairman in Ho Chi Minh City has usually had a Central Committee seat. Of the six chairmen since 1975, four were Central Committee members. Apart from Thanh, the only other chairman not to enjoy this privilege was Nguyen Vinh Nghiep, who held the post from 1989–92.
25 See note 22. In particular, Thanh was alleged to have committed major errors during the war. As always with this kind of rumour, it is difficult to verify its accuracy. It may simply have been concocted to cause political damage.
26 Like all city party companies, Saigon Petro comes under the city party's Financial Management Committee (*Ban tai chinh quan tri thanh uy*).
27 Interview May 1998, day not specified.
28 Saigon Petro's difficulties in securing foreign exchange is discussed in another context in Chapter 4.
29 *Tuoi Tre* 28 April 1998; *Sai Gon Giai Phong* 25 September 1992, 23 November 1997, and 29 April 1998.
30 BBC SWB FE/5181/B5–6 9 April 1976 and FE/8447/C2/12–13 20 December 1986; *Thoi Bao Kinh te Sai Gon* 20–6 August 1992; *Saigon Times Daily* 2 January 1997; interviews April 1998, date unspecified, and 5 July 1999.
31 Linh is sometimes mistakenly identified as a southerner by birth. See William J. Duiker, *Vietnam Since the Fall of Saigon*, updated edition, Monographs in International Studies, Southeast Asia Series, no. 56A, Athens, OH: Ohio University, 1989, p. 49 and p. 337 note 15. I have also encountered Vietnamese who have been vehement that Linh was born in the south.
32 *Sai Gon Giai Phong* 7 July 1992; *Saigon Times Daily* 2 January 1997.
33 BBC SWB FE/5181/B5–6 9 April 1976 and FE/8447/C2/12–13 20 December 1986.
34 BBC SWB FE/5181/B5–6 9 April 1976.
35 Interview 5 July 1999.
36 Sang also served as director of the Forestry Department before becoming district party secretary in Binh Chanh. See *Sai Gon Giai Phong* 7 July 1992.
37 Note that both Vo Tran Chi and Truong Tan Sang came to the party secretary post with a background in agriculture. One source said that such a background used to be considered an important qualification for political office but that this is no longer the case. Interview 5 July 1999.
38 *Tuoi Tre* 30 December 1997.
39 Communist Party of Vietnam, *Seventh National Congress of the Communist Party: Documents*, Hanoi: Foreign Language Publishing House, 1991.
40 Interview 5 July 1999.
41 Truong Tan Sang has since achieved high office. He became a Politburo member in 1996 and was appointed head of the central party's Economics Committee (*Ban kinh te trung uong dang*) after he relinquished his position as party secretary in Ho Chi Minh City in 2000. See *Vietnam Business Journal* January 2000, at www.viam.com.
42 *Saigon Times Daily* 9 February 1998; *Nhan Dan* web site, Hanoi, in Vietnamese 13 January 2000 in BBC SWB FE/3738 B/6 15 January 2000.
43 Prior to being appointed party secretary in Ho Chi Minh City in January 2000, Nguyen Minh Triet served from January 1997 to February 1998 as the permanent deputy secretary of the city party Standing Committee (*pho bi thu thuong truc Thanh uy*). However, this appears to be the sum total of his Ho Chi Minh City experience. See *Saigon Times Daily* 2 January 1997 and 6 February 1998.
44 Mai Chi Tho held the position of party secretary in an acting capacity during the period from Nguyen Van Linh's promotion to the centre in July 1985 and Vo Tran Chi's appointment as party secretary in November 1986. See *Tuoi Tre* 1 and 19 November 1986; and *Sai Gon Giai Phong* 27 April 1999.
45 *Sai Gon Giai Phong* 26 September 1997.

156 *Notes*

46 Bui Tin, *Following Ho Chi Minh: The Memoirs of a North Vietnamese Colonel*, translated from the Vietnamese and adapted by Judy Stowe and Do Van, London: Hurst and Company, 1995, p. 95, p. 99, pp. 173–4 and p. 188; interview 5 July 1999. As interior minister, Mai Chi Tho had the title 'General of Security' (*Dai thuong An Ninh*). No one has had the title since and he does not use it now. The source for this piece of information suggested that the title may have been self-proclaimed.
47 Interview 5 July 1999.
48 Ibid.
49 *Thoi Bao Kinh te Saigon* 27 August–3 September 1997.
50 *Sai Gon Giai Phong* 26 September 1997.
51 Phan Van Khai became a Central Committee member at the Sixth Party Congress in 1991, one year after becoming Ho Chi Minh City People's Committee chairman. See BBC SWB FE/5181/B5–6 9 April 1976; *Sai Gon Giai Phong* 15 October 1980, 27 October 1991, and 26 September 1997.
52 *Sai Gon Giai Phong* 26 September 1997.
53 The possible exception is Vo Viet Thanh, although the evidence is by no means conclusive. Some sources have spoken of a brother-in-law of Vo Tran Chi doing business as the director of a company called Dong Lanh Hung Vuong. Interview 6 May 1998. Others spoke of the children of Vo Van Kiet and Phan Van Khai doing business (interview 23 March 1998). However, these interests developed after Kiet and Khai held office in Ho Chi Minh City.
54 As noted in Chapter 1, being a centrally managed city means that like a province there is no intermediate level between the city authority and the centre.
55 *Sai Gon Giai Phong* 27 October 1991.
56 Vo Viet Thanh had earlier served in Ho Chi Minh City as director of police. While today the police are very active in business, Thanh served mainly in the early/mid 1980s when such behaviour was less common. Moreover, the director of police in Ho Chi Minh City answers directly to the centre, which in terms of Nevitt's thesis would suggest it is not the ideal post to develop one's own business interests. See *Saigon Times Daily* 2 January 1997 and *Thoi Bao Kinh te Saigon* 27 August–3 September 1997.
57 Pham Thanh Phan and Pham Thi Thuy Duong, *Vi Tri, Chuc Namg, Nhiem Vu, Va Quyen Ham Cua Chinh Quyen Xa, Phuong* [The Positions, Function, Responsibility and Power of State Administration At the Village and Quarter Level], Nha Xuat Ban Thong Ke [Statistical Publishing House], Hanoi, 1999, pp. 155–79.
58 In 1996, these included land, housing, construction, communications and transport; planning, investment, agriculture, and rural affairs; municipal trade, economies, finance and banking; and social and cultural affairs. See *Vietnam Investment Review* 5–11 August 1996.
59 All the city's deputy chairmen for whom I have data were born in the south. Of these, by far the majority came from Mekong Delta provinces, while a large number have come from Cu Chi.
60 *Thoi Bao Kinh te Saigon* 8–14 October 1992 and 27 August–3 September 1997; *Sai Gon Giai Phong* 1 July 1992; Murray Hiebert, *Chasing the Tigers: A Portrait of the New Vietnam*, Kodansha International, 1996, p. 121; *Tuoi Tre* 25 March 1997; interview 26 May 1999.
61 BBC SWB FE/6993/C2/1–2 1 April 1982; *Sai Gon Giai Phong* 7 July 1992.
62 The city People's Committee chairman has always been a member of the party Standing Committee.
63 *Thoi Bao Kinh te Saigon* 8–14 October 1992 and 27 August–3 September 3, 1997.
64 *Sai Gon Giai Phong* 26 September 1997; *Phu Nu* 1 November 1986; and *Thoi Bao Kinh te Saigon* 1–7 August 1996.

Notes 157

65 The label technocrat has tended to be used rather indiscriminately when discussing Ho Chi Minh City politicians. I suspect it is often equated with terms such as 'southerner' and 'reformer'. Derek Tonkin, for example, refers to Truong Tan Sang as the 'dynamic technocrat party leader in Ho Chi Minh City'. See Derek Tonkin, 'Vietnam: Market Reform and Ideology', Lecture to the Royal Society for Asian Affairs, 22 January 1997. However, the use of the technocrat label seems misplaced: Sang has no specialist technical knowledge gained through higher education. On the contrary, he rose up through the party ranks on account of having acquitted himself well during the war and through mainstream party and government service (i.e. it would appear a classically 'political' career). By contrast, Tran Thanh Long and Nguyen Thien Nhan – loosely labelled as being of a more technocratic bent – have extensive higher educational qualifications and experience, including gained through study overseas. See *Thoi Bao Kinh te Saigon* 20–6 April 1995; *Saigon Times Weekly* 18 December 1999. However, while people with such qualifications are increasingly desired in political office, I would argue that their political credentials are still key to their advancement. Nhan, for example, is the son of a prominent party doctor who endeared himself to the party elite through good service (interview 24 January 2000). For scholarly treatment of these issues see Shi Chen, 'Leadership Change in Shanghai: Toward the Dominance of Party Technocrats', *Asian Survey*, vol. 38, no. 7, July 1998, pp. 671–87. Shi Chen distinguishes between 'technocracy' and 'political technocracy', which appears to be important in the case of Ho Chi Minh City.

66 The careers of two early People's Committee deputy chairmen, Phan Van Khai and Le Van Triet, would appear to be a case in point. Their experience is quite different from the much more 'homegrown' background of the later generation of People's Committee deputy chairmen. For biographical data on Khai and Triet see Appendix A3.1.

67 *Sai Gon Giai Phong* 25 October 1991; *Thoi Bao Kinh te Saigon* 1–7 August 1996.

68 *Sai Gon Giai Phong* 27 October 1991; *Thoi Bao Kinh te Saigon* 22–8 December 1994; interview 26 May 1999.

69 *Sai Gon Giai Phong* 1 July 1989; *Thoi Bao Kinh te Saigon* 6–12 June 1996.

70 *Phu Nu* 1 November 1986; *Thoi Bao Kinh te Saigon* 25 June–1 July 1992 and 3–9 February 1994. The Trade Department was created out of a merger between the Department of Industry and Trade and the Department of Foreign Economy.

71 *Vietnam Investment Review* 5–11 August 1996.

72 *Sai Gon Giai Phong* 1 July 1989.

73 *Thoi Bao Kinh te Saigon* 9–15 November 1995 and 18–24 January 1996.

74 *Nhan Dan* 22 October 1991; *Sai Gon Giai Phong* 27 October 1991 and 12 July 1992; *Thoi Bao Kinh te Saigon* 26 December 1991–1 January 1992, 15 June–1 July 1992, 9–15 November 1995 and 1–7 February 1996; *Saigon Times Weekly* 18–24 May 1996; *Saigon Times Daily* 2 January 1997 and 24 January 1998. See also Appendix A3.1.

75 *Thoi Bao Kinh te Saigon* 6–12 June 1996 and 3–9 October 1996. In 1999 Do Van Hoang became the management board chairman and general director of the newly created Saigon General Corporation. See *Sai Gon Giai Phong* 24 June 1999.

76 On Epco, see also Chapter 5.

77 *Sai Gon Giai Phong* 27 October 1991; *Thoi Bao Kinh te Saigon* 22–8 October 1992.

78 *Thoi Bao Kinh te Saigon* 17–23 October 1991.

79 *Vietnam Investment Review* 5–11 August 1996.

80 *Sai Gon Giai Phong* 1 July 1989.

81 *Sai Gon Giai Phong* 19 November 1983, 6 November 1986 and 27 October 1991; *Thoi Bao Kinh te Saigon* 26 May–1 June 1994.

82 *Thoi Bao Kinh te Saigon* 2–9 February 1994.

158 *Notes*

83 The Vietnamese language captures such assumptions very nicely. Note, for example, the question asked between friends about the holding of public office: '*Co an khong hoac la chi ghe thoi?*' which translates roughly as 'Does it pay or is it just a seat?' See also Chapter 5.
84 Zachary Abuza, 'Leadership Transition in Vietnam Since the Eighth Party Congress: The Unfinished Congress', *Asian Survey*, vol. 38, no. 12 (December 1998), pp. 1105–21; Carlyle A. Thayer, 'The Regularization of Politics: Continuity and Change in the Party's Central Committee, 1951–86', in *Postwar Vietnam: Dilemmas in Socialist Development*, edited by David G. Marr and Christine P. White, Ithaca: Southeast Asian Program, Cornell University, 1988, pp. 177–93; Carlyle A. Thayer, 'The Regularization of Politics Revisited: Continuity and Change in the Party's Central Committee, 1976–96', a paper presented to a panel on 'Vietnamese Politics in Transition: New Conceptions and Inter-Disciplinary Approaches, Part 2' at the 49th Annual Meeting of the Association for Asian Studies, Chicago, 13–16 March 1997; Thaveeporn Vasavakul, 'Sectoral Politics and Strategies for State and Party Building from the VII to the VIII Congress of the Vietnam Communist Party (1991–96)', in *Ten Years after the 1986 Party Congress*, edited by Adam Fforde, Political and Social Change Monograph 24, The Australian National University, Canberra, 1997, pp. 81–135.
85 Gabriel Kolko, *Vietnam: Anatomy of a Peace*, London and New York: Routledge, 1997, pp. 123–4; Economist Intelligence Unit, *Vietnam Country Forecast*, third quarter 1997, p. 7.
86 Born in 1912 in Hanoi and politically active from the 1930s, Le Duc Tho was the head of North Vietnam's delegation at the Paris peace talks in the early 1970s. After the war he served for many years as the head of the central party's Organisation Department (*ban to chuc trung uong dang*). He retired from both the Politburo and the Central Committee at the Sixth Congress in 1986. See Duiker, *Vietnam*, 1989, p. 345; Porter, *Vietnam*, p. 67, p. 103 and p. 107.
87 *Sai Gon Giai Phong* 15 October 1980; BBC SWB FE/8446/C1/1–2 19 December 1986; Communist Party of Vietnam, *Seventh National Congress*; Bui Tin, *Following Ho Chi Minh*, p. 99, pp. 173–4 and p. 188; *Thoi Bao Kinh te Saigon* 27 August–9 September 1997; interview 5 July 1999.
88 In Vo Tran Chi's case, his emergence as party secretary in District 5 in 1975 is striking, partly because of his relatively low profile during the war as a provincial resistance leader but also because of the fact that appointments in District 5 were considered politically important given its large ethnic Chinese population and sensitivities associated with this. For biographical details on Chi see Appendix Table A3.1.
89 Interview 5 July 1999.
90 A similar point is made about China by Lowell Dittmer. Drawing on work by Lucien Pye he 'rejects the premise that factions are defined by traditional "primordial" ties such as shared generation, class or geographical origins, likewise discarding ties "achieved" in previous bonding experiences, such as school ties, organisational links, or even ideological affinity, pointing to exceptions to each presumptive links'. See Lowell Dittmer, 'Chinese Informal Politics', *The China Journal*, no. 34, July 1995, p. 5.
91 Interview 6 April 1999.
92 *Thoi Bao Kinh te Saigon* 25 June–1 July 1992; *Sai Gon Giai Phong* 1 July and 12 July 1992. Poulo Condore is the name of a prison established by the French on what is now Con Son island. It was used by both the French and later the South Vietnamese government to imprison Communist leaders. See Peter B. Zinoman, 'The Colonial Bastille: A Social History of Imprisonment in Colonial Vietnam, 1862–1940', Ph.D. diss., Cornell University, 1996.

93 Interview 5 July 1999.
94 Two such companies were Imexco and Cofidex. See *Thoi Bao Kinh te Saigon* 26 December 1991–1 January 1992 and *Danh Muc Co Quan Xi Nghiep Tai Thanh Pho Ho Chi Minh*, pp. 39–40.
95 This is echoed in press coverage of such an appointment. See *Thoi Bao Kinh te Saigon* 1–7 October 1992.
96 *Thoi Bao Kinh te Saigon* 9–15 November 1995.
97 *Thoi Bao Kinh te Saigon* 2–8 January 1997.
98 *Thoi Bao Kinh te Saigon* 9–15 February 1995.
99 Interview 21 October 1998. Chau resigned his post as deputy People's Committee chairman a year after becoming chairman of Satra's management board. See *Vietnam Investment Review* 5–11 August 1996.
100 It was also in step with the trend of establishing general corporations (*tong cong ty*) at this time. For literature on general corporations see note 52 in Chapter 2.
101 At least 22 out of 29 were Trade Department companies, according to my own research. One appeared to have originated under the umbrella of the Youth Volunteer Force (*luc luong thanh nien xung phong*) and six could not be identified. See *Ngan Hang Nha Nuoc Viet Nam* [State Bank of Vietnam], *Thanh Pho Ho Chi Minh: Trung Tam Tai Chinh Tien Te Lon Cua Viet Nam* [Ho Chi Minh City: The Great Financial and Monetary Centre of Vietnam], *Nha May In Thong Tan Xa Viet Nam*, 1998, pp. 160–1 and *Danh Muc Co Quan Xi Nghiep Tai Thanh Pho Ho Chi Minh*, pp. 39–40 and pp. 50–1.
102 Not surprisingly such lucrative assets have invited conflict. The struggle for control of these assets will be looked at in Chapter 4.
103 *Saigon Times Daily* 24 January 1998.
104 BBC SWB FE/8446/C1/1–2 19 December 1986; Communist Party of Vietnam, *Seventh National Congress*; *Sai Gon Giai Phong* 6 July 1992.
105 BBC SWB FE/3035 B/1–2 27 September 1997.
106 One source said that Hoa, Chau and Hai served together in Saigon as student leaders. There was a fourth member of their group, Hoa's sister Truong My Le, who Chau married. Truong My Le has not played a part in post-war politics. Interview 5 July 1999.
107 Truong My Hoa was reportedly twice put in the infamous 'tiger cages' during her imprisonment on Poulo Condore. However, according to a press account, she remained steadfast in her support for the party and continued to organise in prison. See *Sai Gon Giai Phong* 6 July 1992.
108 *Phu Nu* 18 October 1986 and *Sai Gon Giai Phong* 6 July 1992.
109 Interview 5 July 1999.
110 Le Thi Van served in Tan Binh district alongside Hoa. Le Thi Van, who later rose to be deputy People's Committee chairman, was called to give evidence in the Tamexco case as someone who had 'relations with the accused'. Although Van denied having received kickbacks from the Tamexco director, she resigned her People's Committee post ahead of the trial and was effectively disgraced.
111 In 1994 there were 81 companies under the Industry Department, down from 112 in 1990. See *Thoi Bao Kinh te Saigon* 18–24 August 1994.
112 *Thoi Bao Kinh te Saigon* 17–23 October 1991 and 3–9 October 1996.

4 Institutional conflict: the city, the centre and the lower levels

1 See for example Ben Kerkvliet's discussion of different ways of conceptualising the state in Vietnam: Benedict J. Tria Kerkvliet, 'Village–State Relations in Vietnam: The Effect of Everyday Politics on Decollectivisation', *The Journal of Asian Studies* 54, no. 2 (May 1995), pp. 396–418. Kerkvliet favours attributing greater weight to the influence of societal influences rather than the customary

emphasis on a strong state. Although the sharp dichotomy between state and society in his account is not something I feel comfortable with, the element of spontaneity is certainly present. Carlyle Thayer has also raised the issue of the need to re-think the period from the 1950s to the 1970s in terms of the influence of local activity and 'everyday politics'. See Carlyle A. Thayer, 'Mono-organizational Socialism and the State', in *Vietnam's Rural Transformation*, edited by Benedict J. Tria Kerkvliet and Doug J. Porter, Boulder, CO.: Westview Press, 1995, pp. 59–61. In addition, there seems to be a parallel between the phenomenon I am describing here and Mark Sidel's characterisation of press freedom in Vietnam as 'highly controlled flexibility' and 'neither full autonomy nor complete censorship'. See Mark Sidel, 'Law, the Press and Police Murder in Vietnam: The Vietnamese Press and the Trial of Nguyen Tan Duong', in *The Mass Media In Vietnam*, edited by David G. Marr, Political and Social Change Monograph 25, Department of Political and Social Change, Research School of Pacific and Asian Studies, The Australian National University, Canberra, 1998, pp. 97–119.
2 Yia-Ling Liu, 'Reform from Below: The Private Economy and Local Politics in Rural Industrialisation', *The China Quarterly*, no. 130 (June 1992), pp. 293–316.
3 Michael Mann, 'The Autonomous Power of the State: Its Origins, Mechanisms and Results', *Archives of European Sociology*, no. xxv (1984), pp. 185–313.
4 Kenneth and Michael Oksenberg Lieberthal, *Policy Making in China: Leaders, Structures, and Processes*, Princeton: Princeton University Press, 1988.
5 For a discussion of the 'developmental state' see Gordon White, *Riding the Tiger: The Politics of Economic Reform in Post-Mao China*, London: Macmillan, 1993, pp. 4–8. While a sense of spontaneity is uppermost, this is not to say that at a certain level one cannot speak of a coherent policy blueprint – if only as the sum total of certain reform measures. However, what comes out at the other end tends to be much less planned and much more a consequence of a range of other influences, of which spontaneous action is an important part. These issues will be discussed more fully in Chapter 6.
6 Jean C. Oi, 'Fiscal Reform and the Economic Foundations of Local State Corporatism in China', *World Politics* (October 1992), pp. 99–126.
7 Communist Party of Vietnam, *Sixth National Congress of the Communist Party: Documents*, Hanoi: Foreign Language Publishing House, 1987.
8 Interview 5 July 1999.
9 Although alleged rivalry between the Ho Chi Minh City party committee and People's Committee was frequently spoken about, it was never very easy to pin down the source of this rivalry. Some argued that it was driven by a personal rivalry between the two incumbents at the time, namely Truong Tan Sang and Vo Viet Thanh. One source made reference to the fact that Vo Viet Thanh gained a Central Committee seat before Sang, only to lose it and see Sang get ahead. Others emphasised the rivalry as being more institutional, deriving from the fact that the precise allocation of tasks between the party and the People's Committee was not clear. Interviews 4 February 1998, 5 July 1999, 24 January 2000.
10 See *Luat To Chuc Hoi Dong Nhan Dan Va Uy Ban Nhan Dan* [Law on the Organisation of the People's Council and People's Committee] in Pham Thanh Phan and Pham Thi Thuy, *Duong, Vi Tri, Chuc Nang, Nhiem Vu, Va Quyen Hart Cua Chinh Quyen Xa, Phuong* [The Positions, Function, Responsibility and Power of State Administration At the Village and Quarter Level], *Nha Xuat Ban Thong Ke* [Statistical Publishing House], Hanoi, 1999, pp. 155–201.
11 Interview 3 July 2000.
12 See also Dang Phong and Melanie Beresford, *Authority Relations and Economic Decision-Making in Vietnam: An Historical Perspective*, Nordic Institute of Asian Studies, 1998, p. 52 and p. 54. For a discussion of the natural Vietnamese tendency to think and behave in a politically dualistic way, see Adam Fforde, *Vietnam:*

Economic Commentary and Analysis, no. 9. Canberra: ADUKI, November 1997, pp. 14–15.
13 Adam Fforde, *Public Administration Reform in Ho Chi Minh City: A Report on the 'Vietnamese Process', with Suggestions for How to Support It*, prepared for the Government Committee on Organisation and Personnel and UNDP Hanoi, unpublished manuscript 1997, p. 6.
14 Some sources suggest that the city party does have some authority over centrally managed enterprises in Ho Chi Minh City but in practice these things have to be worked out on a case-by-case basis. See *Ban Thuong Vu Thanh Uy Dang Cong San Viet Nam Thanh Pho Ho Chi Minh* [Standing Committee of the Ho Chi Minh City Communist Party], *Thanh Pho Ho Chi Minh Hai Muoi Nam (1975–1995)* [Ho Chi Minh City: Twenty Years (1975–1995)], Nha Xuat Ban Thanh Pho Ho Chi Minh [Ho Chi Minh City Publishing House], 1996, pp. 515–16.
15 For literature on state enterprise reform in Vietnam see World Bank, *Vietnam: Public Sector Management and Private Sector Incentives: An Economic Report*, Report No. 13143-VN; World Bank, *Vietnam: Economic Report on Industrialization and Industrial Policy*, Report No. 14645-VN, 17 October 1995; Frank Hiep Huynh, Ng Chee Yuen, Nick J. Freeman (eds), *State-Owned Enterprise Reform in Vietnam: Lessons from Asia*. Singapore: Institute of South East Asian Studies, 1996; Ari Kokko and Fredrik Sjoholm, *Small, Medium, or Large? Some Scenarios for the Role of the State in the Era of Industrialisation and Modernisation in Vietnam*, Swedish International Development Cooperation Agency, 1997.
16 For literature on public administration reform in Vietnam see Thaveeporn Vasavakul, 'Politics of the Reform of State Institutions in the Post-Socialist era', in *Vietnam Assessment: Creating a Sound Investment Climate*, edited by Suiwah Leung. Curzon Press, Institute of Southeast Asian Studies/National Centre for Development Studies, 1996, pp. 42–68 and Thaveeporn Vasavakul, 'Vietnam: The Third Wave of State Building', in *Southeast Asian Affairs 1997*, Institute of Southeast Asian Affairs, 1997, pp. 337–63. For a discussion of administrative reform in Ho Chi Minh City see Fforde, *Public Administration Reform*.
17 There is also a Chief Architect in Hanoi.
18 Interview 18 February 1998.
19 I understand this to mean that the city party committee has a say in the appointment.
20 This is based on interviews (18 February 1998 and 23 June 1999). It proved very difficult to clarify the precise process by which the Chief Architect is appointed. My request for a copy of the relevant decree went unanswered. In describing the Chief Architect's appointment, the press affords the prime minister an even greater role than I was told saying he elects (*bo nhiem*) the Chief Architect. See *Thoi Bao Kinh te Sai Gon* 22–8 October 1992 and 2–8 September 1993. In the case of the deputy Chief Architect, the appointment was described in the press as resulting from the signing of a decree by the city People's Committee chairman. This puts the deputy Chief Architect on a par with departmental directors in the city who are also appointed by a People's Committee decree. See *Thoi Bao Kinh te Sai Gon* 12–18 October 1995.
21 Interviews 18 February 1998 and 23 June 1999.
22 Le Van Nam was born in the Mekong Delta province of Dong Thap in 1938. He went north in 1954 and has studied in Russia, China and Poland. Prior to becoming Chief Architect, he was director of Ho Chi Minh City's Construction Department. He was a member of the Ho Chi Minh City party Executive Committee in 1991 and 1996. See *Sai Gon Giai Phong* 27 October 1991 and *Saigon Times Weekly* 18–24 May 1996.
23 Interview 18 February 1998.
24 Interview 20 February 1998.

25 See *Nguoi Lao Dong* 10 April 1998.
26 This is despite the fact that the Chief Architect, Le Van Nam, came from the Construction Department and was succeeded by his deputy Vu Hung Viet (interview 23 June 1999). These anomalies seem to be commonplace, perhaps emphasising the institutional rather than the personal foundations of conflict.
27 Interview 23 June 1999.
28 *Sai Gon Giai Phong* 23 November 1998.
29 A *Cuc* is a department of a Ministry (in this case the Ministry of Transport). It is not to be confused with the *So*, although this is also translated as a Department. The article is less specific as to who are the interests referred to as the 'public transport branch' in Ho Chi Minh City. It may simply have originated as the southern office of the *Cuc*. An alternative interpretation is that it is interests at the *So giao thong tong chanh*. Interview 30 June 2000 and 3 July 2000.
30 Interview 30 June 1999.
31 The other districts where 'one stop, one stamp' was conducted on an experimental basis were District 5 and Cu Chi. In November 1997 the government called for the project to be extended to all remaining districts in Ho Chi Minh City. See *Thoi Bao Kinh te Sai Gon* 18 March 1999.
32 In the press, people were described literally as having to 'do the run around' (*chay long vong*) while there were frequent references to the existence of negativities (*tieu cuc*) – a catch-all for corruption – and trouble for the people (*phien ha cho dan*). To complete house documentation, it was commonplace for a person to have to visit the district authorities alone some five times. To get a licence to renovate your house could take six months. See *Sai Gon Giai Phong* 16 May 1998.
33 Ibid. and *Nguoi Lao Dong* 15 June and 3 October 1998.
34 See Fforde, *Public Administration Reform*, pp. 33–4.
35 *Nguoi Lao Dong* 10 April 1998 and *Sai Gon Giai Phong* 16 May 1998.
36 Ibid.
37 *Thoi Bao Kinh te Sai Gon* 16 May 1998 and 18 March 1999.
38 *Thoi Bao Kinh te Viet Nam* 29 August 1998. The critique of Satra is in line with the critique of general corporations in general. This emerged clearly in a meeting on the issue chaired by the prime minister a few months later. See *Sai Gon Giai Phong* 2 March and 26 June 1999; *Tuoi Tre* 2 March 1999; *Thoi Bao Kinh te Sai Gon* 4 March 1999.
39 *Sai Gon Giai Phong* 21 October 1998.
40 In the first half of 1999, Satra's total turnover was estimated at 2,922 billion dong, which was only 40 per cent of the year's target. See *Saigon Times Daily* 18 June 1999.
41 *Saigon Times Daily* 4 May 1998.
42 *Saigon Newsreader* 28 October 1998; *Saigon Times Weekly* 12 June 1999.
43 *Saigon Times Daily* 11 March 1999.
44 *Saigon Times Weekly* 2 January 1999.
45 This fits with parts of the Vietnam literature that emphasise periodic efforts at recentralisation. See Adam Fforde and Stefan de Vylder, *From Plan to Market: The Economic Transition in Vietnam*, Boulder, CO.: Westview Press, 1996, pp. 132–3; Adam Fforde, *Vietnam: Economic Commentary and Analysis*, no. 7. Canberra: ADUKI, November 1995, pp. 18–30; Carlyle A. Thayer, 'The Regularization of Politics: Continuity and Change in the Party's Central Committee, 1951–86', in *Postwar Vietnam: Dilemmas m Socialist Development*, edited by David G. Marr and Christine P. White, Ithaca: Southeast Asian Program, Cornell University, 1988, pp. 177–93; Carlyle A. Thayer, 'The Regularization of Politics Revisited: Continuity and Change in the Party's Central Committee, 1976–96', a paper presented to a panel on 'Vietnamese Politics in Transition: New Conceptions and Inter-Disciplinary Approaches, Part 2', the

49th Annual Meeting of the Association for Asian Studies, Chicago, 13–16 March 1997; Thaveeporn Vasavakul, 'Sectoral Politics and Strategies for State and Party Building from the VII to the VIII Congress of the Vietnam Communist Party (1991–96)', in 1997 in *Ten Years after the 1986 Party Congress*, edited by Adam Fforde, Political and Social Change Monograph 24, The Australian National University, Canberra, 1997, pp. 81–135.

46 Christopher Earle Nevitt, 'Private Business Associations in China: Evidence of Civil Society or Local State Power?' *The China Journal*, no. 36 (July 1996), pp. 39–41.

47 It also appears possible to distinguish between effective clampdowns and clampdowns that appear simply as 'going through the motions'. Some of the clampdowns on smuggling have such a feel and hence are not taken very seriously. Contrast, for example, the cynical 'here we go again' response of Ho Chi Minh City's business community to Instruction (*chi thi*) 853 launching a clampdown on smuggling in November 1997 with its response to Decree 18 and Decree 37 as described below. The main concern of business people in response to Instruction 853 was that it would be used as an excuse by officials to harass them. See *Thoi Bai Kinh te Sai Gon* 13 and 20 November 1997; *Vietnam News* 6 January 1998; *Nguoi Lao Dong* 6 January 1998; *Vietnam Investment Review* 29 December 1997–4 January 1998.

48 Reflecting this dichotomy, the IMF has referred to the situation pertaining after 1993 as one of 'quasi-ownership', while the Constitution states that land and all other property that belongs to the state comes under the 'ownership by the entire people' (*thuoc so huu toan dan*) (Article 17). The state manages all land and entrusts it to organisations and individuals for stable and lasting use. They may transfer the right to use the land entrusted to them by the state (*duoc chuyen quyen su dung dat Nha nuoc giao*) (Article 18). See International Monetary Fund, *Vietnam: Recent Economic Developments*. Country Report no. 96/145 1996; *The Constitution of Vietnam: 1946–1959–1980–1992*, Hanoi: The Gioi Publishers, 1995; *Hien Phap Nuoc Cong Hoa Xa Hoi Chu Nghia Viet Nam 1992* [Constitution of the Socialist Republic of Vietnam 1992], Nha Xuat Ban Chinh Tri Quoc Gia [National Political Publishing House], Hanoi 1998.

49 See Article 3 of the 1993 Land Law in *Nha O, Dat Dai Va Thue Nha Dat* [Housing, Land and the Rental of Housing and Land], compiled by Thanh Thao, Nha Xuat Ban Thanh Pho Ho Chi Minh [Ho Chi Minh City Publishing House], 1997, pp. 200–19.

50 *Sai Gon Giai Phong* 22 March 1995.

51 *Lao Dong* 30 March 1995.

52 For the text of Decree 18 see *Nha O, Dat Dai Va Thue Nha Dat*, pp. 248–53.

53 *Thanh Nien* 30 March 1995.

54 *Sai Gon Giai Phong* 22 March 1995 and *Tuoi Tre* 13 May 1995.

55 *Tuoi Tre* 13 March 1995.

56 During 1996–9, the differential varied between 0 and 1,200 dong. Normally it was a few hundred dong.

57 *Thoi Bao Kinh te Sai Gon* 18 December 1997.

58 *Tuoi Tre* 6 January 1998.

59 The relative success of Decree 37 was probably also helped by the prevailing macroeconomic conditions of the time, namely falling demand for dollars as imports contracted with the post-Asian crisis economic slowdown. See Business Monitor International, *Vietnam 1998*, pp. 51–7.

60 *Thoi Bao Kinh te Sai Gon* 19 February 1998. Smuggling, particularly smuggling of gold, tends to push up the black-market dollar price. See *Vietnam News* 6 March 1997; *Saigon Times Daily* 9 January 1997; *Vietnam Investment Review* 26 May–1 June 1997.

164 *Notes*

61 Interview 8 May 1998.
62 Interviewing the head of the General Department of Land, Ton Gia Huyen, one journalist raised the possibility of their being 'distance' (*khoang cach*) between the National Assembly Standing Committee and the government on the merits of Decree 18. The suggestion was that there was a degree of lukewarm-ness towards the decree in prime minister's office. This was vigorously denied. See *Tuoi Tre* 16 March 1995.
63 Two banks defaulted on deferred payment letters of credit during 1997–8. They were Viet Hoa Bank and VP Bank. See *Far Eastern Economic Review* 25 September 1997.
64 The foreign exchange black market was very quiet until late August and September 1998 when market activity picked up significantly. At its peak in the second half of September, the differential between the black and formal exchange rate was nearly 900 dong against the dollar.
65 Sources I spoke to said that by no means all companies were required to convert to leases, while even those that did often did not have to pay rent. Interview 30 January 1999.
66 Interview 22 January 1998.
67 Interview 4 February 1998.
68 *Tuoi Tre* newspaper described the arrest as follows: 'Year of birth 1968, permanent resident in Hanoi, temporary resident in Ho Chi Minh City, of no fixed occupation . . . Pham Van Duc looked like a "king"' (*Tuoi Tre* 20 January 1998).
69 *Nguoi Lao Dong* 28 March 1995.
70 *Thanh Nien* 6 April 1995; *Sai Gon Giai Phong* 22 March 1995.
71 *Thoi Bao Kinh te Sag Gon* 9 July 1998.
72 *Sai Gon Giai Phong* 24 December 1998; *Tuoi Tre* 24 December 1998.
73 Vietcombank claimed this was because Saigon Petro was not one of its usual customers. However, there were also off-the-record suggestions that it thought Saigon Petro was engaging in currency speculation. Later, when pressed, Vietcombank said Saigon Petro could borrow the dollars but it would not do a straight dong-for-dollar swap.
74 *Sai Gon Giai Phong* 16 October 1998 and *Thoi Bao Kinh Te Viet Nam* 21 October 1998.
75 Interview 26 October 1998.

5 The politics of economic decentralisation: the Tamexco and Minh Phung–Epco cases

1 *Phu Nu* 18 October 1996 and *Sai Gon Giai Phong* 6 July 1992. Truong My Hoa became a Central Committee member in 1991 and vice-chairman of the National Assembly in 1997.
2 Le Thi Van served as Tan Binh District People's Committee chairman 1986–94. See *Phu Nu* 1 November 1986 and *Thoi Bao Kinh te Saigon* 22–8 December 1994.
3 *Tuoi Tre* 25 March 1997.
4 Interviews 6 May 1998 and 8 March 1999. The relatively long period Le Thi Van held office in Tan Binh District (eight years) was noted in Chapter 3 as a possible illustration of the emergence of entrenched local business interests during the late 1980s and 1990s.
5 *Tuoi Tre* 25 January 1997.
6 *Thoi Bao Kinh te Saigon* 10–16 October 1991.
7 *Thoi Bao Kinh te Saigon* 18–24 June 1992.
8 *Thoi Bao Kinh te Saigon* 4–10 February 1993.
9 *Thoi Bao Kinh te Saigon* 26 May–1 June 1994.
10 *Thoi Bao Kinh te Saigon* 6–12 October 1994.

11 *Thoi Bao Kinh te Saigon* 5–11 May 1994.
12 *Thoi Bao Kinh te Saigon* 21 January–3 February 1993; *Tuoi Tre* 20 May 1997; *Chan Dung Nhung Doanh Nghiep Thanh Dat* [A Portrait of Business on the March], *Nha Xuat Ban Thanh Pho He Chi Minh* [He Chi Minh City Publishing House], Saigon Times Group, VAPEC, 1997, p. 16.
13 *Thoi Bao Kinh te Saigon* 19–25 August 1993 and *Nguoi Lao Dong* 24 October 1998.
14 *Thoi Bao Ngan Hang* No. 127, 1994. This was confirmed in *Sai Gon Giai Phong* 24 June 1999.
15 *Tuoi Tre* 10 July 1999.
16 *Chan Dung Nhung Doanh Nghiep Thanh Dat* 1997, p. 16.
17 *Thoi Bao Kinh te Saigon* 11–17 March 1993 and 16–22 January 1997.
18 *Thoi Bao Kinh te Saigon* 12–18 December 1991 and *Thoi Bao Kinh te Viet Nam* 18 March 1998. District 3 People's Committee had a 40 per cent stake with the remainder divided between the four individuals.
19 *Nguoi Lao Dong* 26 October 1998. This was according to the statement of Epco's management board chairman, Nguyen Tuan Phuc, who was also a District 3 employee. According to the investigating authorities, there was no material evidence to this effect.
20 *Thoi Bao Kinh te Saigon* 8–14 December 1994.
21 *Nguoi Lao Dong*, 26 October 1998; *Thoi Bao Kinh te Viet Nam*, 18 March 1998.
22 *Thoi Bao Kinh te Saigon* 12–18 December 1991.
23 *Thoi Bao Kinh te Saigon* 23–9 April 1992 and 5–11 October 1995.
24 *Chan Dung Nhung Doanh Nghiep Thanh Dat* 1997, p. 23.
25 *Thoi Bao Kinh te Saigon* 22–8 June 1995 and 26 October–1 November 1995.
26 *Thoi Bao Kinh te Saigon* 5–11 May 1994.
27 *Thoi Bao Kinh te Saigon* Tet edition 1997.
28 *Thoi Bao Kinh te Saigon* 21–7 November 1996.
29 *Thoi Bao Kinh te Saigon* 29 February–6 March 1996.
30 In the end total losses in the Tamexco case were estimated at just under 500 billion dong. See *Thoi Bao Kinh te Saigon* 12–18 August 1999. I attempted to find an equivalent first Vietnamese reference to Pham Huy Phuoc's arrest but without success. This is surprising and I suspect such a reference does exist. After all, English-language newspapers in Vietnam generally rely heavily on their Vietnamese-language counterparts for news and articles.
31 *Vietnam Investment Review* 6–12 May 1996.
32 *Tuoi Tre* 10 October 1996.
33 *Tuoi Tre* 26 October 1996. The twelve others not mentioned by name here were charged with corruption, exploiting their public position, or for gambling. They included people who had held positions within Tamexco or other limited liability companies, or had held public office in Ba Ria-Vung Tan. Some of them were relatives of Pham Huy Phuoc. For full details see *Tuoi Tre*, 1 February 1997.
34 *Sai Gon Giai Phong* 27 May 1996 and *Thoi Bao Kinh te Saigon* 19–25 June 1997.
35 *Vietnam Investment Review* 5–11 August 1996.
36 *Thoi Bao Kinh te Saigon* 19–25 June 1997.
37 *Tuoi Tre* 25 March 1997.
38 *Ngan Hang Nha Nuoc Viet Nam* [State Bank of Vietnam], *Thanh Pho Ho Chi Minh: Trung Tam Tai Chinh Tien Te Lon Cua Viet Nam* [Ho Chi Minh City: The Great Financial and Monetary Centre of Vietnam]. *Nha May In Thong Tan Xa Viet Nam*, 1998, pp. 114–15.
39 *Thoi Bao Kinh te Saigon* 24 October 1996.
40 *Tuoi Tre* 19 December 1996.
41 *Tuoi Tre* 29 October 1996.
42 *Saigon Times Daily* 20 January 1997; *Reuters* 23 January 1997 and *Tuoi Tre* 25 January 1997.

166 *Notes*

43 *Tuoi Tre* 28 January 1997.
44 Ibid.
45 One source suggested almost as a passing comment that it was the then party secretary in Ho Chi Minh City, Vo Tran Chi. Interview 4 February 1998.
46 In fact, eight months after the trial Truong My Hoa was promoted, being appointed vice-president of the National Assembly. See BBC SWB FE/3035 B/1–2 27 September 1997.
47 Accounts of their executions make for particularly gruesome reading. The men were woken at dawn, offered cigarettes and a last meal of steamed buns, chicken and a soft drink, and given an opportunity to write final letters. All three declined the food. One wrote a letter to his wife and children. One took a cigarette. They were then blindfolded and gagged with lemons in their mouths and led to the execution ground. Onlookers said Phuoc appeared to faint. In the final moments, a woman called out his name to which Phuoc responded in brief acknowledgement. Moments later they were shot. See *Death Penalty News* 7 January 1998 at http://venus.soci.niu.edu/~archives?ABOLISH/rick-halperin/jan98/0035.htmi.
48 Announcing the change in Le Minh Hai's sentence Justice Pham Hung said 'Hai's father's deeds were the crucial factor in saving him. Hai himself had done no good for the Party and the State of Vietnam and he is very lucky that he has a hero as a father.' See *Vietnam Investment Review* 22–8 September 1997.
49 *Associated Press* 20 April 1999.
50 *Saigon Times Daily* 25 March 1997 and *Vietnam News Agency* 26 March 1997.
51 For details of the *cong ty con* and *cong ty con con* see *Thoi Bao Kinh te Vietnam* 18 March and *Sai Gon Giai Phong* 23 October 1998.
52 *Reuters* 23 April 1997.
53 *Agence France Press* 4 August 1999.
54 *Saigon Times Daily* 28 April 1997.
55 *Reuters* 15 May 1997.
56 *Kinh doanh va phap luat* 5 June 1997.
57 *Tuoi Tre* 5 June 1997.
58 *Sai Gon Giai Phong* 23 October 1998; *Agence France Press* 4 August 1999. The man who died in custody was Tran Van Suong, who was the director of Cong ty Hoang. According to the official account he had simply died of illness (*chet do benh ly*). The person with psychiatric problems was Du Thi Quoc Phong, formerly director of Cong ty Hiep Thong.
59 *Tuoi Tre* 23 December 1997 and *Saigon Times Daily* 16 February 1998.
60 *Vietnam News* 11 May 1998.
61 *Sai Gon Giai Phong* 20 March 1998.
62 After overrunning the 24 July date, the investigation was again extended in August. See *Sai Gon Giai Phong* 25 August 1998 and 22 October 1998 and *Nguoi Lao Dong* 26 August 1998.
63 *Tuoi Tre* 11 February 1999.
64 *Vietnam Investment Review* 9–15 August 1999.
65 *Nguoi Lao Dong* 23 October 1998.
66 *Vietnam News* 23 May 1997.
67 *Vietnam Economic Times* April 1997.
68 *Tuoi Tre* 20 May 1997.
69 *Thoi Bao Kinh te Saigon* 12 August 1999; *Vietnam Investment Review* 9–15 August 1999. Those who received life sentences were Le Minh Xu (director of Dat Viet Company), Nguyen Hong Hai (director of Dat Thanh Company), Tran Quang Hiep (director of Hiep Y Company), Tran Binh Minh (head of the credit department of Incombank Ho Chi Minh City), Le Tot Nghiep (deputy head of the credit department of Incombank Ho Chi Minh City) and Huynh Van Ut (director Thai Tue Company).

70 *Reuters* 13 January 2000.
71 Interview 7 March 1999.
72 Interview 25 May 1999. A full appraisal of Vietnam's judiciary is beyond the scope of this book or my competence. For a discussion of these issues see Mark Sidel, 'The Re-emergence of Legal Discourse in Vietnam.' *International and Comparative Law Quarterly* vol. 34 (January 1994), pp. 163–74 and Amnesty International, 'Socialist Republic of Vietnam: New debate on the death penalty?', Report ASA 41/04/99 July 1999.
73 *Reuters* 24 January 1997.
74 *Reuters* 23 January 1997.
75 *Wall Street Journal* 26 March 1997.
76 Interviews 8 March 1999; 15 June 1999.
77 For background on state enterprise indebtedness see International Monetary Fund, *Vietnam: Recent Economic Developments*, IMF Staff Country Report no. 96/145 1996, pp. 33–4.
78 For literature on local Chinese business and its relations with the state in Vietnam see Chapter 2, note 9.
79 At the time of Phung and Thin's arrest, the then Ho Chi Minh City party secretary, Truong Tan Sang, said that he did not think Chinese Vietnamese would lose faith in the government as a result: Chinese Vietnamese 'can always feel safe to do business', he said. '[W]e create favourable economic conditions for both Chinese Vietnamese and Vietnamese people to make their wealth in compliance with Vietnam's law'. See *Saigon Times Daily* 7 April 1997.
80 Economist Intelligence Unit, *Vietnam, Country Forecast*, second quarter 1996, pp. 4–5. Allegations of wartime disloyalty is a common way of trying to undermine political rivals. Foreign accounts of Nguyen Ha Phan's fall have tended to take the allegations made against him at face value or at least report them without comment. However, it is recognised among Vietnamese that such tactics have a long history. For foreign accounts of Phan's fall see Mark Sidel, 'Generational and Institutional Transition in the Vietnamese Communist Party: The 1996 Congress and Beyond', *Asian Survey* 37, no. 5 (May 1997), p. 487; Thaveeporn Vasavakul, 'Sectoral Politics and Strategies for State and Party Building from the VII to the VIII Congress of the Vietnam Communist Party (1991–96). Also in *Ten Years After the 1986 Party Congress*, edited by Adam Fforde, Political and Social Change Monograph 24, The Australian National University, Canberra, 1997, p. 99; Zachary Abuza, 'Leadership Transition in Vietnam Since the Eighth Party Congress: The Unfinished Congress', *Asian Survey*, vol. 38, no. 12 (December 1998), pp. 1109. Note also how the whispering campaign against Ho Chi Minh City People's Committee chairman Vo Viet Thanh in the second half of the 1990s, discussed in Chapter 3, centred on alleged wartime errors. During the war, Nguyen Ha Phan was a party leader in Can Tho, where he is now living under house arrest. See Gareth Porter, *Vietnam: The Politics of Bureaucratic Socialism*, Ithaca, NY: Cornell University Press, 1993, pp. 24–5 including note 97.
81 Interviews 28 March 1998 and 23 June 1999.
82 Interview 23 June 1999.
83 *Vietnam Investment Review* 5–11 August 1996.
84 Interviews 3 March and 23 June 1999.
85 *Tuoi Tre* 1 February 1997.
86 Interview 6 May 1998.
87 Interview 23 June 1999.
88 Interview 8 March 1999.
89 As was noted earlier, Minh Phung was investigated in 1993 for real estate irregularities, resulting in a small fine. Some sources have suggested he got off relatively lightly because of his political connections (interview 23 June 1999).

168 *Notes*

90 Ibid.
91 Interview 28 March 1998.
92 Interview 23 June 1999.
93 A sense of fear in the aftermath of the Tamexco case was certainly very real. In an article written in early 1998 entitled 'Finance without Fear: Restoring Financial Strength and Stability', one foreign banker wrote: 'The last year has been traumatic for Vietnamese bank managers. They have, for whatever reason and no matter how justified, been blamed for a variety of wrongs and some of them have suffered severe penalties for their failings. Whilst it is not my place to comment on the justice system, I would point out that this has created an atmosphere of fear, and no banking system can function properly when its decision makers are afraid to make decisions!' See *Vietnam Business Journal* February 1998.
94 In general, the press tends to be more cautious when talking about state institutions or officials.
95 For literature on the Soviet show trials see J. Arch Getty and Oleg V. Naumov, *The Road To Terror: Stalin and the Self-Destruction of the Bolsheviks, 1912–1939*, Newhaven, CT: Yale University Press, September 1999.
96 This comment seems to allude to the distinction between managers and owners in state enterprises and a lack of clarity as to who is responsible. This is discussed in Chapter 6.
97 Interview 28 March 1998.
98 Interview 15 June 1999.
99 *Chan Dung Nhung Doanh Nghiep Thanh Dat 1997*, pp. 16, 23 and 68. This is the source used in Chapter 2. The job of the censor was not done very well and the hidden entries could easily be viewed with the help of a sharp knife.
100 *Nguoi Lao Dong* 10 July 1999. In answer to a question in court about his relationship with Nguyen Van Ha, Tang Minh Phung said that before he died Ha was 'sad' because of something involving Nguyen Ngoc Bich (*Truoc khi chet, anh Ha buon. Nguyen nhan la tu viec lam cua anh Bich*). However, the matter was pursued no further.
101 *Saigon Times Daily* 4 October 1996; *Associated Press* 8 October 1996; *Vietnam Investment Review* 14–20 October 1996.
102 *Vietnam Investment Review* 20–6 October 1997; *Vietnam News* 2 November 1997 and 2 February 1998; *Saigon Times Daily* 17 November 1997, 24 December 1997 and 20 March 1998; *Tuoi Tre* 19 May, 23 May and 10 June 1998; *Nguoi Lao Dong* 10 June 1998; *Reuters* 12 November 1999.
103 *Nguoi Lao Dong* 6 May 1998; *Tuoi Tre* 7 May 1998.
104 *Washington Post* 15 May 1997.
105 *Agence France Presse* 7 May 1997.
106 *Vietnam Investment Review* 5–11 August 1996; *Tuoi Tre* 24 April 1997; *Nguoi Lao Dong* 18 March 1998. Rotating credit schemes (*hui*) are an informal savings and loan mechanism. How they operate varies but the typical pattern is that a group of people make regular payments into a central fund from which they may borrow. When *hui* members borrow they pay interest to the other members of the group. The skill is in deducing the extent of the demand for the money in the fund and pitching one's interest rate accordingly. Consequently, it can be a game of bluff and counter-bluff. See World Bank, *Vietnam Financial Sector Review: An Agenda for Financial Sector Development*, Report No. 13135-VN, 1 March 1995, pp. 78–9.
107 *Saigon Times Daily* 3 February 1997.
108 The exception to this is the deputy People's Committee chairman in District 3, Pham Tan Khoa, although he was given a short prison term.

6 Rethinking reform: property rights and the dynamics of change

1 Partial reforms are to be contrasted with 'big-bang' reforms, which aim to transform simultaneously as many aspects of the economic system as possible. This includes instituting rapid privatisation. The big-bang approach was pursued most notably in Poland in the early 1990s, and to varying degrees in the former Czechoslovakia and Russia. For a discussion of the different approaches to reform see Barry Naughton, *Growing Out Of the Plan: Chinese Economic Reform 1978–93*, Cambridge: Cambridge University Press, 1995, pp. 13–20.
2 During 1994–8 economic growth in the city averaged 13.2 per cent compared with 5.5 per cent in the period 1980–90. Nationwide GDP growth during 1994–8 was 8.5 per cent. See Ho Chi Minh City Statistical Bureau, quoted in *Ban Thuong Vu Thanh Uy Dang Cong San Viet Nam Thanh Pho Ho Chi Minh* 1996, p. 54; *Nien Giam Thong Ke Thanh Pho Ho Chi Minh* 1997 and 1998, pp. 31–2 and pp. 31–2.
3 Jean Oi and Andrew Walder, eds, *Property Rights and Economic Reform in China*, Stanford University Press, 1999, pp. 19–20. See also Jane Duckett, *The Entrepreneurial State in China*, London and New York: Routledge, 1998, pp. 5–11. Duckett favours 'new political economy' over 'neo-liberalism' which she says refers to a wider body of literature. See Duckett, *The Entrepreneurial State*, pp. 188–9, note 3.
4 Janos Kornai, *The Socialist System: The Political Economy of Communism*, Oxford: Clarendon Press, 1992.
5 In government/policy circles, this remains the dominant position, although there is a growing body of literature on China, which challenges this position. See especially Duckett, *The Entrepreneurial State*. On some of the difficulties encountered in relation to 'big-bang' reforms see Naughton, *Growing Out of the Plan*, pp. 16–18.
6 Note, however, the argument made with reference to China that economic growth has been more 'extensive' rather than 'intensive' owing to the gradualist nature of reform. See Dali L. Yang 'Governing China's Transition to the Market: Institutional Incentives, Politicians Choices, and Unintended Outcomes', *World Politics* 48 (April 1996), pp. 448–9.
7 This included the establishment of an informal market in company shares before the official stock market was set up. See *Thoi Bao Kinh te Saigon* 25–31 May 2000. The Ho Chi Minh City-based company Refrigerator Engineering Company (REE) led the way in issuing two-year convertible bonds on an experimental basis in 1996. A former local state company, REE was also one of the first firms to equitise. See Business Monitor International, *Vietnam 1998*, p. 84.
8 By referring to the banking system as state-dominated, I am thinking not only of the state-owned banks but also the fact that so many of the joint stock banks have state institutions as their dominant shareholders. For details see Appendix, Table A2.6.
9 Duckett's thesis that the Chinese state should be regarded as entrepreneurial rests on the fact that individual government departments have established and are operating 'profit-seeking, risk-taking businesses'. She also emphasises the fact that such activities are 'potentially productive', downplaying involvement in profiteering or rent-seeking activity. It is on this basis that she argues her findings contradict the traditional view that officials will necessarily oppose reform. My interpretation differs from Duckett's insofar as it would appear that officials behave in ways that involve simultaneously both 'opposing' and 'embracing' reforms. See Duckett, *The Entrepreneurial State*, pp. 13–15.
10 Walder and Oi, 'Introduction' to Oi and Walder (eds), *Property Rights*, pp. 6–10.
11 Privatisation (*tu nhan hoa*) has been shunned in favour of the more limited equitisation (*co phan hoa*). Here the state retains a significant stake in the

170 *Notes*

company, while the tendency in practice has been for shares to be sold to existing management and those connected to them. During the 1990s the equitisation programme advanced only slowly. Other property forms, such as contracting and leasing, have not been widely applied.

12 This can be seen in the way 'old interests' in a company seem to retain influence even after the controlling institution is formally changed. Phu Nhuan Jewellery Company and Tamexco are good examples.

13 A good example is Huynh Buu Son. Formerly of Saigon Industrial and Commercial Bank (*Sai Gon Cong Thuong*), he was brought across to VP Bank as its general director following financial difficulties there in 1997. See *Thoi Bao Kinh te Saigon* 26 May–1 June 1994 and 17–23 April 1997.

14 Good examples would appear to be Do Van Hoang at Saigon Tourist and Cao Thi Ngoc Dung at Phu Nhuan Jewellery Company. The one-time director of Tamexco, Pham Huy Phuoc, would also appear to fall into this category, although the way he was later brought down highlights the relative fragility of his position.

15 *Thoi Bao Kinh te Saigon* 7–13 November 1991; interview 12 December 1997; *Saigon Times Daily* 5 March 1999.

16 Apart from being director of Saigon Jewellery Company, Nguyen Huu Dinh was management board chairman of Exim Bank, Saigon Finance Company, and International Beverages Corporation. Saigon Jewellery Company was a leading shareholder in all three. See *Thoi Bao Kinh te Saigon* 26 March–1 April 1992; *Ngan Hang Nha Nuoc Viet Nam* [State Bank of Vietnam], *Thanh Pho Ho Chi Minh: Trung Tam Tai Chinh Tien Te Lon Cua Viet Nam* [Ho Chi Minh City: The Great Financial and Monetary Centre of Vietnam], *Nha May In Thong Tan Xa Viet Nam*, 1998, pp. 127–8; and *Saigon Times Weekly* 6 February 1999. For a period during the 1990s, International Beverages Corporation was the joint-venture partner along with a Singaporean firm for Pepsi Cola in Vietnam. In 1999, Pepsi Cola bought out both its joint-venture partners. However, in a further illustration of Nguyen Huu Dinh's apparent influence, it was announced by Pepsi Cola that he would remain on the management board of Pepsi Cola Vietnam.

17 Asked why Nguyen Huu Dinh was on the boards of so many companies and banks, one informant said it was because he was a specialist in banking and finance with an economics degree before 1975. In addition, the informant described Dinh as a 'revolutionary fighter', adding that people could therefore trust him. Furthermore, he said he had enhanced his reputation by making a success of Saigon Jewellery Company. The informant also said he was a former member of the Youth Union, which he described as a 'major channel' for city leaders. Interview 23 June 1999.

18 Walder and Oi, 'Introduction' to Oi and Walder (eds), *Property Rights*, p. 5.

19 This ties in with a point made in relation to China, namely that the decentralisation that has accompanied reform has set limits on the behaviour of government at all levels. While in some respects this can be debilitating, in relation to property rights it provides a level of protection that otherwise would be lacking. See Gabriella Montinola, Yingyi Qian, and Barry R. Weingast (eds), 'Federalism, Chinese Style: The Political Basis for Economic Success in China', *World Politics* 48 (October 1995), especially p. 79.

20 Walder and Oi, 'Introduction' to Oi and Walder (eds), *Property Rights*, pp. 13–15.

21 Examples cited in the China literature are geographically diverse, including a village in Tianjin municipality, a county near Shanghai and a village in Sichuan.

22 David L. Wank. *Commodifying Chinese Communism*. Cambridge University Press, 1999; David L. Wank, 'Private Business, Bureaucracy, and Political Alliances in a Chinese City', *Australian Journal of Chinese Affairs*, 33 (January 1995), pp. 55–71.

23 There is a tendency in the literature to emphasise the way the old economic order managed to retain power. See, for example, the account by Nigel Thrift and Dean Forbes of the early 1980s in Nigel Thrift and Dean Forbes, *The Price of War: Urbanization in Vietnam 1954–1985*, London: Allen and Unwin, 1986. However, the ferocity and ultimately debilitating impact of the moves against so-called 'comprador capitalists' in 1975 and the commercial bourgeoise in 1978 – and in particular the associated surprise currency changes designed to root out those who had squirreled away large sums of money – should not be underestimated. See BBC SWB FE/4900/A3/5–6 10 May 1975; FE/W834/A/35–37 9 July 1975; FE/4955/B/5 15 July 1975; and FE/4932/BS–7 18 June 1975; FE/5014/B/4–6 23 September 1975; FE/5015/13/2–4 24 September 1975; FE/5204/B/2 10 May 1976; FE/5265/B/3 21 July 1976; FE/5804/B/1–2 4 May 1978; FE/5805/B/9–12 5 May 1978; and FE/5810/B/6 11 May 1978.

24 Ho Chi Minh City seemingly attracted the commercial attention of northern cadres from the moment of liberation, as encapsulated in the comment 'the relations came south and the goods went north'. See Bui Tin, *Following Ho Chi Minh: The Memoirs of a North Vietnamese Colonel*, translated from the Vietnamese and adapted by Judy Stowe and Do Van, London: Hurst and Company, 1995, p. 99. Cadres were being disciplined in Ho Chi Minh City for taking bribes in the days immediately following Liberation. See BBC SWB FE/5004/B3–5 11 September 1975. By the time reforms got under way, any ideas embodied in official ideology that looked down upon the city had largely been replaced by recognition that the city had an important part to play in the national economy. See Chapter 1 note 65 for references.

25 On the extent of Viet Kieu investment in Vietnam see *Vietnam Investment Review* 28 August–3 September 2000 and on the restrictions on Viet Kieu activity in the land market see *Thoi bao Kinh te Saigon* 12–18 December 1998. On the exodus of the 'boat people' see Thrift and Forbes, *The Price of War*.

26 In this respect, one could say that the manner in which people left Ho Chi Minh City has had a bearing on the nature of the property arrangements that emerged there after 1975. For periodisation details on Overseas Chinese migration to Vietnam see Tran Khanh, *The Ethnic Chinese and Economic Development in Vietnam*, Indochina Unit, Institute of Southeast Asian Studies, 1993.

27 One example would be Nguyen Huu Dinh mentioned above in connection with Saigon Jewellery Company. See especially note 22. Another would be Huynh Buu Son, also mentioned above in connection with VP Bank. See note 16. Son was an official at the National Bank of South Vietnam before 1975 (interview 5 July 1999). For an account of how the Communists made use of sympathisers within the pre-1975 banking system in South Vietnam to finance their activities, see *Dola Trong Cuoc Khang Chien Chang My Cuu Nuoc* [The Dollar In Our Country's War of Resistance Against the Americans], Nha Xuat Ban Tre [Youth Publishing House], 1996.

28 Naughton, *Growing Out of the Plan*, p. 23.

29 Walder and Oi, 'Introduction' in Oi and Walder (eds), *Property Rights*, pp. 21–2.

30 Naughton, *Growing Out of the Plan*, p. 22.

31 Ibid. p, 21. Naughton says that in the case of the China literature such an interpretation is more prevalent in the media than in scholarly accounts. In the case of Vietnam, such views are often to be found in the scholarly literature as well. This is discussed further later in this chapter.

32 Ibid. p. 5. One might ask whether the coherence of which Naughton writes is more recognisable in the eyes of outsiders or a limited number of trained economists inside Vietnam. I did not get the impression that middle- or lower-level officials have much of a sense of a reform blueprint.

33 Dorothy Solinger argues similarly on China. See Dorothy J. Solinger, 'Urban Entrepreneurs and the State: The Merger of State and Society', in *State and Society in China: The Consequences of Reform*, edited by Arthur Lewis Rosenbaum, Boulder, CO.: Westview Press, 1992, pp. 121–41.

34 This is not to say that they have been the only beneficiaries. For a discussion of the impact of reform on poverty alleviation see World Bank, *Vietnam: Poverty Assessment and Strategy*, Report No. 13442-VN, 23 January 1995.

35 See Chapter 1 note 56 for references.

36 The principal exception to this is writings by Adam Fforde, including a number of texts which he has co-authored with other scholars. See Adam Fforde, 'The Political Economy of "Reform" in Vietnam: Some Reflections', in *The Challenge of Reform in Indochina*, edited by Borje Ljunggren, Cambridge, MA.: Harvard Institute for International Development, 1993; Adam Fforde and Stefan de Vylder, *From Plan to Market: The Economic Transition in Vietnam*, Boulder, CO.: Westview Press, 1996; and Adam Fforde and Steve Seneque, 'The Economy and the Countryside: The Relevance of Rural Development Policies', in *Vietnam's Rural Transformation*, edited by Benedict J. Tria Kerkvliet and Doug J. Porter, Boulder, CO.: Westview Press, 1995. Concepts such as 'pressure from below', 'fence-breaking' and 'spontaneous processes of change', which derive from these texts, are now quite well-known. However, I would argue that in much of the academic literature on Vietnam the implications of these ideas are rarely fully taken on board and are sometimes poorly understood. Jonathan Stromseth makes reference to Fforde and de Vylder's term 'fence-breaking' but then describes it as representing the 'expansion of autonomous transactions by societal actors', when the key point is that fence-breaking is being carried out by state institutions. See Jonathan R. Stromseth, 'Reform and Response in Vietnam: State–Society Relations and the Changing Political Economy', Ph.D. diss., University of Columbia, 1998, p. 21. Carlyle Thayer refers to 'bottom–up economic reforms' while maintaining a sense of the primacy of policy and change being driven by reform. See Carlyle A. Thayer, 'Mono-organizational Socialism and the State', in *Vietnam's Rural Transformation*, edited by Benedict J. Tria Kerkvliet and Doug J. Porter, Boulder, CO.: Westview Press, 1995, p. 39.

37 In some accounts, one encounters an underlying sense that there may be more to change than reform. Borje Ljunggren discusses how the prevailing view in the approach to the Eighth Party Congress was that reforms had stalled but adds that such an analysis tends to underestimate the 'strength of actual tendencies and forces at work'. However, the remark is made in passing and hence is not developed. See Borje Ljunggren, 'Doi Moi in the Year of the Eighth Party Congress: Emerging Contradictions in the Reform Process', in *Vietnam: Reform and Transformation*, conference proceedings edited by Bjorn Beckman, Eva Hansson and Lisa Roman, Centre for Pacific Asia Studies, Stockholm University, 1997, p. 27.

38 For an example see World Bank, *Vietnam: Transition to the Market*, Country Operations Division, Country Department I, East Asia and Pacific Region, September 1993, p. iii.

39 Gareth Porter, *Vietnam: The Politics of Bureaucratic Socialism*, Ithaca, NY: Cornell University Press, 1993, p. 140. For a fuller discussion of the so-called policy debates see also pp. 140–51.

40 Mark Sidel, 'Generational and Institutional Transition in the Vietnamese Communist Party: The 1996 Congress and Beyond', *Asian Survey* 37, no. 5 (May 1997), p. 481; and Zachary Abuza, 'Leadership Transition in Vietnam Since the Eighth Party Congress: The Unfinished Congress', *Asian Survey*, vol. 38, no. 12 (December 1998), p. 1121.

41 Carlyle A. Thayer, 'The Regularization of Politics: Continuity and Change in the Party's Central Committee, 1951–86, in *Postwar Vietnam: Dilemmas in Socialist Development*, edited by David G. Marr and Christine P. White, Ithaca: Southeast Asian Program, Cornell University, 1988, p. 190. For a particularly strong tendency to emphasise the role of individual leaders see Lewis Stern, *Renovating the Vietnamese Communist Party: Nguyen Van Linh and the Programme for Organisational Reform, 1987–91*, Singapore: Institute of Southeast Asian Studies, 1993. See also Neil Sheehan, *Two Cities: Hanoi and Saigon*, London: Picador and Jonathan Cape, 1992, pp. 73–82.
42 Abuza, 'Leadership Transition', pp. 1120–1.
43 Lewis Stern is a past master at this kind of analysis. In an analysis of a particular plenum Stern concludes: 'The plenary resolution . . . referred to the state-run economy playing the leading role: however, it was somewhat less dogmatic about the importance of preserving the pivotal role of the state economic sector and somewhat more prescriptive about the need to enshrine the roles and obligations of state enterprises in clear legislation'. See Lewis M. Stern, 'Party Plenums and Leadership Style in Vietnam', *Asian Survey*, vol. 35, no. 10 (October 1995), pp. 909–21, 'Leading' or 'pivotal'? I am not sure that it is helpful to examine speeches in this way.
44 William S. Turley and Brantly Womack, 'Asian Socialism's Open Doors: Guangzhou and Ho Chi Minh City', *The China Journal*, no. 40, July 1998, pp. 108 and 111.
45 The official account of how reform emerged in Vietnam and Ho Chi Minh City's role in it can be found in the chapters by former Ho Chi Minh City party secretaries Nguyen Van Linh and Vo Tran Chi, in *Ban Thuong Vu Thanh Uy Dang Cong San Viet Nam Thanh Pho Ho Chi Minh* [Standing Committee of the Ho Chi Minh City Communist Party], *Thanh Pho Ho Chi Minh Hai Muoi Nam (1975–1995)* [Ho Chi Minh City: Twenty Years (1975–1995)], *Nha Xuat Ban Thanh Pho Ho Chi Minh* [Ho Chi Minh City Publishing House], 1996, pp. 29–38 and 511–31. For other foreign accounts besides Turley and Womack that talk about reform experiments see Chapter 1 note 62.
46 For literature on Vietnam's so-called private sector see Chapter 1 note 97.
47 This tends to go hand in hand with the view that with the onset of reforms Ho Chi Minh City has 'come full circle' since 1975. Douglas Pike talks about the 'bourgeoisie re-emerging in strength in the south'. However, there is very little analysis of who or what is 're-emerging' when in fact it has very little to do with the pre-1975 period, as can be seen from the depiction of Ho Chi Minh City's post-1975 political economy in this research. See Douglas Pike, 'Vietnam in 1993: Uncertainty Closes In', *Asian Survey*, vol. 34, no. 1 (January 1994).
48 See Carlyle A. Thayer, 'The Regularization of Politics', in Marr and White (eds), *Postwar Vietnam*, pp. 177–93; Carlyle A. Thayer, 'The Regularization of Politics Revisited: Continuity and Change in the Party's Central Committee, 1976–96', a paper presented to a panel on 'Vietnamese Politics in Transition: New Conceptions and Inter-Disciplinary Approaches, Part 2', the 49th Annual Meeting of the Association for Asian Studies, Chicago, 13–16 March 1997; Thaveeporn Vasavakul, 'Sectoral Politics and Strategies for State and Party Building from the VII to the VIII Congress of the Vietnam Communist Party (1991–96)', in *Ten Years after the 1986 Party Congress*, edited by Fforde, Political and Social Change Monograph 24, The Australian National University, Canberra, 1997, pp. 81–135.
49 See my article in the *Vietnam Business Journal* in January 2000, which adopts such an approach in respect to elite political manoeuvring in late 1999 and early 2000.

Bibliography

Books, articles and documents

Abuza, Zachay,. 'Leadership Transition in Vietnam Since the Eighth Party Congress: The Unfinished Congress', *Asian Survey*, vol. 38, no. 12 (December 1998), pp. 1105–21.

Amnesty International, 'Socialist Republic of Vietnam: New Debate on the Death Penalty?', Report ASA 41/04/99 July 1999.

Ban Thuong Vu Thanh Uy Dang Cong San Viet Nam Thanh Pho Ho Chi Minh [Standing Committee of the Ho Chi Minh City Communist Party], *Thanh Pho Ho Chi Minh Hai Muoi Nam (1975–1995)* [Ho Chi Minh City: Twenty Years (1975–1995)], *Nha Xuat Ban Thanh Pho Ho Chi Minh* [Ho Chi Minh City Publishing House], 1996.

Beresford, Melanie, *National Unification and Economic Development in Vietnam*, New York: St Martin's Press, 1989.

—— 'Interpretation of the Vietnamese Economic Reforms 1979–85', in *Researching the Vietnamese Economic Reforms: 1979–86*, Australia–Vietnam Research Project, Monograph Series no. 1, School of Economic and Financial Studies, Macquarie University, Sydney, January 1995, pp. 1–16.

—— and Bruce McFarlane, 'Regional Inequality and Regionalism in Vietnam and China', *Journal of Contemporary Asia*, vol. 25, no. 1 (1995), pp. 50–72.

Blecher, Marc J., 'Developmental State, Entrepreneurial State: the Political Economy of Socialist Reform in Xinji Municipality and Guanghan county', in *The Chinese State In the Era of Economic Reform: the Road to Crisis*, edited by Gordon White, London, Macmillan, 1991, pp. 265–94.

—— and Vivienne Shue, *Tethered Deer: Government and Economy in a Chinese County*, Stanford: Stanford University Press, 1996.

Bottomore, Tom, Laurence Harris, V. G. Kieman and Ralph Miliband (eds), *A Dictionary of Marxist Thought*, second edition, Oxford: Blackwell, 1991.

British Consulate General, 'Official Career Outline of Truong Tan Sang', provided to British Consulate General in Ho Chi Minh City by Vietnamese government, unpublished 1996.

Brocheux, Pierre, *The Mekong Delta: Ecology, Economy and Revolution, 1860–1960*, University of Wisconsin-Madison: Center for Southeast Asian Studies, Monograph no. 12, 1995.

Bui Tin, *Following Ho Chi Minh: The Memoirs of a North Vietnamese Colonel*, translated from the Vietnamese and adapted by Judy Stowe and Do Van, London: Hurst and Company, 1995.

Burns, John P., 'Strengthening Central CPP Control of Leadership Selection: The 1990 Nomenklatura', *China Quarterly*, no. 138 (June 1994), pp. 458–91.

Business Monitor International, *Vietnam 1998*.

—— *Vietnam 2000*.

Shi Chen, 'Leadership Change in Shanghai: Toward the Dominance of Party Technocrats', *Asian Survey*, vol. 38, no. 7, July 1998, pp. 671–87.

Cima, Ronald, 'Vietnam in 1988: The Brink of Renewal', *Asian Survey* vol. 29, no. 1 (January 1989), pp. 64–72.

Chan Dung Nhung Doanh Nghiep Thanh Dat [A Portrait of Business on the March], Nha Xuat Ban Thanh Pho Ho Chi Minh [Ho Chi Minh City Publishing House], Saigon Times Group, VAPEC, 1997.

Communist Party of Vietnam, *Sixth National Congress of the Communist Party: Documents*, Hanoi: Foreign Language Publishing House, 1987.

—— *Seventh National Congress of the Communist Party: Documents*, Hanoi: Foreign Language Publishing House, 1991.

The Constitution of Vietnam: 1946–1959–1980–1992, Hanoi: The Gioi Publishers, 1995.

Cotter, Michael G., 'Towards a Social History of the Vietnamese Southward Movement', *Journal of Southeast Asian History*, no. 9 (March 1968).

Dacy, Douglas C., *Foreign Aid, War and Economic Development: South Vietnam 1955–75*, Cambridge: Cambridge University Press, 1986.

Dang Phong, 'Viewing the Decade 1976–1986 in Vietnam Vertically and Horizontally', in *Researching the Vietnamese Economic Reforms: 1979–86*, Australia–Vietnam Research Project, Monograph Series no. 1, School of Economic and Financial Studies, Macquarie University, Sydney, January 1995, pp. 17–21.

—— and Melanie Beresford, *Authority Relations and Economic Decision-Making in Vietnam: An Historical Perspective*, Nordic Institute of Asian Studies, 1998.

Danh Muc Co Quan xi Nghiep Tai Thanh Pho Ho Chi Minh [List of Commercial Organisations in Ho Chi Minh City], Cue Thong Ke Thanh Pho Ho Chi Minh [Ho Chi Minh City Statistical Office], 1 January 1996.

Dieu Le Dang Cong San Viet Nam [Communist Party of Vietnam Statutes], Ha Noi: Nha Xuat Ban Chinh Tri Quoc Gia [Hanoi: National Political Publishing House], 1996.

Dittmer, Lowell, 'Chinese Informal Politics', *The China Journal*, no. 34, (July 1995), pp. 1–34.

Dola Trong Cuoc Khang Chien Chong My Cuu Nuoc [The Dollar In Our Country's War of Resistance Against the Americans], Nha Xuat Ban Tre [Youth Publishing House], 1996.

Dollar, David, 'Macroeconomic Management and the Transition to the Market in Vietnam', *Journal of Comparative Economics* vol. 18 (1994), pp. 357–75.

Duckett, Jane, *The Entrepreneurial State in China*, London and New York: Routledge, 1998.

Duiker, William J., *Vietnam Since the Fall of Saigon*, updated edition, Monographs in International Studies, Southeast Asia Series, no. 56A, Athens, Ohio: Ohio University, 1989.

East Asia Analytical Unit Department of Foreign Affairs and Trade, 'Vietnam', in *Overseas Chinese Business Networks in Asia*, Commonwealth of Australia, 1995, pp. 80–5.

Economist Intelligence Unit, *Vietnam: Country Forecast*, second quarter 1996.

Bibliography

—— *Vietnam Country Forecast*, third quarter 1997.
—— *Vietnam Country Forecast*, first quarter 2000.
—— *Vietnam: Country Profile 1996–97*.
—— *Vietnam Country Report*, fourth quarter 1999.
Elliott, David W. P., 'Dilemmas of Reform in Vietnam', in *The Challenge of Reform in Indochina*, edited by Borje Ljunggren, Cambridge, MA.: Harvard Institute for International Development, 1993, pp. 53–94.
Esterline, John H., 'Vietnam in 1987: Steps towards Rejuvenation', *Asian Survey* vol. 28, no. 1 (January 1988), pp. 86–94.
Fforde, Adam, 'The Political Economy of "Reform" in Vietnam: Some Reflections', in *The Challenge of Reform in Indochina*, edited by Borje Ljunggren. Cambridge, MA.: Harvard Institute for International Development, 1993, pp. 293–325.
—— and Doug Porter, 'Public Goods, the State, Civil Society and Development Assistance in Vietnam: Opportunities and Prospects', a paper presented to Doi Moi, the State and Civil Society: Vietnam Update 1994 Conference, Canberra, 10–11 November 1994.
—— *Vietnam Economic Commentary and Analysis*, no. 6, Canberra: ADUKI, April 1995.
—— *Vietnam: Economic Commentary and Analysis*, no. 7, Canberra: ADUKI, November 1995.
—— and Steve Seneque, 'The Economy and the Countryside: The Relevance of Rural Development Policies', in *Vietnam's Rural Transformation*, edited by Benedict J. Tria Kerkvliet, Boulder, CO.: Westview Press, 1995, pp. 97–138.
—— and Stefan de Vylder, *From Plan to Market: The Economic Transition in Vietnam*, Boulder, CO.: Westview Press, 1996.
—— 'The Vietnamese Economy in 1996 – Events and Trends – The Limits of Doi Moi?', in *Ten Years after the 1986 Party Congress*, edited by Adam Fforde, Political and Social Change Monograph 24, The Australian National University, Canberra, 1997, pp. 145–80.
—— *Vietnam: Economic Commentary and Analysis*, no. 9, Canberra: ADUKI, November 1997.
—— 'Public Administration Reform in Ho Chi Minh City: A Report on the "Vietnamese Process" with Suggestions for How to Support It', prepared for the Government Committee on Organisation and Personnel and UNDP Hanoi, unpublished manuscript 1997.
Forbes, Dean and Nigel Thrift (eds), *The Socialist Third World: Urban Development and Territorial Planning*, Oxford: Basil Blackwell, 1987.
Frank Hiep Huynh, Ng Chee Yuen and Nick J. Freeman (eds), *State-Owned Enterprise Reform in Vietnam: Lessons from Asia*, Singapore: Institute of Southeast Asian Studies, 1996.
Gainsborough, Martin, 'The Politics of the Greenback: The Interaction Between the Formal and Black Markets in Ho Chi Minh City', in *Urban Tiger*, edited by Lisa Drummond, Thuy Pham and Mandy Thomas, London: Curzon Press, 2002.
Getty, J. Arch and Oleg V. Naumov, *The Road To Terror: Stalin and the Self-Destruction of the Bolsheviks, 1912–1939*, New Haven, CT.: Yale University Press, September 1999.
Goldstein, Avery, 'Trends in the Study of Political Elites and Institutions in the People's Republic of China', *China Quarterly*, no. 139 (September 1994), pp. 714–30.

Hiebert, Murray, *Chasing the Tigers: A Portrait of the New Vietnam*, Kodansha International, 1996.
Hien Phap Nuoc Cong Hoa Xa Hoi Chu Nghia Viet Nam 1992 [Constitution of the Socialist Republic of Vietnam 1992], *Nha Xuat Ban Chinh Tri Quoc Gia* [National Political Publishing House], Hanoi 1998.
Hertz, Ellen, *The Trading Crowd: An Ethnography of the Shanghai Stock Market*. Cambridge and New York: Cambridge University Press, 1998.
Huang, Yasheng, 'Central–Local Relations in China During the Reform Era: The Economic and Institutional Dimensions', *World Development*, vol. 24, no. 4 (1996), pp. 655–72.
International Monetary Fund, *Vietnam: Recent Economic Developments*, IMF Staff Country Report no. 96/145 1996.
—— and World Bank, *Vietnam: Towards Fiscal Transparency*, June 1999.
Jerneck, Anne, *The Role of the State in a Newly Transitionary Economy: The Case of Vietnam's General Corporations*, report prepared as part of a collaboration between Sida, Stockholm, the Department of Economic History at Lund University, and the Embassy of Sweden in Hanoi, Vietnam, September 1997.
—— and Nguyen Thanh Ha, 'The Role of the Enterprise Unions in the Shift from Central Planning to Market Orientation', in *Vietnam In a Changing World*, edited by Irene Norland, Carolyn L. Gates and Vu Cao Dam, London: Curzon Press 1995, pp. 159–80.
Kerkvliet, Benedict J. Tria, 'Village–State Relations in Vietnam: The Effect of Everyday Politics on Decollectivisation', *The Journal of Asian Studies* vol. 54, no. 2 (May 1995), pp. 396–418.
—— and Doug J. Porter (eds), *Vietnam's Rural Transformation*, Boulder, CO.: Westview Press, 1995.
Kokko, Ari and Fredrik Sjoholm, *Small, Medium, or Large? Some Scenarios for the Role of the State in the Era of Industrialisation and Modernisation in Vietnam*, Swedish International Development Cooperation Agency, 1997.
Kolko, Gabriel, *Vietnam: Anatomy of a Peace*, London and New York: Routledge, 1997.
Kornai, Janos, *The Socialist System: The Political Economy of Communism*, Oxford: Clarendon Press, 1992.
Lam Tao-chiu, 'Review of "Tethered Deer: Government and Economy in a Chinese Country", by Marc Blecher and Vivienne Shue', *The China Journal*, no. 38 (July 1997), pp. 179–81.
Law on Foreign Investment in Vietnam (November 1996), Hanoi: National Political Publishing House, 1996.
Li, Linda Chelan, 'Provincial Discretion and National Power: Investment Policy in Guangdong and Shanghai, 1978–93', *China Quarterly*, no. 152 (December 1997), pp. 778–804.
Lieberthal, Kenneth and Michael Oksenberg, *Policy Making in China: Leaders, Structures, and Processes*, Princeton: Princeton University Press, 1988.
Liu, Yia-Ling, 'Reform from Below: The Private Economy and Local Politics in Rural Industrialisation', *The China Quarterly*, no. 130 (June 1992), pp. 293–316.
Ljunggren, Borje, *The Challenge of Reform in Indochina*, Cambridge, MA.: Harvard Institute for International Development, 1993.
—— 'Doi Moi in the Year of the Eighth Party Congress: Emerging Contradictions in the Reform Process', in *Vietnam: Reform and Transformation*, edited by Bjorn

178   Bibliography

Beckman, Eva Hansonn and Lisa Roman, Centre for Pacific Asia Studies, Stockholm University, 1997, pp. 9–36.

Ma, Shu-Yan, 'The Role of Spontaneity and State Initiative in China's Shareholding System Reform', *Communist and Post-Communist Studies* 32 (1999), pp. 319–37.

Mann, Michael, 'The Autonomous Power of the State: its Origins, Mechanisms and Results', *Archives of European Sociology*, no. xxv (1984), pp. 185–313.

McCormick, Barrett L., 'Political Change in China and Vietnam: Coping with the Consequences of Economic Reform', *The China Journal*, no. 40 (July 1998), pp. 121–43.

Montinola, Gabriella, Yingyi Qian and Barry R. Weingast (eds), 'Federalism, Chinese Style: The Political Basis for Economic Success in China', *World Politics* vol. 48 (October 1995), pp. 50–81.

Murray, Martin J., 'White Gold or White Blood? The Rubber Plantations of Colonial Indochina, 1910–40', *Journal of Peasant Studies*, vol. 19, no. 3/4 (April–July 1992).

Naughton, Barry, 'Cities in the Chinese Economic System: Changing Roles and Conditions for Autonomy', in *Urban Spaces in Contemporary China: The Potential for Autonomy and Community In Post-Mao China*, edited by Deborah S. Davis, Richard Kraus, Barry Naughton, and Elizabeth J. Perry, Woodrow Wilson Center Press and Cambridge University Press, 1995.

——*Growing Out Of the Plan: Chinese Economic Reform 1978–93*, Cambridge University Press, 1995.

Nee, Victor, 'A Theory of Market Transition: From Redistribution to Markets in State Socialism', *American Sociological Review*, no. 54 (October 1989), pp. 663–81.

Nevitt, Christopher Earle, 'Private Business Associations in China: Evidence of Civil Society or Local State Power?', *The China Journal*, no. 36 (July 1996), pp. 25–43.

Ngan Hang Nha Nuoc Viet Nam [State Bank of Vietnam], *Thanh Pho Ho Chi Minh: Trung Tam Tai Chinh Tien Te Lon Cua Viet Nam* [Ho Chi Minh City: The Great Financial and Monetary Centre of Vietnam], *Nha May In Thong Tan Xa Viet Nam*, 1998.

Nguyen Dinh Cung, John Bentley, Le Viet Thai, Hoang Xuan Thanh and Phan Nguyen Toan, *Research Report on Improving Macroeconomic Policy and Reforming Administrative Procedures to Promote Development of Small and Medium Enterprises in Vietnam*, United Nations Industrial Development Organisation and Ministry of Planning and Investment, Hanoi, January 1999.

Nguyen Dinh Dau, *From Saigon to Ho Chi Minh City: 300 Year History*, Ho Chi Minh City: Land Service, Science and Technics Publishing House, 1998.

Nguyen Huu Dinh, *Kinh Doanh Vang Tai Thanh Pho Ho Chi Minh: Chinh Sach Va Giai Phap* [The Gold Business in Ho Chi Minh City: Policy and Solutions], *Nha Xuat Ban Thanh Pho Ho Chi Minh* [Ho Chi Minh City Publishing House], Saigon Times Group, Vapec, 1996.

Nguyen Ngoc Tuan, Ngo Tri Long and Ho Phuong, 'Restructuring of SOEs towards Industrialisation and Modernisation in Vietnam', in *State-Owned Enterprise Reform in Vietnam: Lessons from Asia*, edited by Ng Chee Yuan, Nick J. Freeman and Frank H. Huynh, Institute for Southeast Asian Studies 1996, pp. 19–37.

Nha O, Dat Dai Va Thue Nha Dat [Housing, Land and the Rental of Housing and Land], compiled by Thanh Thao, *Nha Xuat Ban Thanh Pho Ho Chi Minh* [Ho Chi Minh City Publishing House], 1997.

Nien Giam Thong Ke 1995 [Statistical Yearbook 1995], Ha Noi: *Nha Xuat Ban Thong Ke* [Hanoi: Statistical Publishing House], 1996.

Nien Giam Thong Ke 1998 [Statistical Yearbook 1998], *Ha Noi: Nha Xuat Ban Thong Ke* [Hanoi: Statistical Publishing House], 1999.

Nien Giam Thong Ke Thanh Pho Ho Chi Minh 1997 [Ho Chi Minh City Statistical Yearbook 1997], *Cue Thong Ke Thanh Pho Ho Chi Minh* [Ho Chi Minh City Statistical Office], 1997.

Nien Giam Thong Ke Thanh Pho Ho Chi Minh 1998 [Ho Chi Minh City Statistical Yearbook 1998], *Cue Thong Ke Thanh Pho Ho Chi Minh* [Ho Chi Minh City Statistical Office], 1998.

Norlund, Irene, 'The Role of Industry in Vietnam's Development Strategy', *Journal of Contemporary Asia*, vol. 14, no. 1, (1984), pp. 94–107.

Nyland, Chris, 'Vietnam, the Plan/Market Contradiction and the Transition to Socialism', *Journal of Contemporary Asia*, vol. 11, no. 4, (1981), pp. 426–49.

Oi, Jean C., 'Market Reforms and Corruption in Rural China', *Studies in Comparative Communism*, vol. 22 (Summer/Autumn 1989).

—— 'Fiscal Reform and the Economic Foundations of Local State Corporatism in China,' *World Politics* (October 1992), pp. 99–126.

—— and Andrew Walder (eds), *Property Rights and Economic Reform in China*, Stanford University Press, 1999.

Oksenberg, Michel and James Tong, 'The Evolution of Central–Provincial Fiscal Relations in China, 1971–84: the Formal System', *The China Quarterly*, no. 125 (March 1991), pp. 1–32.

Owen, Norman G., 'The Rice Industry of Mainland Southeast Asia 1850–1914', *The Journal of the Siam Society*, vol. 59, part 2 (July 1971), pp. 75–143.

Perry, Elizabeth J., 'Trends in the Study of Chinese Politics: State–Society Relations', *The China Quarterly*, no. 139 (September 1994), pp. 704–13.

Pham Thanh Phan and Pham Thi Thuy Duong, *Vi Tri, Chuc Nang, Nhiem Vu, Va Quyen Han Cua Chinh Quyen Xa, Phuong* [The Positions, Function, Responsibility and Power of State Administration At the Village and Quarter Level], *Nha Xuat Ban Thong Ke* [Statistical Publishing House], Hanoi, 1999.

Pike, Douglas, 'Vietnam in 1993: Uncertainty Closes In', *Asian Survey*, vol. 34, no. 1 (January 1994).

—— 'Vietnam: Its Durability and Its Direction', paper presented to a conference on The Durability and Direction of the Four Remaining Socialist Countries: China, Vietnam, Cuba and North Korea, the Korean Association of International Studies and the Research Institute for National Unification, 27–8 May Seoul, 1994.

Porter, Doug J., 'Economic Liberalization, Marginality, and the Local State', in *Vietnam's Rural Transformation*, edited by Benedict J. Tria Kerkvliet and Doug J. Porter, Boulder, CO.: Westview Press, 1995, pp. 215–46.

Porter, Gareth, 'The Politics of "Renovation" in Vietnam', *Problems of Communism*, vol. 39 (May–June 1990), pp. 72–88.

—— *Vietnam: The Politics of Bureaucratic Socialism*, Ithaca, NY: Cornell University Press, 1993.

Rambo, Terry, 'A Comparison of Peasant Social Systems of Northern and Southern Viet-Nam: A Study of Ecological Adaption, Social Succession and Cultural Evolution', Ph.D. diss., University of Hawaii, 1972.

Riedel, James and Chuong S. Tran, *The Emerging Private Sector and Industrialisation in Vietnam*, report on the project: Vietnam's Emerging Private Sector and Promising Private Companies, James Riedel Associates, Inc., April 1997.

180 Bibliography

Shu-Yun Ma, 'The Role of Spontaneity and State Initiative in China's Shareholding System Reform', *Communist and Post-Communist Studies* 32 (1999), pp. 319–37.

Shue, Vivienne, *The Reach of the State: Sketches of the Chinese Body Politic*, Stanford, CA: Stanford University Press, 1988.

Sidel, Mark, 'The Re-Emergence of Legal Discourse in Vietnam', *International and Comparative Law Quarterly*, vol. 34 (January 1994), pp. 163–74.

—— 'Generational and Institutional Transition in the Vietnamese Communist Party: The 1996 Congress and Beyond', *Asian Survey* vol. 37, no. 5 (May 1997), pp. 481–95.

—— 'Law, the Press and Police Murder in Vietnam: The Vietnamese Press and the Trial of Nguyen Tan Duong', in *The Mass Media In Vietnam*, edited by David G. Marr, Political and Social Change Monograph 25, Department of Political and Social Change, Research School of Pacific and Asian Studies, The Australian National University, Canberra, 1998, pp. 97–119.

Sheehan, Neil, *Two Cities: Hanoi and Saigon*, Picador and Jonathan Cape, 1992.

Solinger, Dorothy J., 'Urban Entrepreneurs and the State: The Merger of State and Society', in *State and Society in China: The Consequences of Reform*, edited by Arthur Lewis Rosenbaum, Boulder, CO.: Westview Press, 1992, pp. 121–41.

—— 'Despite Decentralisation: Disadvantages, Dependence and Ongoing Central Power in the Inland – the Case of Wuhan', *China Quarterly*, no. 145 (March 1996), pp. 1–34.

Spoor, Max, 'Reforming State Finance in Post-1975 Vietnam', *Journal of Development Studies*, vol. 24, no. 4 (July 1988), pp. 102–14.

Stern, Lewis M., 'The Overseas Chinese in the Socialist Republic of Vietnam, 1979–82', *Asian Survey* 25, no. 5 (May 1985), pp. 521–36.

—— *Renovating the Vietnamese Communist Party: Nguyen Van Linh and the Programme for Organisational Reform, 1987–91*, Singapore: Institute of Southeast Asian Studies, 1993.

—— 'Party Plenums and Leadership Style in Vietnam', *Asian Survey*, vol. 35, no. 10 (October 1995), pp. 909–21.

Stromseth, Jonathan R., 'Reform and Response in Vietnam: State–Society Relations and the Changing Political Economy', Ph.D. diss., Columbia University, 1998.

Thanh Pho Ho Chi Minh [Ho Chi Minh City], Nha Xuat Ban Thanh Pho Ho Chi Minh [Ho Chi Minh City Publishing House], 1983.

Templer, Robert, *Shadows and Wind: A View of Modern Vietnam*, London: Little, Brown and Company, 1998.

Thayer, Carlyle A., 'The Regularization of Politics: Continuity and Change in the Party's Central Committee, 1951–86', in *Postwar Vietnam: Dilemmas in Socialist Development*, edited by David Marr and Christine P. White, Ithaca: Southeast Asian Program, Cornell University, 1988, pp. 177–93.

—— 'Political Reform in Vietnam: Doi Moi and the Emergence of Civil Society', in *The Developments of Civil Society in Communist Systems*, edited by Robert F. Miller, Allen and Unwin 1992, pp. 110–29.

—— 'Mono-organizational Socialism and the State', in *Vietnam's Rural Transformation* edited by Benedict J. Tria Kerkvliet and Doug J. Porter, Boulder, CO.: Westview Press, 1995, pp. 39–64.

—— 'The Regularization of Politics Revisited: Continuity and Change in the Party's Central Committee, 1976–96', paper presented to a panel on 'Vietnamese Politics in Transition: New Conceptions and Inter-Disciplinary Approaches, Part 2', the 49th Annual Meeting of the Association for Asian Studies, Chicago, 13–16 March 1997.

Thrift, Nigel and Dean Forbes, *The Price of War: Urbanization in Vietnam 1954–1985*, London: Allen and Unwin, 1986.
Tonkin, Derek, 'Vietnam: Market Reform and Ideology', Lecture to the Royal Society for Asian Affairs, 22 January 1997.
Tran Khanh, *The Ethnic Chinese and Economic Development in Vietnam*, Indochina Unit, Institute of Southeast Asian Studies, 1993.
Turley, William S., 'Vietnam: Ordeals of Transition', in *Asian Contagion: The Causes and Consequences of a Financial Crisis*, edited by Karl D. Jackson, Boulder, CO.: Westview Press 1999, pp. 268–99.
—— and Brantly Womack, 'Asian Socialism's Open Doors: Guangzhou and Ho Chi Minh City', *The China Journal*, no. 40, (July 1998), pp. 95–119.
Ungar, E. S., 'The Struggle Over the Chinese Community in Vietnam, 1946–84', *Pacific Affairs* vol. 60, no. 4 (Winter 1987–88), pp. 596–614.
Unger, Jonathan and Anita Chan, 'China, Corporatism, and the East Asian Model', *The Australian Journal of Chinese Affairs*, no. 33 (January 1995), pp. 29–53.
Vasavakul, Thaveeporn, 'Politics of the Reform of State Institutions in the post-socialist era', in *Vietnam Assessment: Creating a Sound Investment Climate*, edited by Suiwah Leung, Curzon Press, Institute of Southeast Asian Studies/National Centre for Development Studies, 1996, pp. 42–68.
—— 'Sectoral Politics and Strategies for State and Party Building from the VII to the VIII Congress of the Vietnam Communist Party (1991–96)', in *Ten Years After the 1986 Party Congress*, edited by Adam Fforde, Political and Social Change Monograph 24, The Australian National University, Canberra, 1997, pp. 81–135.
—— 'Vietnam: The Third Wave of State Building', in *Southeast Asian Affairs 1997*, Institute of Southeast Asian Affairs, 1997, pp. 337–63.
Vietnamese Studies, *Saigon From the Beginnings To 1945*, no. 45, Hanoi: Foreign Languages Publishing House, 1977.
Vu Tuan Anh, *Development in Vietnam: Policy Reforms and Economic Growth*, Indochina Unit, Institute of Southeast Asian Studies, 1994.
Walder, Andrew, *Communist Neo-Traditionalism, Work and Authority in Chinese Industry*, Berkeley and Los Angeles: University of California Press, 1986.
—— 'Local Bargaining Relationships and Urban Industrial Finance', in *Bureaucracy, Politics and Decision Making in Post-Mao China*, edited by Kenneth G. Lieberthal and David M. Lampton, Berkeley: University of California Press, 1992, pp. 308–33.
Wank, David L., 'Private Business, Bureaucracy, And Political Alliances in a Chinese City', *Australian Journal of Chinese Affairs*, no. 33 (January 1994), pp. 55–71.
—— *Commodifying Chinese Communism*, Cambridge University Press, 1999.
Webster, Leila, *SME's in Vietnam: On the Road to Prosperity*, Private Sector Discussions No. 10, Mekong Project Development Facility.
—— and Markus Taussig, *Vietnam's Under-Sized Engine: A Survey of 95 Larger Private Manufacturers*, Mekong Project Development Facility, 4 June 1999.
Werner, Jayne, 'The Problem of the District in Vietnam's Development Policy', in *Postwar Vietnam: Dilemmas in Socialist Development*, edited by David G. Marr and Christine P. White, Ithaca: Southeast Asian Program, Cornell University, 1988, pp. 147–62.
White, Gordon, *Riding the Tiger: The Politics of Economic Reform in Post-Mao China*, London: Macmillan 1993.

Wong, Christine P. W., 'Central–local Relations in an Era of Fiscal Decline: The Paradox of Fiscal Decentralisation in Post-Mao China', *The China Quarterly*, no. 128 (1991), pp. 691–714.

Woodside, Alexander, 'Nationalism and Poverty in the Breakdown of Sino–Vietnamese Relations', *Pacific Affairs* vol. 52 (Fall 1979), pp. 381–409.

World Bank, *Transforming a State Owned Financial System: A Financial Sector Study of Vietnam*, Report No. 9223-VN, 15 April 1991.

—— *Vietnam: Transition to the Market*, Country Operations Division, Country Department I, East Asia and Pacific Region, September 1993.

—— *Vietnam: Public Sector Management and Private Sector Incentives: An Economic Report*, Report No. 13143-VN, 26 September 1994.

—— *Vietnam: Poverty Assessment and Strategy*, Report No. 13442-VN, 23 January 1995.

—— *Vietnam Financial Sector Review: An Agenda for Financial Sector Development*, Report No. 13135-VN, 1 March 1995.

—— *Vietnam: Economic Report on Industrialization and Industrial Policy*, Report No. 14645-VN, 17 October 1995.

—— *Vietnam: Fiscal Decentralisation and the Delivery of Rural Services: An Economic Report*, Report No. 15745-VN, 31 October 1996.

—— *Vietnam: Deepening Reform for Growth: An Economic Report*, Report No. 17031-VN, 31 October 1997.

—— *Vietnam: Preparing for Take-off? How Vietnam Can Participate Fully in the East Asian Recovery*, an Informal Economic Report of the World Bank Consultative Meeting for Vietnam, Hanoi, 14–15 December 1999.

Wright, Gwendolyn, *The Politics of Design in French Colonial Urbanism*: Chicago University Press, Chicago, 1991.

Yang, Dali L., 'Governing China's Transition to the Market: Institutional Incentives, Politicians Choices, and Unintended Outcomes', *World Politics* vol. 48 (April 1996), pp. 424–52.

Zhang, Le-Yin, 'Chinese Central–Provincial Fiscal Relationships, Budgetary Decline and the Impact of the 1994 Fiscal Reform: An Evaluation', *The China Quarterly*, no. 157 (March 1999), pp. 115–41.

Zinoman, Peter B., The Colonial Bastille: A Social History of Imprisonment in Colonial Vietnam, 1862–1940, Ph.D. diss., Cornell University, 1996.

Books, articles and documents

Vietnamese language

Dau Tu [Investment]
Kinh Doanh Va Phap Luat [Business and Law]
Lao Dong [Labour]
Ngan Hang [Banking]
Nguoi Lao Dong [The Worker]
Phu Nu [Women]
Sai Gon Giai Phong [Liberated Saigon]
Thanh Nien [Youth]
Thoi Bao Kinh te Saigon [Saigon Economic Times]
Thoi Bao Kinh te Viet Nam [Vietnam Economic Times]

Thoi Bao Ngan Hang [Banking Times]
Tuoi Tre [Youth]

English language

Agence France Presse
Associated Press
BBC Summary of World Broadcasts
Death Penalty News
Far Eastern Economic Review
Financial Times
Reuters
Saigon Newsreader
Saigon Times Daily
Saigon Times Weekly
South China Morning Post
Vietnam Business Journal
Vietnam Economic Times
Vietnam Investment Review
Vietnam News
Wall Street Journal
Washington Post

Index

Abuza, Z. 107
Ai, Nguyen Cong 128
An, Nguyen Ngoc 53, 56, 124, 128
appointments, and business interests 49–50; changes in 46–7; Chief Architect 62, 161n; and clientalist network 42–3, 53–6; complexity of 43–5; controversial 46; and democratic centralism 40–3, 56–8; and department directors/district chiefs 52; and Deputy People's Committee chairmen 50–2, 154n, 155n; from the centre 43–4; organisational participation in 44; and party secretaries 47–8; and People's Committee chairmen 45, 48–9; political/business patterns 53, 61

Ba Thi model 7, 141n
Bamboo Garden rotating credit 96, 168n
Bank for Foreign Trade *see* Vietcombank
banks 149n, 151n; and access to credit 103; credit constraints 152n; expertise in 104; and foreign exchange 76–7; formation of 22; fraudulently obtaining credit 37; investigations into 84, 168n; lending by 31, 62; profiteering/speculation by 39; and property/land 71; shareholding structure 121–3; as state-dominated 100, 169n; and use of Communist sympathisers 171n; vulnerability of 74
Ben Thanh Tourist 29
Bich, Nguyen Ngoc 89, 90
Bitis 18
black market 60, 72–3, 149n, 164n

Burns, J. 42
Business Law 148n

Cadastral, Land and Housing Department 19, 75, 147n
Canh, Le Duc 84, 86–7
Central Party Organisation Department 44
centralisation 1, 135n; vs decentralisation 8–9, 143n
change *see* reform
Chau, Le Minh 51–2, 55–6, 67, 75, 124, 128, 159n
Chau, Pham Thanh 89
Chi, Nguyen Van 53, 67, 124, 128
Chi, Vo Tranh 47, 48, 93, 158n
Chief Architect 77; office 62–3, 161n, 162n
City Party Organisation Department 44
clientalism 42–3; examples of 55–6; existence of 54; identification of 53–4; instances of 54–5
colonialism 2–3
companies 16, 146n; bureaucratic/political background 28–32, 39; and capital 31, 152n; central state 17, 18; and contracts 30–1, 151n; controlling institution 17–19, 146n; emergence of diversified corporations 24, 150n; foreign 17; high growth sectors 21–4, 148n; joint ventures 17, 18, 80; and land 31–2, 152n; and licenses 30, 151n; limited liability 20–1; local state 17, 18–21; management in 28, 117; military/police involvement 19, 147n; and movement of managers 101,

170n; new opportunities with reform 19–21; non-state 17–18; open to reform 99–100; ownership 116; political advantages 100; and property rights 24–5, 28, 102; protection of 29, 151n; and raising of capital 100, 169n; response to Decree 18 72, 75; top 100 118–20
Con, Tran Ngoc 57, 124
corruption 60, 62, 102, 106

Day, Duong Van 53, 129
decentralisation 1, 62, 135n; company examples 79–95; effect on local government 11–12; and market reform 2–3; politics of economic 78–9, 95–7; and property rights 170n; vs centralisation 8–9, 143n
democratic centralism, and appointments system 40–3; official picture 43; under planning 42; under strain 43–6; undermined 56–8
Demsetz, H. 24
Department of Land and Housing 75
developmental state 60, 160n
Dinh, Nguyen Huu 101, 170n
District 3 Seafood Production Import-Export Company (Epco) 16, 18, 20, 23, 31, 100; fall of 87–90, 165n; and high-level political manoeuvring 91–2; key developments 133–4; and loss of political backing 92–3; proving guilt of 94–5; reasons for downfall 90–4; rise of 81–2
Duckett, J. 10, 11, 39, 100
Dung, Cao Thi Ngoc 170n

Economic Department 44
Eden Service and Trading Company 20, 22, 29, 55, 68
Eighth Party Congress 107, 172n
employment 7, 9, 115, 141n–2n, 143n
entertainment 23–4
Epco *see* District 3 Seafood Production Import-Export Company

Fahasa 147n
Fforde, A., and de Vylder, S. 8, 142n; and Seneque, S. 11
Fimexco 22, 23; links with foreign real-estate companies 32
Financial Management Department 148n

foreign exchange market, and Decree 37 72–3, 74, 163n
Foreign Services Company (Fosco) 22, 55, 67
Fosco *see* Foreign Services Company

General Land Department 73, 164n
gold market 38–9

Ha, Nguyen Van 87, 95
Hai, Do Hoang 52, 53, 55, 56, 75, 79, 125, 129, 159n
Hai, Le Minh 83, 86–7
Hai, Le Thanh 51, 124, 129
Health Department 20, 147n
Ho Chi Minh City 1, 135n; administration in 4; anti-urban bias toward 5–6; appointments in 40–58; as bastion of reformism 108, 173n; bureaucratic/political background 28–32; business growth 21–4, 148n; demographics 3, 6, 137n, 140n; development of 3–4, 6, 136n, 139n–40n; dynamics of change in 98–109; economic potential of 7, 141n, 142n; economic statistics 111–12; enhanced power/authority in 8, 142n; expansion of state in 106; and fiscal resources 9, 143n–8n; GDP 113, 116; increased autonomy of 6–8; lack of investment in 6, 139n; local state sector employment in 7, 141n–2n; planning of 5–6; policy debates in 109; political economy of 4, 16–19, 98, 138n; prime commercial sites in 22; property arrangements in 102–4, 171n; share of nationwide output 113–14; socialist 'new order' in 5, 138n; state institutions in 59–77; and trade 6
Ho, Ngo Van 85
Hoa, Pham Van 84, 86
Hoa, Truong My 56, 79, 92, 125, 159n
Hoang, Do Van 52, 125, 130, 170n
Hon, Pham Hao 130
Hong, Pham Nhat 89, 90
Huan, Nguyen Van 92
Huy Hoang 18, 21, 22, 29; diversification of 27; land holdings 32
Huyen, Ton Gia 72

Imexco 52, 147n
Industry Department 19

186 *Index*

institutions, and affinity between People's Committees/city authorities 69; central control 61–2, 68, 161n; and clampdowns 60, 70–4, 163n; and conflict between People's Committees/departments 69–70; and corruption 60, 62, 102, 106; and dual accountability 61, 70, 160n; dynamics of 60; and jurisdiction 60–1, 62, 64; limits to the centre's writ 76–7; pressures on 68–70; rivalry between 59, 60–5, 77, 160n; and state interventions 60
International Beverage Company 20

Khai, Phan Van 48, 49, 54, 75, 76, 125, 156n
Khmer Rouge 5
kickbacks 33
Kiem, Cao Sy 86, 87
Kiem, Le Van 21, 29
Kiet, Vo Van 8, 47, 54, 96, 125, 142n, 156n
Kornai, J. 99

land market 13, 21–2, 75, 145n, 148n, 171n; and Decree 18 71–2, 74, 75, 163n; speculation in 35–7
Legamex 96, 168n
Lieberthal, K. and Oksenberg, M. 60
Lien, Nguyen Dang 82
Ling Liu 11
Linh, Nguyen Van 8, 47, 107, 126, 142n, 155n
Linh, Tran 84
Liu, Y.-L. 60
Lo, Nguyen Duy 84, 85–6, 95
local government 1, 135n; autonomy of 8; business interests of 17, 18–21; characteristics of 9–11; corporate 10, 144n; developmental 9, 144n; disaggregation of 11–13; and employment 7, 9, 141n–2n, 143n; entrepreneurial 10, 11, 144n; less favourable view of 10–11, 145n; as rent-seeking/corrupt 10, 11; strengthening of 2
Long, Tran Thanh 126

McCormick, B. 10
Mann, M. 60
Mekong Delta 8
Minh Phung 18, 21, 46; fall of 87–90;

key developments 132–3; proving guilt of 94–5; rise of 80–1

Nam, Le Van 53, 63, 126, 130, 161n, 162n
Naughton, B. 104–5, 106, 171n
Nevitt, C.E. 12–13
New Economic Zones 5–6
Nghiep, Nguyen Vinh 48, 126, 155n
Nhan, Nguyen Thien 126
non-state companies *see* private sector

Oi, J.C. 11, 42; and Walder, A. 24
Overseas Chinese 103–4, 171n

People's Committee, affinity with city authorities 69; and clampdowns 60, 70–3, 163n; and compromising of authority 68; and one stop, one stamp 65–6, 69, 70, 99, 162n; Organisation Department 44; relations with districts/departments 65–8, 69–70, 162n; response to Decree 18 75
Petroleum Service Company 67
Phan, Nguyen Ha 91–2, 167n
Phieu, Le Kha 75, 107
Phnom Penh 5
Phong, Nguyen Xuan 90
Phu Nhuan Jewellery Company 16, 20, 22, 23, 24, 147n–8n; and capital 31; diversification of 27; sources of gold 38; success of 28
Phuc, Nguyen Tuan 89, 90
Phung, Tang Minh 21, 80–1, 82, 89–90, 92–3, 95, 167n, 168n
Phuoc, Pham Huy 79, 80, 81, 83–5, 86–7, 95, 166n, 170n
Pike, Douglas 2
politicians, biographical data 124–30
Porter, G. 107
Poulo Condore prison 55, 158n, 159n
private sector, antagonism toward 148n; and equitisation programme 150n; and local state business 19, 20, 21, 25, 28, 100, 106; nature of 145n–6n; and property rights 16, 25, 28, 100, 106, 108, 169n–70n, 173n; and siphoning off of public funds for 100–1; size of 14
profiteering 33–4
property rights 98, 109; capital-centred 103–4; changes in 24–6, 28, 100–1, 104, 150n; control, income, transfer

24–5; enforcing 101–2; entrepreneur-centred 102–3; formally sanctioned 25; government-centred 101; informal 25; and local elite privatisation 25, 28, 100, 106; siphoning off of public funds/assets 28
Public Transport Department 19

recentralisation 3
reform 1; big-bang 99; and business interests 62; critiquing literature on 106–8; and decentralisation 2–3; economic/political 107; experiments 109; and 'fence'breaking 172n; meaning of 105–6; and momentum of change 104–5; and moves against comprador capitalists 171n; opposition to 99–100; partial 98, 169n; as policy 106–7, 108, 109; public administration 62, 66, 161n; spontaneous 109; of state enterprise 59–60, 62, 161n; as synonymous with change 107
Refrigerator Engineering Company (REE) 169n
regionalism 2–3
rent-seeking 1, 10, 11, 14, 39, 62, 99, 100, 106, 135n, 169n
Road Vehicle Inspection 99

Sagimexco *see* Saigon General Trading and Import-Export Company
Saigon *see* Ho Chi Minh City
Saigon Finance Company 20–1, 28
Saigon General Trading and Import-Export Company (Sagimexco) 23
Saigon Jewellery Company 16, 19–20, 20, 22, 23, 24, 28, 55, 67, 100, 101, 170n; and capital 31; diversification of 26; links with foreign real-estate companies 32; sources of gold 38
Saigon Petro 46, 76–7, 155n
Saigon Tourist 16, 20, 21, 22, 28, 100; and capital 31; diversification of 26; links with foreign real-estate companies 32
Saigon Trading Company (Satra) 52, 55, 75, 102; reorganisation of 66–8, 162n
Sang, Truong Tan 43, 45, 47, 48, 51, 54, 93, 126, 148n
Satra *see* Saigon Trading Company
Shue, V. 2
Sidel, M. 107

smuggling 25, 153n; efforts to control 73, 163n; party/state involvement in 37–8, 60; and sourcing gold without import quotas 38–9, 153n
social evils 29, 151n
Solinger, D. 151n
Son, Ho Hong 46, 76
Son, Huynh Buu 170n
Son, Nguyen Xuan 38
southern settlement 2–3, 5, 135n–6n, 139n
speculation 34–5, 39; in foreign exchange 35; in land 35–7
state institutions 6, 139n; autonomy of 7, 140n–1n; dependence on 7, 141n; equitisation programme 25, 150n; and local elite 100; off-plan business activities of 6; transfers 114
state-society approach 14, 59–60, 146n, 159n–60n

Tacombank 80, 85
Tam, Dang Cong 85
Tamexco *see* Tan Binh Import-Export Company
Tan Binh Housing and Development Company 75
Tan Binh Import-Export Company (Tamexco) 16, 20, 23, 31, 100; fall of 83–7, 165n, 168n; and high-level political manoeuvring 91–2; key developments in 131–2; and loss of political backing 92–3; proving guilt of 94–5; reasons for downfall 90–4; rise of 79–80
Tan Truong Sanh 25
tax 6, 139n
technocrats 51, 157n
Thanh, Huynh Van 88
Thanh, Vo Viet 43, 92, 126
Thao, Pham Phung 127
Thayer, C. 107
Thin, Lien Khui 82, 89, 90, 167n
Tho, Le Duc 54, 158n
Tho, Mai Chi 48–9, 54, 61, 127, 155n, 156n
Thoai, Doan Thanh 68
Thuong, Tran Thi 81
Thuy, Nguyen Manh 84
Tianjin 12–13, 39, 50, 145n
Tocontap 151n
tourism 23–4, 67
Trade Department 19, 20, 55–6, 147n

trade, foreign/domestic 22–3
transition economies 2, 3, 9, 135n
Tribeco 18, 20, 28
Triet, Le Van 51, 127
Triet, Nguyen Minh 43, 47, 48, 50, 155n
Truc, Pham Chanh 51, 127
Turley, W.S. and Womack, B. 108

urbanisation 5–6

Van, Le Thi 51, 57, 79, 86, 92, 127, 159n
vehicle inspections 64–5, 162n
Vien, Nguyen Khac 5

Viet Hoa Bank 18
Viet Kieu 103, 171n
Viet, Thanh, Vo 45, 48, 49, 51, 154n, 155n, 156n
Viet, Vu Hung 127
Vietcombank 76–7, 82, 84, 149n, 164n
Vinh, Tran Quang 86–7

Yen, Luong Van 85
Youth Volunteer Force 22, 149n
Yteco 147n

Zedong, Mao 5